Reflection in
CBT

⑤SAGE | 50 YEARS

SAGE was founded in 1965 by Sara Miller McCune to support the dissemination of usable knowledge by publishing innovative and high-quality research and teaching content. Today, we publish more than 850 journals, including those of more than 300 learned societies, more than 800 new books per year, and a growing range of library products including archives, data, case studies, reports, and video. SAGE remains majority-owned by our founder, and after Sara's lifetime will become owned by a charitable trust that secures our continued independence.

Los Angeles | London | New Delhi | Singapore | Washington DC

Reflection in
CBT

Beverly Haarhoff *and* Richard Thwaites

with a foreword by
James Bennett-Levy

$SAGE

Los Angeles | London | New Delhi
Singapore | Washington DC

⑤SAGE

Los Angeles | London | New Delhi
Singapore | Washington DC

SAGE Publications Ltd
1 Oliver's Yard
55 City Road
London EC1Y 1SP

SAGE Publications Inc.
2455 Teller Road
Thousand Oaks, California 91320

SAGE Publications India Pvt Ltd
B 1/I 1 Mohan Cooperative Industrial Area
Mathura Road
New Delhi 110 044

SAGE Publications Asia-Pacific Pte Ltd
3 Church Street
#10-04 Samsung Hub
Singapore 049483

Editor: Susannah Trefgarne
Assistant editor: Laura Walmsley
Production editor: Rachel Burrows
Marketing manager: Camille Richmond
Cover design: Lisa Harper-Wells
Typeset by: C&M Digitals (P) Ltd, Chennai, India
Printed and bound by CPI Group (UK) Ltd, Croydon, CR0 4YY

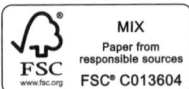

Library of Congress Control Number: 2015939829

British Library Cataloguing in Publication data

A catalogue record for this book is available from
the British Library

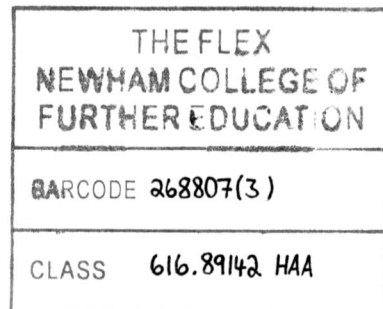

MIX
Paper from responsible sources
FSC
www.fsc.org   FSC® C013604

ISBN 978-1-4462-5888-0
ISBN 978-1-4462-5889-7 (pbk)

At SAGE we take sustainability seriously. Most of our products are printed in the UK using FSC papers and boards.
When we print overseas we ensure sustainable papers are used as measured by the PREPS grading system.
We undertake an annual audit to monitor our sustainability.

CONTENTS

ABOUT THE AUTHORS AND CONTRIBUTORS

Dr Beverly Haarhoff is a clinical psychologist and Senior Lecturer in the School of Psychology at Massey University, Auckland, New Zealand, where she was instrumental in setting up the first Postgraduate Diploma in CBT in the southern hemisphere. For the past 14 years she has trained and supervised both CBT and clinical psychology trainees. Her research has focused primarily on Self-Practice/Self-Reflection (SP/SR) as a mechanism to support and improve therapist skill acquisition in CBT therapists at all levels of development. Dr Haarhoff has a private clinical practice and regularly presents CBT training workshops. She was co-author of the first published SP/SR manual (Bennett-Levy, Thwaites, Haarhoff & Perry, 2015).

Dr Richard Thwaites is a consultant clinical psychologist and CBT therapist who serves as Clinical Director for a large National Health Service psychological therapies service in the United Kingdom. In addition to delivering therapy, he provides clinical leadership, supervision, training, and consultancy in CBT, including around the implementation of Self-Practice/Self-Reflection (SP/SR) programmes. He has been involved in a number of research projects looking at the effectiveness of SP/SR in skill development and belief change across a range of populations, including trainee and experienced CBT therapists and, more recently, low intensity practitioners. He was co-author of the first published SP/SR manual (Bennett-Levy, Thwaites, Haarhoff & Perry, 2015).

Peter Armstrong read Philosophy & English before training as a teacher and qualifying as a mental health nurse in the 1980s, then as a cognitive therapist, under Ivy Blackburn, in the early 1990s. He worked in in-patient psychiatry services, and the Newcastle CBT Centre as therapist, supervisor and teacher, finishing his NHS career as head of training there. With Mark Freeston and colleagues he has developed models of clinical supervision, training and interpersonal processes in CBT. He is also a poet, publishing in magazines and anthologies since 1978 and with five solo collections to his name.

Professor Paul Farrand works at the University of Exeter, where he is an Associate Professor and Director of Postgraduate Low Intensity CBT (LI CBT) programmes within Clinical Education, Development and Research (CEDAR) Psychology. He undertakes research in this area, specifically examining LI CBT for the treatment of mental health problems in people with long-term physical health conditions. He has sat on several national and international committees associated with LI CBT. Clinically he has held several posts in hospital settings, working as an accredited CBT therapist specialising in mental health problems in people with medical problems affecting their head and neck.

Dr James Hawkins specialises in the treatment of psychological difficulties and in helping people enhance their health and wellbeing. James has worked as a medical doctor and also has extensive training in psychotherapy. He is particularly interested in how emerging research can help health professionals become more helpful for their clients. He publishes a bimonthly evidence-based newsletter and has lectured widely to health professionals both nationally and internationally.

Kat Rayson Having previously worked in the forensic psychology field as a therapist on Sex Offender Treatment Programmes, Kat trained as a Psychological Wellbeing Practitioner (PWP) in 2010 and worked as an accredited PWP and Senior PWP. She has worked at the University of Exeter since 2012, initially as an Associate Lecturer on a range of PWP postgraduate and undergraduate programmes and now as Associate Research Fellow. Kat's research interests are in the training of practitioners in delivering evidence-based low intensity CBT interventions and the development of bespoke low intensity CBT interventions to meet the unmet needs of specific patient groups.

Laura Lovis began her training in IAPT as a Psychology Wellbeing Practitioner in 2010. She has since worked at the University of Exeter as an Associate Lecturer on both undergraduate and postgraduate training programmes, delivering teaching on the Low Intensity CBT method. During this period Laura was also involved in a pilot research trial exploring the acceptability of a self-help programme supported by carers for the treatment of depression in people with dementia. Laura's main interest is working with patients using the low intensity method and she is currently working in a service in London as a PWP.

FOREWORD

This is an important book in the journey of CBT. A book that has needed to be written. With the greatest of pleasure I can report that Bev Haarhoff and Richard Thwaites have done an admirable job.

What Haarhoff and Thwaites have achieved – for the first time in CBT – is to start to map the length and breadth of reflection in CBT. They identify the key role of reflection in processes ranging from supervision, self-supervision, and therapist training, through to effective use of client feedback and cultivation of effective therapeutic relationships, through to the development of cultural competency, low intensity competency, and the promotion of self-care. The practical experience and clinical wisdom of the authors enshrined in the case examples shines through, giving the reader confidence that they are in the hands of experts.

Haarhoff and Thwaites marshal evidence from a variety of sources to make a convincing case for the central role of reflection in therapist skill development. Although empirical evidence for the importance of reflection in training and supervision is still in its infancy, a consideration of the literature from such diverse sources as feedback-informed therapy, outcome studies of therapist effects, acquisition of cultural competency, adult learning theory, and therapist skill development and supervision models points to the crucial role of reflection. How could it be otherwise? Once therapists have acquired the basic conceptual, technical and interpersonal skills of a therapy such as CBT, the major learning is to know when, how, why, and with whom to use those skills (what has been termed 'when-then rules'). How do we do this? Not so much by going to occasional workshops – though it certainly helps if we reflect well on these afterwards. Rather, it is by reflecting on our day-to-day clinical experience, including that of our supervisors and supervisees: working out what worked well and what did not; identifying key factors; and practicing and evaluating doing things differently in circumstances where outcomes were not as desirable as we might have hoped. Having a good supervisor who emphasises the value of reflective practice certainly helps in this regard.

Every chapter is replete with a breadth of understanding, born out of the wealth of clinical, training and supervision experience that Haarhoff and Thwaites have acquired through working 'on the ground' with trainees, supervisees and clients. In the process they manage to translate declarative understandings into accessible, practical procedural rules and skills for the reader. The authors have also been astute in bringing in other writers – James Hawkins, Peter Armstrong and Paul Farrand and colleagues – to contribute their expertise in the specific areas of client feedback, CBT training and low intensity practitioners.

Not only do all these authors provide much needed guidelines and strategies for therapists wondering 'how to do reflection', but along the way this wide-ranging text will help future researchers and clinicians get clearer about what reflection is and what it isn't; what the many forms of reflection are, and how they can best be conceptualised and developed. As someone who has been ploughing the reflection/ CBT path alongside of Thwaites and Haarhoff for some years, I find myself standing back and admiring what they have achieved with this book. It manages at the same time to be both interesting and user-friendly, and, though there is still a relatively small literature on reflection in CBT, the book is firmly rooted in empiricism. I found myself constantly stimulated and at times positively excited as I stumbled upon ideas which may have flipped across my consciousness at one time or another, but were now fully articulated and elaborated.

To take one example: self-supervision. Richard Thwaites and I did touch on the importance of self-supervision in our book chapter 'Self and self-reflection in the therapeutic relationship' (Bennett-Levy & Thwaites, 2007), but we did not go into great detail. On reading Thwaites and Haarhoff's Chapter 3 here, I found myself astonished that CBT therapists – in fact all therapists – have paid so little attention to self-supervision. Once the spotlight is shone on self-supervision, it becomes blindingly obvious that self-supervision should not be regarded as some kind of peripheral venture (if it is thought about at all). Self-supervision is something that every therapist should do – on a continuous basis. And therapists should be routinely trained in it! It's no good therapists waiting around for our weekly (if we are very lucky) or monthly supervision session and expecting all our learning to take place then. Typically, in clinical supervision, we might present one or two of our patients. What about all the other patients? What about all the other conceptual, technical or interpersonal skills that we don't get time to address in that session? Should they simply be put aside to await that supervision session in 3 month's, 6 month's, or 1 year's time when the same problem emerges again? Of course not! How else are we to acquire and refine skills if we don't develop a self-supervision practice?

We learn from the chapter that self-supervision may take one of two forms: it may either be an 'ad hoc' reflective practice in response to acute therapeutic problems that alarm us sufficiently to devote some thought and time to the issue; or it can be a structured reflective practice, regularly implemented, that routinely monitors and is sensitive not only to major difficulties, but also to 'subacute problems' that may become major unless we give them attention at earlier stages. Which should it be? Which form of self-supervision do we think might lead to more effective outcomes for clients? Is there not a clear message for all of us therapists?

Chapter 5, 'Reflecting on our socio-cultural background', also struck a personal chord for me. As our societies become progressively multicultural, it behoves thera-pists to examine their own cultural assumptions. As Haarhoff and Thwaites show, many of those from dominant cultures are culturally blind as to the subtle – or not so subtle – impacts of their background. They may believe themselves to be 'culture neutral' or culturally sensitive without ever having examined and questioned their cultural assumptions. Some therapists may attend lectures or read books that refer to cultural factors. But how do we move from declarative knowledge that 'culture may be important in therapy' to procedural skills that have encompassed the therapists' own biases and prejudices and lead to attitude change and different ways of relating? It simply cannot be done without self-reflection. I found myself reflecting at a deeper level on the cultural values that have motivated me as a therapist. How much has my strong reactivity against my father's ancestral assumptions of British upper middle class superiority induced a permanent sense of guilt and a 'need' to right this by working with disadvantaged communities? If it has, is that a bad thing? Or does it carry with it some attitudes and behaviours, born of middle class guilt (e.g. excessive latitude, lack of challenge, and unquestioned acceptance of behaviours such as non-attendance and ongoing self-abusive behaviours), which might not be helpful for either the patients or myself?

Hawkins, Thwaites and Haarhoff's Chapter 6, 'Client feedback', is another tour de force. By the end of the chapter we are left wondering how non-reflective therapists, or therapists who do not consistently seek patient feedback on process and monitor patient outcomes, manage to achieve any decent results at all. Scarily, the answer is that perhaps they don't. There appears to be far more variance in patient outcomes across therapists than between different therapies, which suggests that there has been an excessive research emphasis on therapy outcomes rather than therapist outcomes. Hawkins et al. make a strong case that routine sessional alliance assessment and outcome monitoring and a focus on cases that are not 'on track' should be fundamental to both clinical supervision and self-supervision. Once the patient data are collected and inspected, what's the next thing? Reflection, of course.

I could visit each of the chapters of this book and give my personal reflections, but the Foreword would get very long. In a nutshell, what Haarhoff, Thwaites and colleagues have achieved is a book that illustrates through practical advice and meaningful examples the very essence of what reflective practice is all about. As you go through the book, I would suggest one thing: 15 years of research on self-practice/self-reflection (SP/SR) in therapist training have taught us that to get the most benefit, you will need to move your reading from the declarative to the procedural; to *engage experientially* with the exercises and *reflect in writing* on your experience. Then you will 'get reflection' from the inside out. Unfortunately, there are no short cuts. A reflective space needs to be created, and time set aside. The journey is demanding and exciting in equal measure. But the personal rewards are many. And, perhaps most tellingly, the research is increasingly indicating that it may make a major difference not only for yourself, but to the outcomes for your patients.

Enjoy this treasure of a book. I wish you a stimulating, challenging and practice-changing journey.

James Bennett-Levy
July 2015

ACKNOWLEDGEMENTS

We would like to thank Windy Dryden for initially proposing that SAGE publish a book on reflection in CBT, and the Sage counselling and psychotherapy editors including Alice Oven, Susannah Trefgarne, Kate Wharton, Rachel Burrows, Camille Richmond and Edward Coats for nurturing the book through all the publishing steps. Particular thanks go to Laura Walmsley who supported us in the final push to complete the book.

The input of James Bennett-Levy has been important to both of us. We have appreciated his infectious enthusiasm, humour, intellectual challenge, support and friendship across various related projects over the last decade. His Declarative-Procedural-Reflective model and initial development of SP/SR have both been long-term influences on the genesis of this book.

Many colleagues have inspired our interest in reflection in CBT over the years notably Mark Freeston, Anna Chaddock, Craig Chigwedere, Melanie Davies, Derek Milne, Debbie Wood, and Nick Kazantzis. Helen Perry, Paul Cromarty, Robyn Vertongen, Angela McNaught, Lynley Stenhouse, Samantha Spafford, James Martyn, Ryan Askey-Jones, Laura Lockhart, Dave Sandford, Laura Cairns, Laura Johnston, Ria Lowrie, Andrea Robinson, and Melanie Turner have worked with us on various projects involving reflection in CBT.

Special acknowledgement goes to Christine Padesky, Kathleen Mooney and Pamela Hays for their encouragement and permission to adapt and include their valuable work. Particular thanks go to Dave Sandford for his significant input in the development of our longitudinal formulation template for therapist beliefs in Chapter 10.

Heartfelt thanks go to all the Massey University Postgraduate CBT students in New Zealand and the CBT therapists and Psychological Wellbeing Practitioners in the UK who, since 2004, have worked through various iterations of SP/SR workbooks as part of their CBT training and enthusiastically and honestly reflected on many aspects of their CBT practice in supervision and during training. We have learnt so much from you.

Finally, to our partners Sarah and Errol, who have cheerfully supported us through what at times has seemed a very long journey, thank you for being there.

INTRODUCTION

Many years ago, Richard had a highly intelligent and proficient colleague (and later a good friend) who was also a clinical psychologist and CBT therapist. During a research meeting, Richard was in the position of advocating a piece of research which involved implementing a Self-Practice/Self-Reflection programme for therapists. This meant therapists practising elements of CBT on themselves and then reflecting on the implications for themselves as therapists, supervisors and human beings. Many in the group appeared unconvinced by his passionate arguments and finally his colleague, no doubt in frustration, fired back at him "*Why should therapists reflect? Plumbers don't need to reflect!*" Richard did not believe for a moment that his colleague actually believed this; it was more an "invitation" to explain himself more clearly!

If you've picked this book off the shelf, there is a good chance that you already believe reflection is important for CBT therapists and you are interested in ways to improve your own reflective skills, or the reflective skills of your supervisees or students. On the other hand, you may be sceptical, or even curious, as to what reflection is and why it should be important to you as a CBT practitioner. This book aims to give a convincing and comprehensive answer to the question regarding the role of reflection posed all those years ago and show how reflection functions as a key metacompetence or higher order competency which is important in the professional development of CBT trainees and experienced therapists.

WHY SHOULD CBT THERAPISTS REFLECT?

Returning to the question posed by Richard's colleague, would you want a plumber fixing your waterworks who was only able to implement the specific techniques learnt during his or her training in a rote fashion? Imagine a plumber who had no ability to learn from new experiences and, when faced with similar situations, was unable to generalise from previous pieces of work and the successful solutions that were reached. Would you want a plumber who, faced with a blocked U-bend, kept repeating the same unsuccessful strategy again and again? Or, imagine a plumber who had no ability to deal with difficult customers or to understand how his or her personal attitudes and behaviours contributed to the discussions or arguments about the project. The answer we are sure would be "On no account!"

Given the "plumber" analogy, how much more important is it for mental health practitioners and therapists to be able to reflect? We would hope that therapists are able to learn effectively from experience, notice what is happening, and on this basis, adapt future responses. We would also generally expect therapists to recognise the impact of therapist beliefs and behaviours on the therapeutic relationship. None of this can be achieved without reflection.

STRUCTURE OF THE BOOK

The first part of the book addresses the way in which reflective practice can be integrated and enhanced in those areas of clinical practice which have relevance to all CBT practitioners whether practising high or low intensity CBT, trainee, novice, experienced or expert. The first chapter introduces the Declarative Procedural Reflective model as the theoretical spine of the book and the subsequent chapters on self-reflection in supervision, self-supervision, the therapeutic relationship, the importance of utilising regular client feedback, and the influence of socio-cultural factors are all discussed in the context of reflective practice for all. Chapters 7, 8 and 9, however, each have a more specific focus and describe the role of reflection for specific groups of CBT practitioners, such as low intensity practitioners or therapists undergoing training (whether basic training or workshops later in their career). In this part of the book Self-Practice/Self-Reflection (SP/SR) as an experiential learning strategy is also presented as a unique process to guide and enhance therapist self-reflection. The final chapter emphasises reflection on therapist self-care as a fundamental activity relevant to all CBT therapists, whatever the context.

MASTERING THE BASICS: THE DECLARATIVE PROCEDURAL REFLECTIVE MODEL OF THERAPIST SKILL ACQUISITION

Imagine basic CBT skills being learned by rote and applied with robotic conformity, without the ability to reflect on the cues and new information received from the client. As we will discuss later in this book, some acquisition of "dry" knowledge might be possible without reflection, but how is the learner to turn this into an applicable set of skills and rules for practice? And how would CBT, delivered in this way, be experienced by the client? Would the client feel validated and understood by the therapist? Would the client's individuality and uniqueness be respected? Chapter 1 lays out the theoretical and empirical framework that supports and underpins the importance of reflection for the acquisition of therapeutic skill and competency.

SUPERVISION AND SELF-SUPERVISION

Reflective skills are not just required when we are with our clients. It is likely that all supervisors could search their hearts and find examples of when their supervision was lacking in reflection, either when they failed to use their reflective skills as a supervisor or when their supervision was unsuccessful in evoking a useful amount of reflection in their supervisee. For most supervisors this is likely to be due to passing influences, such as tiredness, overload, worry about a risk issue, supervisory drift or even frustration with the supervisee. These are all normal and unavoidable. But what about a supervisor who *repeatedly* fails to help his or her supervisees reflect, perhaps due to lack of training or lack of understanding about the most helpful ways for supervisees to learn?

Whatever the cause, supervision without reflection is likely to feel over-safe, uninspiring, non-challenging and potentially simply a monitoring or supportive process, rather than a forum that develops the supervisee as a practitioner. Lack of reflection from supervisor *and* supervisee can even lead to comfortable collusion within the supervisory relationship that may support poor practices (Milne, Leck & Choudhri, 2009). We believe that high-quality supervision, with a strong emphasis on reflection as part of the learning process, is an essential element supporting optimum therapist development. In Chapter 2 we will explore the role of reflection in clinical supervision and suggest ways to improve the reflective content of your supervision as both a supervisee and supervisor. Chapter 3 examines the role of reflection in establishing your own effective self-supervision processes.

THE THERAPEUTIC RELATIONSHIP

The task of delivering psychological therapies is a complex one where interpersonal dynamics and abstract factors such as values and expectations have to be taken into account. An unreflective therapist would, at the very least, be limited to delivering therapy by rote, relying on a narrow set of interventions. Being able to adapt, adjust and tailor interventions to particular clients at particular times would be severely restricted and we would see little clinical artistry or creativity, the qualities identified time and time again in therapists considered most competent and effective. It is very likely that the unreflective therapist would be thrown off course by the inevitable misunderstandings that occur in the often intensely interpersonal context of therapy.

Even if someone had just enough reflective ability to learn and apply the basics of CBT after some initial training, what would happen during the first therapeutic rupture? If there was a misunderstanding and the therapist felt attacked or criticised, how would the unreflective therapist even start to make sense of his or her personal emotional and behavioural response? We would suggest that such a therapist would be unlikely to step back from the problematic situation long enough to "unhook" from automatic ways of responding, reflect on the current situation and be able to formulate the rupture in CBT terms, integrating relevant theory with actual practice.

The examples presented above are somewhat exaggerated to demonstrate worst case scenarios for the unreflective therapist. It is not, however, as black and white as this. Most therapists have areas of strength and weakness and this also applies to their ability to reflect. Some may be able to routinely reflect within therapy but have certain types of client where, for a range of reasons, they are unable to step back from and observe their own contribution to the interaction and, on this basis, behave differently. It can be a client that reminds us of a significant other in our lives, or expresses thoughts or feelings that are uncomfortable for us as individuals (e.g. some therapists may struggle with sadness and depression, others may struggle to cope with uncertainty). Our examples suggest that deficits in reflective skill can prevent therapists from behaving in optimal ways for clients. In Chapter 4 we will examine the role of reflection in formulating and appropriately responding in the therapeutic relationship, especially during the moments where a rupture is possible.

REFLECTION ON THE INFLUENCE OF SOCIO-CULTURAL FACTORS

As Western societies become increasingly culturally diverse, the possibility of cultural bias in the therapist has to be seriously entertained as a factor that can potentially interfere with therapy. In Chapter 5 we examine the role of social and cultural influences on us as therapists and ask how we can use reflection to understand these and ensure that our values do not insidiously impact on the therapy that we provide.

REFLECTING ON CLIENT FEEDBACK

An extremely important aspect of therapist reflection involves being open to learning from client feedback. While this is a truism, eliciting and responding appropriately to client feedback is often a blind spot in some CBT therapists. Learning to reflect on and respond to the routine use of sessional feedback is important for improving therapist effectiveness. Additionally, targeting supervision to focus on clients who are not improving at predicted rates is an area of considerable interest. Chapter 6 discusses the importance of eliciting and responding appropriately to client feedback.

MAXIMISING REFLECTION IN TRAINING PROGRAMMES

Some readers will deliver, or anticipate delivering, training as part of their role, whether brief sessions on a focused topic (e.g. training GPs how to do a basic CBT formulation) or as part of an advanced CBT training course. While most trainers will be familiar with Kolb's learning cycle (Kolb, 1984), it is unlikely that the majority of trainers plan their training courses by identifying the key areas of knowledge and/or skills they want the trainee to develop and then tailor evidence-based training strategies more likely to lead to these desired outcomes. Although evidence-based literature regarding training remains sparse, there is some evidence that different training strategies are differentially effective in the acquisition of different types of knowledge and skills (Bennett-Levy, McManus, Westling & Fennell, 2009). Three types of systems relevant to the acquisition of knowledge and skills are identified, namely declarative or "book" knowledge, procedural knowledge (when… then… or if… then… rules built up over the course of clinical experience), and the reflective system. Procedural skills are particularly difficult to teach using traditional didactic methods and there is evidence to suggest that the ability to use reflection skilfully is one pathway to developing such skills. Bennett-Levy, McManus et al. (2009) found that "reading, lectures/talks and modelling were perceived to be most useful for the acquisition of declarative knowledge, while enactive learning strategies (role-play, self-experiential work), together with modelling and reflective practice, were perceived to be most effective in enhancing procedural skills" (p. 571).

Reflection is key here, both on the part of the trainer in designing and implementing their training, but also as a component of training therapists in the sophisticated procedural skills so necessary for successful therapy interventions. The interaction of these three systems is conceptualised in the Declarative Procedural Reflective model, fully described in Chapter 1. In Chapter 7 we contextualise the role of reflection in training and ask how reflective processes can be integrated in different types of training, ranging from half-day workshops to postgraduate CBT Diploma courses.

SELF-PRACTICE/SELF-REFLECTION

Both authors have been involved in developing and researching a specific learning strategy called Self-Practice/Self-Reflection, in which therapists practise CBT techniques on themselves and reflect on this to improve their understanding of both the therapy and themselves as therapists and individuals (e.g. Bennett-Levy, Lee, Travers, Pohlman & Hamernik, 2003; Bennett-Levy, Turner, Beaty, Smith, Paterson & Farmer, 2001; Chaddock, Thwaites, Bennett-Levy & Freeston, 2014; Davis, 2008; Davis, Thwaites, Freeston, Bennett-Levy, 2015; Haarhoff, Gibson & Flett, 2011). Usually delivered in a workbook format, SP/SP is increasingly finding a place in CBT training and professional development. There is a growing body of evidence that SP/SR can help develop procedural skills (especially those of an interpersonal nature) and also lead to belief change (relating to therapist self or the personal self). The anecdotal feedback from SP/SR participants is that this is usually one of the most powerful learning experiences of their career, and that they truly feel that they have experienced CBT from the inside. Chapter 8 describes the use of SP/SR workbooks to support reflection in CBT, describing and providing examples taken from actual SP/SR training programmes.

LOW INTENSITY PRACTITIONERS

We have found that reflective practice is important for mental health practitioners practising in a variety of different roles and contexts. Low intensity CBT or Psychological Wellbeing Practitioners are a relatively recent addition to the National Health Service in England. This group of practitioners is currently spearheading a broader worldwide movement to address the treatment gap by improving access to evidence-based psychological therapies on a wider and more efficient basis through the delivery of high-volume specific interventions. Chapter 9 outlines ways in which the development of reflective skills in a workforce with variable levels of mental health experience on entry to training presents several challenges. Reflective practice is highly relevant to this group during training but, in addition, developing or enhancing the capacity to reflect offers a way to help further learning from experience and to maximise competency, and subsequent post-qualification artistry.

SELF-CARE

Mental health practitioners consistently report high levels of occupationally-related stress, resulting in physical and/or psychological problems for those affected in this way (Tyler & Cushway, 1998). These challenges include caring for vulnerable clients, needing to make decisions in situations that are often ambiguous, and sometimes coping with high levels of risk, for example, client self-harm and, in some instances, suicide (Kottler, 2012). In the final chapter, we consider the role reflection has in facilitating the CBT therapist's active choice to maintain optimum levels of self-care in professional situations. We have positioned this chapter at the end of the book to emphasise that all practitioners owe it to themselves and, more importantly, to their clients to reflect on how best to take care of themselves in their role as therapist.

CONCLUSION

Historically, reflection has been poorly defined in the evidence-based therapies and many CBT therapists may perceive reflective practice as navel-gazing or being too self-focused. We hope our initial arguments have supported the need for CBT therapists to engage in reflection for a variety of reasons and across a number of different contexts. The purpose of the book is to motivate CBT therapists to improve the way they use reflection in clinical practice and to make reflection manageable by providing a number of structures and frameworks for self-reflection across different contexts. The ultimate aim of reflective practice, and indeed this book, is improved therapist competence and, most importantly, client care. We conclude by asking: "If you were a patient seeing a CBT therapist, would you prefer to see a therapist who had had: *'twenty years of experience or one year of experience twenty times'*" (Skovholt, Rønnestad & Jennings, 1997, p. 365). We come down firmly in favour of 20 years of varied experience, and concur with these authors, who cite reflection as making the difference.

1

REFLECTION IN CBT:

Becoming Better Therapists, Supervisors and Trainers

Beverly Haarhoff and Richard Thwaites

LEARNING AIMS

- To introduce the Declarative Procedural Reflective (DPR) model of therapist skill development as the theoretical spine of the book
- To highlight the importance of reflection for the training, ongoing professional development and professional lives of all CBT therapists

INTRODUCTION

When at work, with my clients, supervisor or colleagues, I can sometimes feel bored, angry, sad, anxious, guilty, scared, hopeless, uncertain, or out of control. Why is this? Is it them or is it me? What should I do next? Have I made the right decision? How is it that my intervention didn't work? Why did I fall into that old pattern of reacting? How will I cope? What should I do next? What if the client gets worse? I can't stand working with depressed/angry/anxious/older/younger/suicidal clients. Am I a good enough therapist? Why did my client suddenly drop out of therapy? Could I have done something different? How can I improve as a therapist?

These are all familiar questions that occur from time-to-time for therapists (and other professionals) dealing with complexity, ambiguity, multiple sources of information, risk, and evaluation on a daily basis. Ever since the publication of Donald Schön's ground-breaking book *The Reflective Practitioner* in 1983, reflection and reflective practice have been recognised as important processes which can be helpful in unpacking, managing and responding to these questions, and to the situations that generate them (Schön, 1983). In addition, Schön also identified reflection as playing an important role in education and professional development. In a nutshell, he challenged the accepted notion that there was a body of empirical knowledge that professionals from various disciplines could learn at university and then apply with confidence, once qualified, to guide problem-solving and decision-making. He observed that the day-to-day nature of professional responsibility frequently entails the ability to cope with complexity, uncertainty, ambiguity, conflicts of values, and ethical and moral dilemmas. Being professionally effective, he insisted, requires not only the mastery of the theoretical principles and knowledge base connected to the profession, but being able to apply this knowledge in flexible, adaptive and creative ways. He identified *reflection on experience* as the primary key to unlocking what he describes as "professional artistry", the ability to skilfully unite theory and scientific facts with practical experience. To do this the professional practitioner needs to be able to reflect on what they are doing as they do it (reflection-in-action) and also reflect on what they have done (reflection-on-action) and plan to do in the future. Reflection is now considered a core competency by many professional bodies, and practitioners from different professions are often required to demonstrate their reflective ability in the form of written reflective accounts of their practice in order to maintain their professional registration. This is particularly prevalent in the "helping" professions, such as nursing, social work and psychotherapy. Numerous academic courses also have a reflective component as part of course work, which is often assessed and evaluated.

REFLECTION IN CBT

Historically, CBT is firmly rooted in the empiricist tradition, evolving as it did from the behavioural therapies developed by academic psychologists in opposition to the powerful psychoanalytic models of human development and psychopathology (Watson & Rayner, 1920; Wolpe & Lazarus, 1966). CBT is now widely recognised as the foremost evidence-based psychotherapy, with a proven track record of effectiveness with an ever-increasing range of diagnostic presentations (Butler, Chapman, Forman & Beck, 2006). CBT practitioners are expected to consistently deliver evidence-based interventions tailored to the client's diagnostic presentation and there is considerable evidence to suggest that the closer CBT practitioners stick to the evidence-based protocols, the more successful the therapy is likely to be (Schulte & Eifert, 2002). To some degree this history has engendered a misperception that CBT therapists are technically-focused practitioners applying proven interventions in a "cookbook" manner, not recognising or utilising reflection as an important element of training and professional development (Bennett-Levy, Thwaites, Chaddock & Davis, 2009). Although reflection and reflective practice has not, traditionally, been explicitly integrated into CBT training and professional development programmes in the same

way as it has been in professions such as nursing and social work, this perception is
not accurate and reflection has always been tacitly incorporated in CBT, as shown in
the following examples:

- Socratic enquiry ("What do you make of that?" "How do you make sense of what hap-
  pened given your belief about this?")
- Reflecting on the outcome of behavioural experiments
- Supervision models
- The use of informal self-practice and self-reflection in training programmes ("How did
  you experience keeping an activity diary?")
- The emphasis on collecting and responding to feedback from clients and supervisors

In addition, since 2000, Self-Practice/Self-Reflection (SP/SR), as an experiential
adjunct to CBT training, has become integrated into a growing number of training programmes and professional development opportunities (Bennett-Levy et al.,
2001; Haarhoff et al., 2011). Furthermore, since CBT has expanded to provide
therapy for more severe and complex presentations, such as clients diagnosed
with a personality disorder, CBT therapists have been advised to reflect on the
interaction between therapist and client assumptions, beliefs and compensatory
behaviours (Beck, 2011; Laydon, Newman, Freeman & Morse, 1993; Leahy, 2001;
Young, Klosko & Weishaar, 2003). Reflection on the therapist's own beliefs, feelings and actions is now seen as essential in the development and maintenance of
therapeutic relationships, particularly when addressing alliance ruptures (Safran &
Segal, 1990). Personal therapy, the therapist's therapy, is the form reflection often
takes in many psychotherapeutic modalities (Laireiter & Willutski, 2003), and
although personal therapy is not generally a compulsory part of CBT training
in most English-speaking countries, many CBT therapists independently seek
out personal therapy as a self-reflective forum (Orlinsky, Norcross, Rønnestad &
Wiseman, 2005).

   In this book we build on and extend the wide-ranging reflective practice already
inherent in the principles of CBT. Our overall aim is to show how reflection and
reflective practice can, and should, play a key role in the training, professional development and the ongoing daily professional life of all CBT therapists (whether novice or
expert), supervisors and trainers, in many different contexts and formats. Our goal is
to clearly identify the different forums of reflection in CBT and provide clear structured
procedural guidelines for practice in each.

   In this introductory chapter we clarify the ways in which we will be describing
the various components of reflection, namely reflective practice, skill and process.
We also introduce the Declarative Procedural Reflective (DPR) model of therapist
skill acquisition (Bennett-Levy, 2006) as our guiding theoretical model and highlight
reflection as a metacompetency underpinning all other therapeutic competencies.
Remaining true to our empirical roots, we summarise the evidence collected over
the past decade that consistently suggests that certain forms of reflection are useful in
specific CBT skill acquisition, conceptual understanding and more skilful management
of the interpersonal dimensions of therapy.

CBT practitioners can often have very different reactions to the requirements and expectations around reflection. Some will embrace and delight in the activity, others may feel somewhat unnerved or confused, possibly worried that they have no idea how to go about engaging in such activities, especially if during training this involves meeting institutional expectations. Each chapter therefore concludes with some suggestions regarding the ways that reflection can be taken forward and implemented by the CBT therapist. This introductory chapter will conclude with some guidelines concerning how best to use this book.

UNDERSTANDING AND DEFINING REFLECTION IN CBT

There are many definitions of reflection. From a common-sense perspective, however, reflection is: "thinking about something that has happened [*usually in a complex, difficult or ambiguous situation*] and considering the implications in more detail" (Moon, 1999, our italics). While this makes sense, it has been noted that the language of reflection in the context of psychotherapy could benefit from clarification as the term covers a number of different and discrete aspects of reflection (Bennett-Levy, Thwaites, et al. 2009). These authors distinguish four usages of the term, which are described below:

Reflective practice refers to reflecting on clinical experience that includes the personal reactions of the therapist. This may happen in supervision, self-supervision, through reflective journals and Self-Practice/Self-Reflection. Reflective practice can also involve reviewing therapy tapes, attending to client or supervisor feedback and reviewing client progress measures.

Reflective skill encompasses *general reflective skills* (the ability to reconstruct and explore events) and *self-reflective skills* (the observation and exploration of self, for example the therapist's own thoughts, emotions and behaviours).

The **reflective system** is part of the Declarative Procedural Reflective (DPR) model of therapist skill acquisition developed by Bennett-Levy and colleagues (Bennett-Levy, 2006; Bennett-Levy & Thwaites, 2007). This model will be discussed in greater detail below. Briefly, however, **declarative knowledge** refers to theoretical and practical knowledge gained through traditional pedagogical channels, such as reading and attending lectures – technical knowledge in Schön's terms (Schön, 1983). Declarative knowledge is abstract knowledge. For example, knowledge about the therapeutic relationship can exist without actually ever having been part of a therapeutic relationship (e.g. "*It is a good thing to foster collaboration in CBT*"). **Procedural knowledge and skills** we build up over time in a more complex manner and this relies on the ability to utilise experience in a meaningful manner, detecting patterns and processes. In the therapeutic context, procedural knowledge and skills are often observed to differentiate experienced from novice clinicians. Experience allows the clinician to build up a series of implicit rules, for example, "*When this happens, then I do x, y or z*". The reflective system is characterised as being at the centre of therapist knowledge and skills, containing no permanent knowledge but functioning as an "engine" which drives the other two systems, integrating knowledge from both declarative and procedural systems, helping the therapist obtain answers to questions such as "*How does this theory or practical intervention work out with this particular client?*" In therapy, an effective reflective system should focus and integrate information derived from what is happening in therapy with the client, and what is happening in the therapist's head, with appropriate evidence-based declarative and procedural knowledge. For example, if a client is struggling to complete an intervention such as a thought diary, the therapist can bring to mind other similar experiences to shed potential light on how to manage the current difficulty (for example, some clients find writing and spelling difficult and need reassurance that this is not important, some clients have a belief that writing thoughts down makes them more likely to occur). Strengthening the reflective system has particular relevance for the development of interpersonal skills which are essential in the delivery of sensitive and flexible interventions and which can reduce the likelihood of client disengagement and aid the therapist in addressing inevitable therapeutic alliance ruptures (Bennett–Levy & Thwaites, 2007).

Reflection as a process is seen as having three parts:

- Focused attention on a problem. This can be stimulated by a rupture in therapy, an unexpected or overfamiliar emotional reaction, curiosity, or a mismatch between client and therapist goals and expectations;
- The ability to reconstruct and observe the event. Reconstruction can rely on imagery, role-play or mindful observation; and finally,
- The event is conceptualised and synthesised by a process of self-questioning, logical analysis and problem-solving strategies.

To summarise, our understanding of the scope of reflection includes the *practice* of reflection together with the general and self-focused *reflective skills* involved. We also consider the *reflective system* as the key element or engine driving the Declarative Procedural Reflective model of therapeutic skill acquisition. Finally, the *process of reflection* entails attention, reconstruction and conceptualisation, which ideally can be used by the CBT therapist in ways that extend understanding and ideally also change emotional reactions and behaviours.

THE DPR MODEL OF THERAPIST SKILL ACQUISITION

In the original representation of the DPR model (Bennett–Levy, 2006), each of the systems was depicted as of equal size. Subsequently, however, the model was redrawn to centralise and privilege the contribution of the reflective system now described as the "engine" driving lifelong learning, demonstrating the role of reflection as a regular process within iterative learning cycles (Bennett–Levy, Thwaites et al., 2009) (see Figure 1.1). In addition, in the model adapted for this chapter, the relationships between the reflective system and declarative knowledge and procedural skills are clearly marked as a two-way process. For more experienced CBT therapists, their knowledge and skills will be both an input and an output to the ongoing process of reflection in the development of expertise (Bennett-Levy, 2006). This is to be contrasted with the novice therapist who will possess more limited therapy-related declarative knowledge and potentially even less procedural skills. For such an individual there is likely to be a greater role for the reflective system producing therapy-specific knowledge and skills and a lesser role for knowledge and skills feeding into the process of reflection.

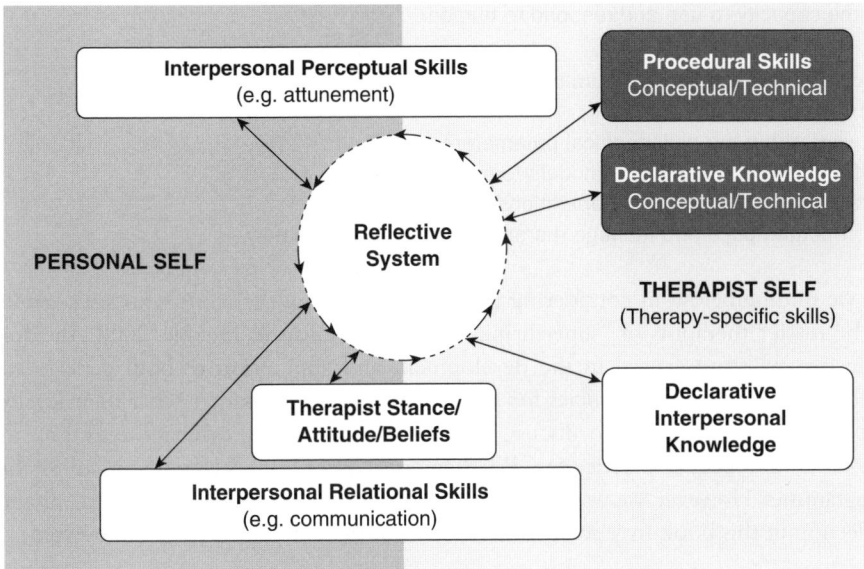

FIGURE 1.1 *A perspective on the DPR model highlighting the central role of reflection on therapist skill development (adapted from Bennett-Levy, Thwaites, Chaddock & Davis, 2009, p. 119)*

Ideally, the reflective system focuses on all aspects of therapy practice, including the "therapist self". Appropriate inputs include the client presentation, therapeutic relationship, case conceptualisation, interventions, assessment measures, client feedback, etc. Therapist self-reflection means recognising that the self-as-therapist, self-as-supervisor, or self-as-trainer interact with, and are influenced by, the personal self of the therapist. This is particularly necessary during alliance ruptures when more self-referent material might be evoked (e.g. "*You're an awful therapist and don't care about me at all*").

REFLECTION AS A METACOMPETENCY

It is often observed with the accumulated knowledge of many decades of psycho-therapy research, that successful therapy requires tailoring interventions to the idiosyncratic needs of diverse clients. This means that the implementation of CBT can at times feel more like an art than a science (Whittington & Grey, 2014). Responding to this challenge, a set of metacompetences (higher order competencies) have been proposed as necessary to decide what works best for whom, in what circumstance, and how to apply it (Roth & Pilling, 2007a). These authors have identified generic and CBT-specific metacompetences.

Generic metacompetences are:

- clinical judgement
- the ability to adapt interventions in response to client feedback
- the capacity to use and respond to humour.

Specific CBT metacompetences are the ability to:

- work within the philosophical parameters of CBT
- formulate and apply CBT models to individual clients
- apply appropriate CBT interventions
- structure, pace and manage therapy obstacles appropriately.

As we outline below, in considering the characteristics of therapists who are regarded to be master therapists or "supershrinks" (Miller, Duncan & Hubble, 2008), therapist reflective skills are crucial in the development and application of both generic and specific CBT metacompetencies for all CBT therapists, no matter what their level of experience. As we go on to discuss, most of the supporting evidence regarding the usefulness of reflective practice to CBT therapists comes from the evaluation of SP/SR programmes. However, we would hypothesise that the other tools suggested to enhance reflection in this book may achieve an impact on the same domains to some extent.

EVIDENCE SUPPORTING THE IMPORTANCE OF REFLECTION IN CBT TRAINING AND PROFESSIONAL DEVELOPMENT

Although there is widespread proof and acceptance that psychotherapy is effective (Wampold, 2001), and that CBT is one of the most successful of these therapies (Butler et al., 2006), it is also true that many individuals (even those receiving CBT), do not benefit as much as we would wish (Clark, 2011). Furthermore, progress towards improving the status quo concerning therapeutic outcomes established 30 years ago, has been limited (Lambert, 2013). However, what we do know is that some therapists, across the various established models of psychotherapy, achieve consistently better outcomes than other therapists. This is increasingly being considered as relevant in the quest to improving psychotherapeutic competency (Green, Barkham, Kellett & Saxon, 2014). As we argue below, reflection appears to be a pivotal factor in differentiating excellent or master therapists from those who achieve average or below average outcomes (Jennings, Goh, Skovholt, Hanson & Banerjee-Stevens, 2003).

Searching for psychotherapeutic expertise has been described as an "elusive goal" (Tracey, Wampold, Lichtenberg & Goodyear, 2014) and questions regarding psycho-therapeutic expertise, how expertise develops, and what can be done to improve expertise remains the subject of continued debate. That said, we do have some pointers regarding the factors that combine to produce psychotherapeutic expertise and Table 1.1 summarises the characteristics found in master therapists, those therapists who achieve markedly better outcomes with their clients. These findings come from a number of diverse studies summarised by Jennings et al. (2003).

TABLE 1.1   *Characteristics of master therapists (adapted from Jennings et al., 2003)*

Personal characteristics	The ability to form good interpersonal relationships in challenging, emotionally-charged situations with complex or difficult clients. Master therapists are intellectually astute, emotionally mature, self-aware, congruent, attendant to self-care, have highly developed interpersonal skills, have the ability to self-regulate, be congruent, have a sense of humour, and are inspiring and fun.
Tolerance of ambiguity	Master therapists have a "nuanced ethical compass", and are therefore able to tolerate ambiguity and uncertainty, accept risk and "remain flexible in the face of chaos".
Openness to change	Master therapists possess curiosity and a "drive to mastery" (recognising that there is always more to learn).
Cultural competence	The ability to work effectively with cultural diversity is identified as an important component of expertise missing from the literature focused on identifying expertise.
Reflective practice	Rønnestad and Skovholt (2003) concluded that these therapists displayed unusually high levels of reflectivity that enabled them to maintain awareness of complexity, continuously reflect on difficulties and resist premature therapy closure.

Holding in mind the characteristics that define master therapists, such as strong self-reflective capacity and excellent interpersonal skills, we outline the results of the research that has evaluated the impact of reflection on CBT therapists' psycho-therapeutic skill acquisition. Studies have evaluated the experiential learning strategy Self-Practice/Self-Reflection (SP/SR), reflective journaling, trainee and practitioner reflections on their professional learning and, in one instance, a comparison between personal therapy and SP/SR. SP/SR remains the most widely researched CBT-focused form of reflective practice and the reader is referred to Chapter 8 in this volume for a comprehensive summary of the main research findings regarding the positive impact of SP/SR on all the components of the DPR model described above. Of particular note is the impact that SP/SR has been found to have on the inter-personal aspects of therapy, such as increased empathy and understanding of what it is like to be a client and the difficulties involved in undergoing therapy, heightened self-awareness and the recognition and regulation of personal and therapy-related beliefs (Gale & Schröder, 2014). The fact that SP/SR as a reflective method enhances interpersonal competence aligns with the qualities identified in master therapists (for example, the ability to form good interpersonal relationships in challenging, emotionally-charged situations with complex or difficult clients). Personal therapy (PT) is named by some psychotherapy models as the key to developing interpersonal awareness. However, a recent quantitative study comparing SP/SR and PT, using an opportunistic sample made up of CBT trainees and counselling psychology doctorate trainees in Ireland, showed SP/SR to be an equivalent and, in some ways, a superior training intervention to PT (Chigwedere, Fitzmaurice & Donohoe, 2014). SP/SR has also been shown to increase therapists' confidence in their ability to actually use CBT with clients and the recognition that reflection should be incorporated into regular practice, again mirroring the master therapists' attention to self-care and reflexivity. It should also be noted that SP/SR has been judged as useful by CBT therapists ranging from trainee to experienced therapists (Bennett-Levy et al., 2001; Davis et al., 2015; Haarhoff et al., 2011).

Reflective journals, as another form of written self-reflection, have been also been evaluated and found to be helpful in supporting increased empathy and self-awareness, once again underlining reflection as being important in developing interpersonal awareness. In contrast to SP/SR, participants in this study did express the desire for more structure when engaging with reflective journaling as part of training (Sutton, Townend & Wright, 2007).

One study enquired into which training or supervision methods had been most effective in enhancing different types of therapy-related skills or knowledge (Bennett-Levy, McManus et al., 2009). This study again identified reflective practice and self-experiential work as being particularly helpful in developing procedural knowledge and consolidating and improving interpersonal skills, aspects crucial to developing psychotherapeutic expertise.

The past decade has seen an increasing number of studies, across different countries and contexts, evaluating the impact of reflective practice on the competency and expertise of CBT therapists at various stages in their professional development (Gale & Schröder, 2014). These studies have consistently supported reflection, particularly SP/SR, as improving important competencies and metacompetencies, notably those in the interpersonal domain. As mentioned in the Introduction of this book, Schön (1983) recognised reflection as being fundamental to negotiating the challenges of professional life, such as working with ambiguity, uncertainty, risk, and complex interpersonal situations. Master therapists who achieve high levels of competence and metacompetence have been shown to both value and practise reflection. It seems logical, therefore, to work towards enhancing the ability to reflect "well" in all CBT practitioners and it is hoped that the chapters in this book will inspire further research in this important area.

HOW TO GET THE BEST FROM THIS BOOK

As we have highlighted in the Introduction, the majority of chapters in this book are relevant for all CBT therapists. After Chapter 1, however, the reader can pick and choose in terms of individual interest and each chapter can be read independently of the others. Our aim is to present a comprehensive view of what we consider to be the main forums for developing and supporting reflection in CBT, namely supervision, self-supervision, the therapeutic relationship, socio-cultural issues, therapist attention to client feedback, training and self-care. Two chapters address more specialised areas, namely SP/SR and the optimal use of reflection in the context of low intensity CBT. The book is designed to be of practical use to CBT therapists, providing exercises, clinical examples, tools and conceptual frameworks which we hope will be useful to practitioners wishing to develop or improve professional reflective practice.

We would also emphasise that recognising the importance of reflection in the practice of CBT is only the first step. Integrating meaningful self-reflection as a routine part of professional life is a different matter. Much like maintaining a healthy lifestyle, exercising regularly and eating healthy food, reflective practice requires planning, preparation and practice. Time is always identified as an obstacle to reflection (Haarhoff et al., 2011; Haarhoff, Thwaites & Bennett-Levy, 2015; Spafford & Haarhoff, 2015). The obstacle "time" can only be overcome by prioritising reflection and by formally allocating and scheduling reflective time. Studies evaluating SP/SR underline the fact that to achieve benefit, engagement in the reflective process is necessary, and that engagement means *making* time (Bennett-Levy & Lee, 2014). Scheduling a regular appointment with yourself to reflect is one solution. Better still, joining a group or working with a "buddy" or colleague can provide motivation. Research findings also suggest that sharing self-reflections in a safe context can significantly enhance the experience. All of these suggestions are elaborated on in the book.

Some of the reflective exercises we have suggested may take the reader out of their comfort zone and, on occasions, strong and sometimes unexpected emotions can be evoked. There will also be times when reflection seems to create even more ambiguity and uncertainty. Remember, there is no right or wrong way to feel. As CBT therapists we work with the emotions of our clients and understanding and managing our own response is part of this. Trust the process and discuss your reactions with people you trust.

Each chapter ends with a "Taking it forward" section to encourage the reader to take some of the ideas forward into practice and we also include a suggested reading section where appropriate.

TAKING IT FORWARD

What *declarative knowledge* have you learned from reading this chapter?

- Has anything stood out for you?
- How would you explain the Declarative Procedural Reflective model to a colleague?
- Identify one thing that you have learned about the role of reflection in developing either basic CBT skills or mastery and artistry in CBT?

Identifying your own *procedural rules*

- Think about a set of knowledge or skills you hold outside your professional life where you have a degree of mastery or expertise (e.g. DIY, child care, photography, cooking, car maintenance, knitting). How did you learn to become proficient or excellent in this area?
  - Can you identify any procedural (when... then...) rules that you have been following, either explicitly or implicitly?
  - Has reflection played any part in the development of these?
  - How could reflection help you to improve your skills in this area?
- Returning to your CBT practice, try to bring to mind one example of your current procedural rules (when... then...) that help you to deliver effective evidence-based CBT?
- Put this rule into words and try to identify how you developed or learned this rule (e.g. reading, teaching, supervision, clinical experience).

Engaging your *reflective system* as you read the chapters in this book

- Thinking about both your work and wider personal life, what helps you to engage and use your reflective skills? What might you need to put in place to effectively reflect on the ideas, tools and exercises in this book?
- What might act as a potential barrier to effective reflection? For example, time, pressure, distraction, tiredness, memory. How might you take action to troubleshoot these potential barriers?

SUGGESTED READING

Bennett-Levy, J. (2006). Therapist skills: a cognitive model of their acquisition and refinement. *Behavioural and Cognitive Psychotherapy*, 34(1), 57–78.

2

BRINGING CBT SUPERVISION ALIVE:

Maximising the Role of Supervisor and Supervisee Reflection

Richard Thwaites and Beverly Haarhoff

LEARNING AIMS

- To develop declarative knowledge concerning the key role of reflection across a range of CBT supervision models
- To understand the key roles of supervisor and supervisee in maximising the reflective component of supervision
- To develop your own procedural rules that make reflection more likely to occur within your supervision as a supervisee (and also as a supervisor, if applicable)

INTRODUCTION

Reflection has regularly been identified as one of the key process within effective learning (Bennett–Levy, 2006; Kolb, 1984) and therefore as an essential element of effective supervision (Milne, 2009). This was supported by a survey of UK CBT course leaders (Townend, 2008) which suggested that reflection was one of the processes "at the heart of decision making within cognitive behavioural psychotherapy supervision, and thus linked to the learning processes of supervision" (p. 334).

The role of reflection can be seen to be central to each aspect of supervision. For example, consider the definition of supervision developed by Milne (2007) which details the management, support, development and evaluation of therapy in the context of a supervisory relationship. Reflection is required on the part of the supervisee and supervisor in order to maximise the effectiveness of the supervisory relationship (and troubleshoot when it runs into difficulties), reflection is absolutely essential to using supervision to learn from clinical experience, and reflection is one source of information to support the evaluation and governance function of supervision. This assertion of the key role of reflection in outcome supervision has been supported by competency frameworks for supervisors (e.g. Roth & Pilling, 2007b), ratings scales of supervisory competence (e.g. James, Blackburn, Milne & Freeston, 2004) and a small number of research studies (Milne, Aylott, Fitzpatrick & Ellis, 2012; Townend, 2008).

The DPR model of skill development, which is at the core of this book (see Chapter 1), emphasises the role of reflection within supervision in a number of ways (Bennett-Levy, 2006; Bennett-Levy & Thwaites, 2007). For example, it proposes that supervision allows time for the supervisee to focus their attention on the clinical content of their sessions, or reflection-on-action, as described by Schön (1983), and to identify and develop the "when… then…" and "if… then…" rules that guide their behaviour during sessions. This might involve experiential methods such as modelling or role-playing (Bennett-Levy, McManus et al., 2009), which would be combined with reflection and planning to allow the learning to be assimilated and put into practice in a future session. Later in the chapter we will provide specific examples of how the DPR model can help the supervisor and supervisee be guided by a structured, six-stage process to optimally engage the reflective system, identify and formulate a focus for supervisory intervention, and establish a way forward.

Although this chapter clearly argues the case for reflection being essential for effective supervision, a word of caution needs to be applied around the limits of reflection in developing skills and knowledge within clinical supervision. Kilminster and Jolly (2000) warn that while reflection is central to supervision, "total reliance on reflection may not always be appropriate in supervision because beginners need direction" (p. 831). Reflection is only one of the components required for effective supervision, particularly for novices, who are likely to require more direction and scaffolding in order to be able to use reflection effectively (James, Milne & Morse, 2008). Other important processes include conceptualising, experiencing, experimenting and planning (Milne, 2009; Milne, Aylott, Fitzpatrick & Ellis, 2012). However, as we will see, reflection would be required as an element of these other activities to some degree.

In this chapter we will review some of the main CBT models of supervision and examine the role of reflection within these. We will identify what supervisors and supervisees can do to ensure that their supervision promotes active reflection both *within* the session and *outside* the session. What use is therapist reflection if it only happens once per week (or worse, once per month) within clinical supervision? One of the aims of clinical supervision has to be the enhancement of the supervisee's ability to reflect before, during and after clinical sessions. Chapter 3 provides a framework for supervisees to use outside clinical supervision to apply similar principles via a self-supervision framework.

This chapter also examines how reflective processes can be enhanced by both supervisor and supervisee stance and behaviours. Although the chapter focuses in the main upon one-to-one CBT supervision, some thought will be given to the roles for reflection in other supervision contexts, such as group or pair supervision and clinical case management supervision.

CURRENT CBT SUPERVISION MODELS

The standard format

The standard format of a CBT supervision session would include many elements that parallel CBT therapy, for example an identification of a focus or problem and subsequent goals, an agenda, guided discovery, behavioural experiments and tools to clarify understanding and evoke initial reflection round an identified focus (e.g. discussion of therapist beliefs, role-plays, usage of recordings, self-ratings, thought diaries, etc.) (Blackburn et al., 2001; Grey, Deale, Byrne & Liness, 2014).

One of the earliest descriptions of CBT supervision clearly acknowledges the role of what we would see as reflection (while not necessarily using the term) (Padesky, 1996). The initial questions recommended establish the most helpful content and method for that supervision session (e.g. "*How can I help you today?*", "*How would you prioritise your concerns?*", *What mode or focus of supervision do you think would be most helpful?*"). These questions ask the supervisee to start reflecting from the very start of the supervision session (or before).

Once a focus and method has been agreed, Padesky encourages the further use of reflective questions to identify and formulate potential blocks to the successful process of CBT ("*What is happening or not happening in therapy that leads to your question?*", "*At what point do your interventions break down?*") For example, she refers to the use of experiential methods such as a role-play of a specific intervention with a client, and then follows this up with reflective questions around how such interventions would usually proceed and how difficulties arise with that particular client. So far she has established a situation where both supervisee and supervisor are primed to access specific detail about the supervisee's knowledge and skills, and the implementation of these with a specific client. Padesky then suggests that the supervisee should be asked to consider "what client beliefs or interpersonal process might be impeding progress" (Padesky, 1996, p. 283). At this point, the supervisee is being asked to bring together, and assimilate, their knowledge of the client (including potential client beliefs) and their knowledge of CBT models. Future models of CBT supervision remain broadly consistent with this original description but have become more specific, structured and detailed based on developing theory and, to a lesser extent, the slowly-developing evidence base around supervisory processes.

Evidence-Based Clinical Supervision model

Over the past decade, Milne and colleagues (e.g. Milne, 2009; Milne et al., 2012) have attempted to examine clearly and define both the evidence base for clinical supervision and also the evidence for specific methods and strategies within supervision. Milne places Kolb's (1984) influential experiential learning model at the heart of his various supervision models (e.g. Milne & James, 2005), including his most recent model of Evidence-Based Clinical Supervision (EBCS) (Milne, 2009). The EBCS aims to be applicable to a wider range of therapeutic orientations. It examines research from across the supervision field but remains consistent with the principles of CBT supervision.

The EBCS delineates 12 key supervision principles around all aspects of supervision. Of particular note is its discussion of the learning cycle which reformulates Kolb's model to include later models of learning. One major distinction is the move towards five aspects of the learning cycle, these being: *experiencing* (with the emphasis on emotion), *reflecting, conceptualising, planning* and *experimenting* (with the emphasis on action). Milne also acknowledges criticisms of Kolb's model, such as its lack of emphasis on the system within which learning occurs and that it is too psychological (specifically, too cognitive), problems which both the EBCS model and the Newcastle "cake stand" model (discussed below) (Armstrong & Freeston, 2006) attempt to address. Although Milne suggests that *cognitive reflection* is one of the key elements in effective supervision (e.g. to create tension or a dialectic, to make meaning or generate solutions), he also acknowledges that the model does not have to follow a linear process. Using our wider definition of reflection (see Chapter 1), the act of reflection would also be consciously promoted by effective supervisors in the other learning cycle stages described by him, such as heightening affective awareness (experiencing), connecting to the knowledge-base (conceptualisation) and also in applying to ongoing work (experimenting). In each of these stages, reflective and self-reflective skills will be required and we would see his example questions as reflection-promoting questions, for example, "*What were you feeling when the client wept?*", "*Which negative reactions do you have to this event?*" (Milne, 2009, p. 124). Clinical supervision, when correctly carried out according to this manualised supervision protocol, is likely to be rich in reflective processes.

Newcastle "cake stand" model

Another recent multi-layered model of CBT supervision, the Newcastle "cake stand" model (Armstrong & Freeston, 2006), has described a comprehensive framework of supervision covering all aspects of supervision, from the primary inputs to the moment-by-moment learning process. Space does not allow us to go into such a complex model in this chapter. However, reflection is a fundamental part of all four layers of this model (learning processes, dynamic focus, parameters and primary inputs), which emphasises the explicit acknowledgement of both content and process. In common with many supervision models, Armstrong and Freeston emphasise the process of reflection within a Kolbian learning cycle (Kolb, 1984) at the level of **learning process**. However, the level below, of **dynamic focus** (tracking the moment-to-moment focus with the session), forces supervisee and supervisor to reflect on, and ideally be explicit about, the content on which the process is focusing. Foci for supervision include: the context, the supervision process, the supervisee, the therapeutic relationship, the therapeutic task and safety.

At the initial level of **primary inputs**, Armstrong and Freeston acknowledge the role of the context, supervisee, supervisor and client, and the need to be aware of what is unchangeable (e.g. gender, service demands), but also what is *chosen* to be brought to the supervision session. Reflecting on the characteristics and beliefs, for example, of the supervisor and supervisee, allows both to explicitly acknowledge the potential for under- or over-match and where this may lead to problems. The explicitness of this model can be used to enhance reflection for both parties. It provides a shared framework and language within which awareness of content and process can be brought to attention and discussed.

Cognitive-interpersonal supervision model

In addition to the main CBT supervision models, the influence of Jeremy Safran (e.g. Safran, 1998; Safran & Muran, 2000) cannot be underestimated, especially with respect to the role of the therapeutic relationship and associated ruptures (see Chapter 4 for a fuller description of the Cognitive-Interpersonal model). While Safran does not necessarily refer to reflection, his writings emphasise what we would describe as therapist reflection both within clinical and supervision sessions. For example, he describes the "therapist's observational stance" and the inner work of the therapist in reflecting on material that is evoked during therapy. Safran and Muran (2000) highlight the process of mindfulness and its three components, namely attentional focus, remembering and non-judgemental awareness, arguing that these are required for the therapist to become aware of thoughts, feelings and action tendencies (before acting on them) in order to avoid being "pulled into" cognitive-interpersonal cycles or reciprocal roles. For them, increased self-awareness on the part of the therapist is required to identify their own experience, to formulate and to avoid unhelpful interactions (or to act skilfully to repair therapeutic ruptures from previous actions). As a result, their focus for supervision is largely on self-exploration of the supervisee experience.

While CBT supervision would tend to have a far wider focus than the interpersonal process, much of Safran's work remains highly relevant to CBT practitioners, particularly for those working with clients with more enduring interpersonal problems. Many of the ways of learning described in this approach would be recommended in reflective CBT supervision, from the use of audio- and visual recordings to the use of awareness-oriented role-plays and supervisors and therapists "thinking aloud", that is reflecting on and commenting on their internal processes (e.g. emotions and procedural knowledge, such as when…then rules) during a role-play or while reviewing a recording.

Interestingly, Safran and Muran (2000) also suggest that a similar model applies to impasses within the supervisory relationship and the need for both parties to collaboratively examine their own contributions to these. This is a theme that we will return to in a later section examining the ways that supervisors and supervisees can use reflection to maximise the benefit for supervision.

Six-stage process model

A six-stage model has been developed based on the DPR model of skills development (Bennett-Levy, 2006). This model was developed largely to address difficulties in the therapeutic relationship, but is to a high degree applicable to any "stuck scenario" when the integration of theory and client- and therapist-specific information is required (Bennett-Levy & Thwaites, 2007). The reflective system is at the heart of this model. Figure 2.1 provides a representation of the various stages of this model. Table 2.1 describes the various stages and provides an example of how the model can be operationalised to address an impasse identified by a supervisee working with an individual with health anxiety.

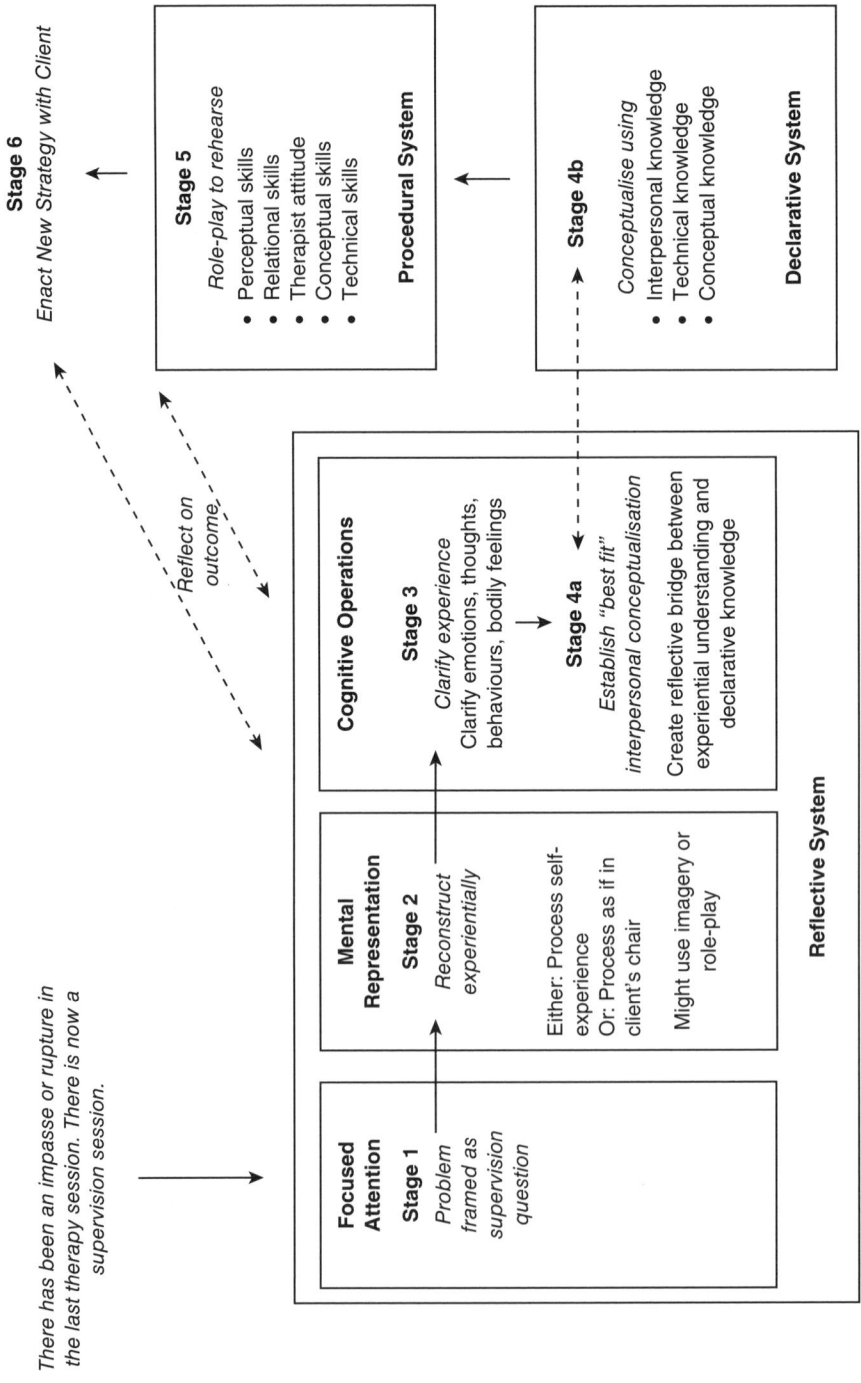

FIGURE 2.1 *The six-stage process model (adapted with permission from Bennett-Levy & Thwaites, 2007, p. 266)*

TABLE 2.1 *Using the six-stage model in practice (adapted from Bennett-Levy & Thwaites, 2007)*

Stage	Stage description	Example
Stage 1: Focus on and frame the problem	The supervisee arrives at the session with some sense of a problem with a client. It may be that the supervisee senses there has been a problem or difficulty within the session (even if they cannot recognise what it was) or it may be that the client response to treatment is differing from what they expected. At this stage the supervisee and supervisor need to reflect on their shared knowledge, of both the client and *supervisee*, to attempt to identify a focus for the supervision.	Joseph came to supervision slightly confused but aware that there was a problem in his therapy with Tara, a client with a diagnosis of health anxiety that he had been working with for six sessions. In discussion, Joseph identified that he felt annoyed and disappointed, stating that "the client wasn't working hard enough and I'm not sure that she wants to get better." He felt frustrated and thought Tara might be on the verge of dropping out.
Stage 2: Evoke mental representation of the experience	During this stage (*mental representation*), the issue is brought to mind. The key task is for the supervisor to help the supervisee to evoke a direct experiential awareness of the feelings, thoughts and behaviours activated at the time of the session. Here the supervisor helps the supervisee to reconstruct his/her experience during the session, e.g. using role-play, imagery work or reviewing recorded material with a specific focus.	Sam (supervisor) suggested that it might be useful for Joseph to show her a short clip from a recent session where he felt most frustrated. During the viewing of this clip, Joseph was prompted to close his eyes and observe what he was feeling (emotionally and physically) and thinking. He was able to describe *his* planned goals for the session and also notice that the client was not following "the plan" (his plan) for the session. During one interaction where Tara explained that she had been unable to refrain from seeking reassurance during the week (and then proceeded to seek reassurance from Joseph in the session), Joseph was able to identify that he felt his whole body tense up, he had a churning feeling in his stomach and felt annoyed and angry at Tara.

(Continued)

TABLE 2.1 (Continued)

Stage	Stage description	Example
Stage 3: Clarifying the experience	During Stage 3, the aim is for the supervisee to be supported to reflect upon, and clarify, their experience in the session. The supervisor can help the supervisee to experience the session from either the therapist's or client's perspective in a subjective, experiential, "how-it-felt" mode. The aim is to increase both the supervisee's and the supervisor's understanding of the emotions and cognitions experienced during the session.	Joseph was encouraged to reflect upon his experience and notice his physical sensations, feelings and thoughts. During this exercise, he was able to identify his own annoyance and anger, which he could track back to thoughts around the client (e.g. *"She's just not trying hard enough", "Why should I have to keep covering the same ground, I'm wasting my time", "She's not following my plan"*). Further probing around how this felt revealed that the anger was probably to some extent due to Joseph's thoughts about himself as a therapist, which led to considerable in-session anxiety (*"This is my fault, I just don't know enough about health anxiety", "I'm just not good enough"*). In addition, time was spent exploring the client experience. Joseph was asked to close his eyes and describe Tara's early experiences of difficult parental deaths (using information he already had). He was also asked to describe the client's day-to-day experience of health anxiety and then asked to define what the client might say about her difficulties in reducing her reassurance-seeking during the preceding week. Finally, Joseph was asked to describe how Tara might have been feeling during their interaction. He identified that there were signs that Tara felt criticised and potentially shamed by her "failure", and that she might have started to withdraw somewhat.
Stage 4: Conceptualising the experience	During Stage 4, there is a shift in the mode of processing from the experiential mode of Stage 3 to a more conceptual mode. The key process is bringing the Reflective (Stage 4a) and Declarative Systems together (Stage 4b) to create a "reflective bridge." This allows the supervisee to use the enhanced experiential understanding together with declarative knowledge to create a conceptualisation of the problem.	Sam and Joseph were able to create an understanding of the process which brought together Joseph's considerable declarative knowledge with his experience with n the session. Although Joseph had had experience and success in working with other anxiety disorders, he had had little experience of health anxiety and struggled to generalise his learning. As an experienced therapist, he felt pressure to be knowledgeable and struggled with this gap in his experience of this particular disorder. He coped with this by planning the sessions in detail, which caused him to become rigid in his style and unable to hear what the client was saying or have an experiential understanding of the client's problems (despite intellectually understanding the difficulties). Unusually, he felt annoyed with Tara rather than feeling his usual warmth. The failure of the therapy was causing him to plan more tightly, and hear Tara even less, which led to a point at which she was probably close to disengagement.

Stage	Stage description	Example
Stage 5: Practice procedural skills	Conceptualisation of the situation, using Interpersonal and Conceptual Knowledge, allows the supervisor and supervisee to identify potential ways of addressing the problem. Such a plan uses a role-play to rehearse putting the appropriate procedural skills into practice.	Joseph had decided to explicitly discuss the last session with Tara. He and the supervisor used a role-play to practise this in supervision. During this role-play he described watching the recording of the session and noticing that he had felt frustrated and hadn't really fully heard what Tara had been saying or how difficult she was finding it to reduce her reassurance-seeking. He explained that he wanted to apologise and wondered how it had felt for her.

Role-playing Tara, the supervisor was touched by the genuineness and openness of Joseph's response and fed this back to him. Joseph planned to acknowledge his role in any rupture, check out Tara's experience and also "loosen" his planning of future sessions. |
| **Stage 6: Try out new strategy** | Once a strategy has been identified and refined, it can be tried out with the client (Stage 6). | At the next session Joseph implemented his plan. He reported noticing an immediate softening and relaxing in Tara's body language. While she acknowledged that she had felt criticised, she was surprised and refreshed by the honesty of the therapist. They agreed on a plan about discussing how to address such feelings if they came up again. As therapy progressed, further discussion regarding this topic was not needed and the therapy proceeded smoothly towards a successful outcome. |
| **Beyond Stage 6** | Following implementation of the previous stages, the supervisee can often gain further benefit from examining whether the problem is part of wider pattern within (or also outside) therapy sessions. This can lead to further self-focused work within self-supervision (see Chapter 3). | Joseph was able to identify that in his new role as a supervisor he had felt pressure to "know everything" and was feeling outside his usual comfort zone. He had noticed that the thought of not being "good enough" as a CBT therapist (*Therapist Attitude/Belief*) had been more frequent recently, both with clients and also with supervisees, and that his responses had tended to be counterproductive, inhibiting his usual productive style.

Joseph explained that he had noticed that some of the anxious feelings about not being good enough reminded him of how he had felt as school, where he struggled academically. He was aware that these thoughts were not new and that he had a range of behaviours he used to cope with this (e.g. avoid new activities that he wasn't good at, or try too hard or aim for perfection). He made a plan to work on noticing such thoughts in other situations and then plan and review some specific behavioural experiments in his self-supervision. This is similar to the notions of "developmental" and "transformational" learning, as described by Carroll (2010). |

As the example demonstrates, reflection can play a key role within supervision in terms of clarifying, formulating and addressing therapeutic difficulties. In the above example, this was made easier by the fact that Sam and Joseph had a history of working together (and a subsequent high degree of mutual trust and respect), which provided an environment in which Joseph felt safe enough to be honest about his own role in the "stuckness". He was also brave and honest enough to acknowledge his role in the situation to the client without any defensiveness. During the next section we will examine the roles of both supervisees and supervisors in maximising reflection within supervision, both when it is going well and also when there are ruptures in the supervisory relationship.

WHAT CAN SUPERVISEES AND SUPERVISORS DO TO ENHANCE REFLECTION IN SUPERVISION?

Supervisor role

"Become a facilitator for learning; teach if you must." (Carroll, 2009)

Contracting for reflection

For supervisors, maximising reflection within supervision starts with the first supervisor–supervisee conversations and the establishment of the supervision contract. Even if the supervisor has previously supervised large numbers of supervisees, they need to ask key questions not just about the declarative and procedural knowledge already held by the supervisee (and subsequent gaps and aims for supervision), but also about the process and learning style of the supervisee. Carroll (2009) provides examples of potentially useful areas for reflective discussion that can be adapted for the stage and language of the supervisee, including: "*What is your learning style?*", "*How can I help you learn and support you?*", "*What blocks your learning?*", "*How might differences between us impact on your learning?*" and "*In brief, how can I best supervise you?*" Scaife (2010) further suggests specific questions, such as "*How will you let me know when you want me to enquire into your ideas and when you want me to tell you what I think?*", and questions around how best to give feedback and avoid or address ruptures, for example "*Would you prefer to invite me to give you feedback or give me a free rein?*", "*How might you react if I were to hurt your feelings?*". These questions indicate a transparency around the process (encouraging honesty and openness) but also provide useful information for both parties about potential relationship rupture markers. At this point, the groundwork can be established to ensure both that an appropriately honest and reflective relationship is established and that supervision is appropriately individualised for the supervisee, in the same way that we would adapt therapy to the client according to their individualised formulation.

Establish a relationship within which reflection can flourish

Although there is clear professional consensus on the value of the supervisory relationship or alliance, to date the research evidence is limited. However, in line with the majority of therapists, supervisors and theorists, we make the assumption that the supervisory alliance is crucial in ensuring the effectiveness of supervision, specifically the reflective component of supervision. While the supervision will be based on the learning needs of the supervisee, the supervisor has significant responsibility for establishing an effective supervisory relationship within which reflection can flourish. A key question that supervisors may ask is "*What kind of supervisory relationship do we need to develop and how do we do this?*" Although there is a range of views on this, there is surprising consensus across theorists and researchers on what kinds of relationship need to be developed for effective reflection to occur. The main themes are:

- Having a clear structure, including transparency around the process
- Providing a "safe base" and creating a climate of trust and safety: Milne (2009) suggests that this can be achieved by having shared expectations, empathic and emotional connections (e.g. self-disclosure), being warm and responsive to learning needs, and avoiding criticism
- Showing commitment to the process by demonstrating interest and enthusiasm (Milne 2009), being prepared and giving full attention (Scaife, 2010)
- Creating an environment where "not knowing" is permissible or even encouraged – "manufacture uncertainty" (Carroll, 2009)
- Thoughtfully managing feedback (Scaife, 2010)
- Being aware of potential cultural differences and being proactive in addressing these (see Chapter 5)
- Ensuring experiential learning (Armstrong & Freeston, 2006; Carroll, 2009; Milne, 2009)
- Evaluating, monitoring and addressing the supervision process (Carroll, 1996)
- Seeking feedback on your supervision (Armstrong & Freeston, 2006; Carroll, 2009; Milne, 2009).

Misunderstandings and ruptures *will* occur in supervision despite the above. Reflecting on the process of supervision, especially when a block is reached, may lead to particularly reflective and powerful learning experiences (for both parties). The above suggestions provide a clear structure and increase the permissibility of reflecting on, and formulating, the supervisory relationship. However, this can be challenging and requires an open, non-defensive stance from both supervisor and supervisee to explore what might be occurring within the supervisory relationship at that point. Many of the principles for addressing interpersonal ruptures within therapy remain applicable here, for example identify markers, try and step back (or disembed) from the current process, establish a sense of "we-ness" or shared responsibility, and explore the experience emphasising one's own subjectivity and responsibility (Safran & Muran, 2000). If difficulties within supervision are taken to the supervisor's own supervision, the six-stage model (Bennett-Levy & Thwaites, 2007) previously discussed can be used to formulate and plan how these can be addressed. For an example of this, see Milne, Leck and Choudhri (2009).

Specific actions that can enhance reflection

While supervision is based around the needs of the supervisee, sometimes the supervisor is best placed to identify specific learning needs or gaps in knowledge or skills. A key task of the supervisor is to raise certain issues for discussion around whether these need to become a focus for supervision. Markers of a potential requirement for reflection could include: negative client feedback, high rates of non-attendance or unplanned endings, a client failing to respond or deteriorating, a therapeutic rupture, difficulty in discharging a client or strong feelings about a client. These markers could be related to a specific client or, in some instances, could be broader, for example, declarative knowledge, procedural skills or attitudes or beliefs around a specific diagnosis or aspect of CBT (e.g. contracting, formulation, agenda setting, behavioural experiments). Haarhoff and Kazantzis (2007) have examined these processes in detail for the supervision of homework setting by trainee therapists. They provide an example of a CBT formulation of a potential supervisee, including thoughts (e.g. "*Homework tasks will make the client feel overstructured and controlled*", "*Homework assignments will be overwhelming for clients who are distressed*"), feelings (e.g. anxiety, frustration) and behaviours (e.g. avoiding assigning homework or assigning homework in a suboptimal way that perpetuates the belief). They provide examples of how this can subsequently be addressed in supervision using standard CBT tools, but also using mini-examples of self-practice and self-reflection. Haarhoff (2006) and Haarhoff and Kazantzis (2007) explore how supervision can be used to identify both automatic thoughts around aspects of CBT and how they may at times be indicative of more generalised beliefs, whether relating to the "therapist self" or the "personal self".

It is essential that supervision is able to meet the learning needs of the supervisee, and a number of writers have emphasised the work of Vygotsky, in particular the Zone of Proximal Development (Vygotsky, 1978). With this in mind, Gordon (2012) has stressed the need to check the supervisee's level of understanding, which serves to ensure that the supervisor does not tell them what they already know, and does not assume an understanding that is not present. For example, if a supervisee were to bring to supervision a client diagnosed as suffering from OCD whom they were struggling to treat using exposure and response prevention (ERP), it would be reasonable to check on their understanding both of OCD and ERP principles before attempting to troubleshoot any stuck points. James, Milne and Morse (2008) have emphasised the use of questions and platforms (e.g. summaries, feedback, integrative statements) as forms of scaffolding that ensure that reflection and learning opportunities are at a level that the supervisee can effectively utilise. For example, they would suggest following the previous examples of questions with further platforms to build on what the supervisee already knows. Using this example, it might be that the supervisee has very little knowledge of the maintenance of anxiety disorders, to the extent that the supervisor has to provide information. Ideally, however, the supervisor would be able to ask reflective questions to bring into the supervisee's awareness relevant information that can act as scaffolding. For example, the supervisor might ask the supervisee what they know about other anxiety disorders and about the processes that maintain a sense of threat in those disorders. Once the supervisee had a clear idea about the level of supervisee understanding, they could use a probe question to make the link with OCD, for example *"Given what you have just told me, can you think of any ways that these processes could be relevant in maintaining this individual's OCD?"*, *"In what ways is this similar?"* *"In what ways is this different?"* This could then lead on to agreement around a treatment plan and the role-playing of a potential way forward.

Supervisees can also use structured reflective forms to capture supervisor feedback and any learning that has occurred within the supervision session. Such tools can provide scaffolding around learning from supervision and also make it more likely that learning will be enacted and embedded. See Ularntinon and Friedberg (2015) for an example of such a tool.

Reflecting on your own supervisory skills

It almost goes without saying that supervisors need to reflect on their supervision in order to ensure it is safe and effective, but also to continue developing as supervisors. This can occur within or after the session, but also within supervision of supervision. The self-supervision tools and methods discussed in Chapter 3 can also be adapted for this purpose.

Supervisee role

Until relatively recently the supervision literature paid scant attention to the role of the supervisee in ensuring supervision was an effective learning process. This was partly rectified by recent chapters and books by Caroll and Gilbert (2011), Knapman and Morrison (1998), Milne (2009) and Grey, Deale, Byrne and Liness (2014), which clearly describe the role and responsibilities of the supervisee in effective supervision. In this book we emphasise the active nature of effective reflection and it is clear that both supervisor and supervisee play an important role in ensuring that supervision becomes and, more challengingly, remains a place where genuine reflection takes place. Without reflection, supervision is limited in its ability to be a learning experience, and while it can guide people with individual cases, it is unlikely to help the practitioner develop metacompetence, as Roth and Pilling (2007b) make clear:

> The **ability to "reflect"** and to undertake accurate self-appraisal is a critical part of adult learning. This implies a capacity both to be open to experience while it is happening, and to review – and hence learn – from experience after it has occurred. This is critical because reflection is one of the ways in which learners learn for themselves; without this skill they will find it hard to shift from a position of being dependent on others. (Roth & Pilling, 2007b, p. 11)

The supervisee has their own significant contribution to make towards supervision becoming a place for genuine reflection and new learning.

Ensuring optimal inputs to supervision

Supervision can only function effectively with the appropriate inputs. For reflection to be facilitated the supervisee needs to provide the "raw material". There is considerable variation in the usage of therapy recordings, but one consistent observation is that supervisees (whatever their reluctance or anxieties about recording sessions) almost invariably report that sessions utilising such recordings are more effective and more productive than those relying on therapist recall and report alone. At the very least, in the absence of a recording, the supervisee would ensure that supervision included sufficient clinical information for genuine reflection and discussion, such as clinical notes, letters, a reflective diary or post-session reflective notes (e.g. *"What did I notice during the session?"*, *"How did I feel?"*, *"What did I feel in my body?"*, *"Was there anything I avoided saying or doing?"*, *"Did anything get in the way of my therapeutic behaviour?"*, *"Did I feel pulled into behaving a certain way?"*) The supervisee would then formulate a supervision question, whether around a general clinical theme or a specific client. This automatically engages the supervisee in reflecting about what they want to get out of the supervision session and what it is they need to know, do or experience. In order to ensure the successful bridging between supervision sessions and effective learning, the supervisee will also need to have reflected on the previous supervision session and subsequent actions and learning.

Contributing to a relationship within which reflection can flourish

Clinical supervision is a collaborative process where supervisor and supervisee share responsibility for the process and outcome (Grey et al., 2014). One of the bedrocks of the process is honesty on the part of the supervisee – honesty about difficult feelings, such as anxiety or thoughts of not being good enough or needing to appear a certain way to the supervisor. Without the courage to admit that they don't know something or that maybe they got something wrong, there is a limit to potential new learning. Some supervisees admit to bringing their best tapes to supervision rather than those of stuck sessions or perceived mistakes. While there is a place within supervision for the celebration of successful sessions (a lot can be learnt from such sessions), being honest about the purpose of such discussions or review is essential. So as a supervisee, when something has gone well, discuss this in supervision and examine what can be learnt (e.g. *"What did you do?"*, *"How can the learning be applied in future?"*). If the session has not gone well or there has been stuckness or a less than optimal display of competence during a moment in the session, then this is also grist for the mill. A willingness to trust the supervisor and suspend excessive worry about their potential judgement is fundamental.

Being willing to acknowledge (and stay with) our thoughts and feelings

If supervision is always comfortable (or predictable), it is probably not a good use of either the supervisee's or the supervisor's time. While we would not underplay the supportive aspects of supervision, it can be about using that supportive relationship in the service of therapist development, for example, developing an increasing awareness of previously avoided thoughts or feelings that are getting in the way of successful therapy, or challenging the supervisee to think about different ways of doing things (increasing creativity rather than maintaining a therapeutic rut). At times it can be about thinking about the clients that the supervisee chooses not to bring to supervision, perhaps those with potential elements of collusion (for example, where avoidance of discharge is outweighing current therapeutic benefit) or shame (for example, the therapist is stuck and thinks they *should* know what to do). This is one of the benefits of clinical case management supervision (discussed later in the chapter) where all clients are discussed.

Providing honest feedback on supervision

A specific aspect of maintaining an effective supervision relationship is honest feedback on useful, and less useful, aspects of the supervision session. All supervisees are different, with differing learning styles, and being clear and explicit with a supervisor will enable the supervisor to tweak what they do to maximise future learning.

ENHANCING REFLECTION ACROSS ALL TYPES OF SUPERVISION

This chapter has focused largely on traditional one-to-one clinical supervision. However, we recognise that this is only one type of supervision. Many CBT courses utilise group or dyadic supervision. The nature of supervision is also influenced by training course, service and national context (Armstrong & Freeston, 2006). For example, Milne (2009) has suggested that in the UK the Improving Access to Psychological Therapies Programme (IAPT) (Department of Health, 2008) has "shifted attention away from the supervisor and explicitly onto the patient" (p. 51), with a change in emphasis from supervision as being "a series of caring and supportive interactions" to ensuring "treatment fidelity, in order to maximise the welfare and safety of all clients". This shift is in line with the roots of the IAPT programme, which emphasised faithfully delivering evidence-based therapies as one would expect within a research trial. However, despite this focus, the national guidance of the IAPT programme does specifically refer to "Staff support and the prevention of burn out" as a secondary function of supervision (Turpin & Wheeler, 2011).

Anecdotal evidence suggests that the change in emphasis predicted by Milne (2009) has occurred but the challenge remains for services to deliver supervision which supports treatment fidelity, develops the clinical skills and knowledge of staff while also fulfilling the supportive functions which prevent burnout within a medium to long-term, high-volume environment. Outside the IAPT programme and the UK, this challenge is likely to be replicated in the context of improving outcomes with decreased health expenditure. The key question we ask, and hope to start to answer, within the final section of this chapter is how we can ensure that the reflection component of supervision does not become lost or sidelined as a result of contextual demands? With this in mind, we review the role of reflection across a broader range of supervision types.

Supervision dyads

Within this section we are using the term "supervision dyads" to refer to a pair of supervisees, we are not referring to "peer supervision", in which there is no clearly identified supervisor (Milne, 2009). Most CBT therapists will have been supervised as part of a pair at some point in their training. Although this is often used due to ratios of available supervisors to supervisees, there are also significant benefits to this method of supervision, including exposure to the therapeutic style of another individual, the normalisation of therapeutic blocks, acceptance of therapist error and the space to reflect on therapeutic issues without the added complication of the involvement of the self. We have observed that while novice supervisors often deliver paired supervision as if it were individual supervision with an audience of one, which then rotates after an hour, experienced supervisors are able to fully utilise the pair in the service of the learning and development of both parties. Paired supervision provides the relatively rare context in which a supervisee is able to reflect on direct clinical content that does not involve their own content. If handled creatively and skilfully, this can provide a unique learning experience. The supervisor has a range of options which should be guided by the learning needs of:

1. The supervision dyad (e.g. Do they need encouragement to support each other? Do they need encouragement in critically challenging each other?)
2. The primary supervisee at that point (e.g. Are they struggling with empathy for the client? Are they missing key information which might inform their formulation? Are they able to reflect on therapy content but not on self-referent material, such as their own thoughts and feelings?)
3. The secondary supervisee at that point (e.g. Do they need to become more attuned to particular forms of client communication, such as body language? Can they learn specific technical aspects from their fellow supervisee, such as agenda setting or asking for feedback? Are there specific procedural rules that they can best learn outside a self-referent context, i.e. when their emotional state may be more neutral?)

For example, if the primary supervisee is struggling to understand the experience of the client during their clinical session, when watching the visual recording, the two supervisees could be allocated differing tasks: the primary supervisee (whose recording it is) could focus on trying to remember and key into their own emotional state and thoughts on a moment-by-moment basis, while the secondary supervisee could attempt to do something similar for the client. The recording could be paused and observations and suggestions could be shared at key moments throughout the session. This would allow a range of formulation options to be considered. Or, to achieve a similar aim, the primary supervisee could be tasked with trying to understand the emotional state of the client moment-by-moment, while the secondary supervisee might be tasked with specifically observing the therapist and trying to hypothesise what their therapeutic aims were at each moment in order to evoke discussion about procedural rules and how these are related to the moment-by-moment experience of the client.

The supervisory options are endless and limited only by the imagination of the three people in the room. Hopefully, over time the supervisees themselves might be able to suggest reflective tasks for each other that link in with their learning needs at that particular moment. In comparison with individual supervision, such supervision dyads allow for a different range of reflective experiences, assuming of course that the supervisor has been able to develop and maintain a reflective environment within the dyad, which would include "a sense of safeness, non-judgemental acceptance, affirmation, empathy, care, warmth and encouragement to explore..." (Bennett-Levy & Thwaites, 2007, p. 264).

Group supervision

For the purposes of efficiency (and often availability of experienced supervisors), many services and courses utilise group supervision for practitioners. Similar principles apply to those discussed in the previous section on individual supervision and supervision dyads, but with far greater challenge. The supervisor is required to create and maintain an environment within which reflection can be encouraged and mistakes and gaps in knowledge and skills are permissible and can be discussed in a non-judgemental manner. Scaife (2010) has suggested that reflection and focus are likely to be enhanced by a clear group structure (supported by contracting) in which "everyone has the opportunity to participate in ways that suit them, to ensure that ideas are critiqued, and that all contributions are treated respectfully" (p. 184). As Safran and Muran (2000) observe, "group supervision and case conference formats are particularly conducive to competitive attempts to come up with clever or insightful formulations" (p. 216). They suggest that care has to be taken to create an environment in which "'not knowing' is valued as much as 'knowing' in order for exploration to occur.

Again, different members or groups within the group can be tasked with specific reflective activities to ensure maximum learning. Supervisees can be encouraged to ask reflective questions of each other rather than instantly offering suggestions. If there is a shared and explicit Kolbian model (Kolb, 1984) underlying the group, supervisees can be socialised to support their colleagues in working around the learning cycle on any particular issue (from observing, to reflecting through, to planning and experience). The main tasks of the supervisor are to identify learning needs, provide structure, manage the group dynamics and provide scaffolding when required to support the learning (for example, by bringing in new information that the group does not have and reminding supervisees of information they already hold but have been unable to bring to mind and apply within that context).

Clinical case management supervision

As discussed earlier, the expansion of CBT-based low intensity interventions in the UK (Department of Health, 2008) has emphasised a new form of clinical supervision called clinical case management supervision (CCMS). This is defined as:

> the regular review of the caseloads of practitioners providing low intensity interventions within IAPT stepped care services. It is undertaken at regular (usually weekly), timetabled intervals and is informed by automated IT-based case management systems. A large number of cases will usually be discussed in any one supervision session. Discussions in case management supervision always include supervisee presentations of patients at pre-determined stages in their care pathway and/or who have particular clinical characteristics. (Turpin & Wheeler, 2011, p. 6)

This type of supervision is usually complemented with more traditional skills-based supervision which concentrates on the "development and maintenance of competence" (Turpin & Wheeler, 2011, p. 6). See Keegan (2013) for a fuller discussion of both types of supervision for low intensity practitioners. This type of supervision is also being utilised for CBT therapists as a way to ensure all clients are discussed, rather than just the ones that the therapist chooses to bring to traditional clinical supervision. This ensures that the clients that the therapist is avoiding reflecting on or bringing to supervision are still discussed and allows both supervisor and supervisees to check whether more detailed discussion is required.

The question of to what extent clinical case management supervision should, or could, include a reflective component requires discussion. The key aims of case management supervision are to maintain fidelity to the research base, ensure safe practice and to support clinicians in their decision-making. Such supervision is challenging due to the volume of clients that are required to be discussed within a relatively short space of time. Of course for some clinicians, learning about decision-making will implicitly occur from the discussion of individual clients, but the question remains of how to maximise case management as a learning experience for the practitioner which can develop and strengthen their decision-making capacity. Despite the challenges of such supervision, can we include brief elements of reflection which will aid the practitioner in learning from the clients discussed and the decisions made? What might this look like?

We suggest that there are a number of brief and simple ways in which learning can be maximised:

1. When discussing proposed decisions (e.g. stepping up to a different practitioner, referring to a different service) or treatment plans, always explicitly discuss what the rationale and aims for this would be. Although simple, it can often feel as if there is not enough time for this when trying to discuss 20 or more clients in one hour. Remembering to discuss rationales and aims makes it easier for the clinician to become aware of the rules guiding their decision-making and can also lead to discussion about their own thoughts and feelings on this topic.

2. When making suggestions or providing guidance, always check what the practitioner thinks the rationale for this might be, or, if time is limited, always clearly communicate the supervisor's rationale for decisions.
3. Finally, if time is available, spend just a few minutes at the end of the session reflecting on any particular themes that came up during case management and whether any of the discussions surprised or challenged the supervisees, brought up any significant feelings for them or led to new learning. If particular issues were identified, they may need to be taken to the more developmentally-focused clinical supervision for more detailed discussion.

CONCLUSION

Supervision is absolutely crucial in both facilitating reflection and developing reflective capacity. Both supervisor and supervisee have a responsibility for creating a structured supervisory relationship within which the supervisee feels safe enough to acknowledge mistakes, uncertainty or not-knowing. The supervisor is responsible for adapting and personalising supervision so that it is geared not just to the learning needs of the supervisee, but also to their individual learning style. We have reviewed the major CBT models and observed the shared emphasis on active reflection not only within a Kolbian learning cycle, but also on wider inputs to supervision, for example cultural and organisation factors.

Both parties are responsible for addressing ruptures and supervisory blocks in an honest and reflective manner. While supervision delivered in ways other than the standard one-to-one model may present some challenges, we hope that this chapter has provided some creative ideas and suggestions about how reflection may be maximised in less traditional supervision formats.

TAKING IT FORWARD

What *declarative knowledge* have you learnt from reading this chapter?

- What has stood out for you in reading this chapter? Has anything strongly resonated with (or challenged) a view of supervision you already held?
- Identify one thing that you have learnt?

What *procedural rules* are you starting to change or develop having reflected on this chapter?

As a supervisee

- Can you identify your contribution to your most helpful and productive supervision sessions? What exactly did you do? How did you prepare? What behaviours did you exhibit?
- Identify one clear "when… then…" rule that can guide your future behaviours in supervision sessions.

As a supervisor (if relevant)

- Think of a specific supervisee with whom you have experienced recent stuckness? As a supervisor, what specific action could you take to help this supervisee reflect more deeply on their clinical work?
- What specific actions might you need to *stop* doing to help them reflect?
- Does this apply with any of your other supervisees?
- Identify one clear '"when… then…" rule that can guide your future supervisory behaviours.

What are you going to put in place to facilitate the engagement of your *reflective system*?

As a supervisee

- What specific actions could you take to increase your reflection within clinical supervision?
- What circumstances or feelings act as barriers to reflection or "hijack" the supervision?

As a supervisor (if relevant)

- What helps you to reflect "in-action" during a supervision session? How could you facilitate this?
- How might you increase your access to information that enhances reflection on the supervision you provide? For example, can you ask for specific feedback, use supervisor rating scales, or use post-session reflection forms? How could you best use them to enhance your reflection on your supervisions sessions?

SUGGESTED READING

Corrie, S., & Lane, D. (2015). *CBT Supervision*. London: Sage.

Grey, N., Deale, A., Byrne, S., & Liness, S. (2014). Making CBT supervision more effective. In A. Whittington & N. Grey (Eds.), *How to become a more effective CBT therapist: mastering metacompetence in clinical practice* (pp. 269–283). Chichester, UK: Wiley.

Milne, D. (2009). *Evidence-based clinical supervision: principles and practice*. Chichester, UK: British Psychological Society/Blackwell.

3

DEVELOPING YOUR SELF-SUPERVISION PRACTICE:

Using Reflection to Increase Therapeutic Effectiveness and Enhance CBT Skill Development

Richard Thwaites and Beverly Haarhoff

LEARNING AIMS

- To understand the concept of self-supervision and identify how you can introduce this into your practice in order to troubleshoot stuck points in therapy and maximise your development of therapeutic skills and knowledge
- To understand and reflect on the three main phases of self-supervision:
  - Identifying a marker of a potential problem
  - Translating this into a focus or question for self-supervision (e.g. on a specific client, with regard to wider therapeutic patterns, or for therapist self-care)
  - Using self-supervision to combine clinical information and previously held CBT knowledge in order to come to a new understanding and plan for action to address the identified focus

INTRODUCTION

Reflection has been described as a metacompetence in itself, but also as a prerequisite to being able to develop other metacompetences (Thwaites, Bennett-Levy, Davis & Chaddock, 2014). Within sessions, reflection is needed to adapt evidence-based CBT protocols with skill, creativity and artistry, while remaining faithful to the underlying research (Whittington & Grey, 2014). Reflection also helps CBT therapists to identify when their self-referrent thoughts, feelings and behaviours have been evoked by client material (whether these are related to a specific client or to a wider therapeutic issue), and to notice whether this is having an unhelpful impact on their personal wellbeing and their ability to effectively provide therapy.

Clinical supervision is the usual structure to support such necessary reflection (see Chapter 2). However, many therapists receive supervision as little as once per month and, even when supervision is more frequent, some clients may never be discussed during the supervision hour. We would argue that the most effective therapists have developed the ability to "self-supervise", not as a replacement for, but as an adjunct to, traditional supervision, for the times prior to session, in-session or post-session where supervision is needed but is not available. Most definitions of self-supervision are very explicit about the limitations of self-supervision. They emphasise the role of self-supervision in identifying what content actually needs to be addressed further within traditional supervision (Chen & Englar-Carlson, 2003; Kottler, 2003).

We think that there is merit in the "resurrection" and definition of the concept of self-supervision in CBT. We do this by explicitly labelling a range of actions as self-supervision and providing clear procedural guidance on when, and how, to best engage in these. Our aim is to make it more likely that CBT therapists will engage in effective reflection during self-supervision and develop their reflective abilities within this framework. Increasing the reflective skills and problem-solving abilities of therapists *during self-supervision* is likely to lead to therapists being more able to use such skills *during therapy*, and thus to be able to troubleshoot moment-to-moment or even anticipate potential blockages or ruptures.

Previous definitions of self-supervision

In the supervision literature, self-supervision has been referred to since the late 1970s across a range of fields and, in the world of psychological therapies, across a number of therapeutic orientations. There have been occasional mentions of self-supervision in the CBT literature (e.g. Bennett-Levy & Thwaites, 2007; Leith, McNiece & Fusilier, 1989) but not necessarily with the degree of definition and guidance required to support novice CBT therapists in developing their own procedural rules about when and how to best engage in self-supervision.

Many definitions of self-supervision emphasise the self-monitoring elements of self-supervision, for example seeing self-supervision as "a process whereby therapists self-monitor their therapeutic behaviour, comparing this behaviour with some model of effective behaviour, with the intent of changing their behaviour to resemble this model more closely" (Todd, 1997, p.18). Jones and Harbach similarly emphasise the self-monitoring aspect, but also two additional key features of the process, formulating it as "a *systematic* process in which professionals work *independently* to *monitor* and direct their own professional development" (Jones & Harbach, 2003, p. 52, italics added).

There is also considerable overlap between definitions of traditional supervision (Milne, 2007) and self-supervision. Both are case-focused and contain elements of education and training, and both share similar functions (e.g. quality control, developing competence, helping therapists to work effectively). However, there is an important difference, namely, self-supervision lacks the governance function and external viewpoint of clinical supervision. The most obvious limitation here is that a therapist may lack self-understanding or self-awareness, resulting in blind spots. For example, a therapist may not be aware that there is a therapy problem to be addressed, or that their behaviour is unhelpful, or perhaps a therapist is ignorant of specific skills or has general skill deficits (Kottler, 2003).

As one would expect, definitions of self-supervision for psychological therapists often contain therapeutic orientation-specific aspects in addition to shared themes. For example, a psychoanalytic conceptualisation of self-supervision would emphasise increased self-awareness (Langs, 1979), and a solution-focused perspective would place greater emphasis on the recognition and development of therapeutic strengths over time (Morrissette, 2001). While there is not a great deal written about self-supervision within CBT to date, one description has been provided by Leith, McNiece and Fusilier (1989, p. 18):

> It is here that she determines the effectiveness and efficiency of her treatment program. It is here that she makes adjustments and corrections in her therapy. She adjusts her therapy to meet the ever-changing needs, attitudes, emotions, and physical state of her client. She adjusts to shifts in the client's motivation, attitudes towards therapy, cooperation, and other factors that influence therapy.

TOWARDS A NEW WORKING DEFINITION OF SELF-SUPERVISION WITHIN CBT

Our working definition of self-supervision captures previous relevant thinking in this area but is also sufficiently CBT-specific to lead to clear procedural guidance. Our definition includes case-based self-supervision and also the longitudinal elements that support the long-term development of therapist skills, knowledge and self-care. The definition also emphasises an increased awareness of thoughts (client- and self-referent), feelings, behaviours and physiology, types of client, and disorders. Most of all, a working definition of self-supervision in CBT needs to be specific enough to support individual therapists in developing their own procedural guidance on how best to engage in self-supervision and receive benefit from this.

Bennett-Levy, Thwaites et al. (2009) have previously defined reflection in CBT as "the process of intentionally focusing one's attention on a particular content; observing and clarifying this focus; and using other knowledge and cognitive processes (such as self-questioning, logical analysis and problem-solving) to make meaningful links" (p. 121). We agree with this definition of reflection and see it as one of the key activities within effective self-supervision. However, self-supervision encompasses a number of other features. In line with this, we use the term "self-supervision" within CBT to describe:

a regular, systematic self-directed process in which a therapist (using a range of inputs from self-monitoring and other feedback sources) identifies a need for different action and then intentionally focusses their attention on a particular content; observing and clarifying this focus; and using other knowledge and cognitive processes (such as self-questioning, logical analysis and problem-solving) to make meaningful links, which then lead to plans for activity (e.g. in a specific session, future sessions or a wider development activity or self-care activity). These plans are reviewed, evaluated and adjusted at a specific future point.

This definition emphasises some key features, including:

- the **regular** and **systematic** nature of self-supervision and suggests scheduling and adhering to self-supervision in the same way as traditional supervision (Jones & Harbach, 2003)
- the use of **self-monitoring** as a way of identifying the need for consideration of a particular client, disorder or professional issue
- the use of **reflection to access relevant material** (particularly self-reflection around self-referent material)
- the use of **various cognitive processes** to bring together sources of information and current knowledge
- the **planning of further action** (whether that be in a specific session, across sessions or out of session, for example seeking further information or supervision, taking part in a self-care activity)
- the **review, evaluation and adjustment** of actions at a specified future point.

HOW CAN A THERAPIST RECOGNISE THAT SELF-SUPERVISION IS INDICATED?

One of the initial tasks for a therapist interested in developing their own practice of self-supervision is to identify when this is most needed. A common challenge for many therapists will be finding time in their busy week to reflect on their clients outside their sessions. In our experience, this is one of the main barriers identified by staff (along with a lack of understanding of how to go about this). This chapter will provide a clear structure on how to self-supervise, but first the therapist has to find a way to make time for this during their working week. While reading this chapter, we would advise the reader to start to think about practical ways to implement any of the ideas that feel potentially useful. How will you make time for this? What activities could you drop to free up time? How will you remember to do what you think might be useful? Although it might feel like you haven't got enough time to reflect, think of it as an investment that will pay off in terms of skill development, effectiveness and your own wellbeing.

Some writers have suggested scheduling a planned time which is then adhered to in the same way that standard supervision would be, even in the face of workplace pressure (Jones & Harbach, 2003). This is particularly important for therapists beginning to apply the principles of self-supervision, where feeling overwhelmed or unsure of how to start the process could lead to avoidance.

Whether you are formally scheduling a self-supervision session or intending to use the principles in a more informal way, the first stage is to recognise when you need to put some time aside to self-supervise. The primary self-monitoring cues or markers are behavioural, affective and cognitive (Shepard & Morrow, 2003). The cues could be in relation to individual sessions, specific clients or wider practice issues (see Bennett-Levy and Thwaites (2007) and Sburlati and Bennett-Levy (2014) for additional information on this topic). Table 3.1 identifies important domains which can cue the need for self-supervision and provides examples.

TABLE 3.1 *Potential markers or cues indicating a need for self-supervision*

Marker domain	Example
Clinical measures (see Chapter 6)	• Client is failing to demonstrate any progress on clinical outcome measures • Mismatch between client report on measures and observed problem (suggesting under- or over-reporting)
Client feedback	• Client expresses doubts about the therapist's competence • Client contacts the service and asks to change their therapist • Client negatively comments on therapist once discharged (e.g. on client experience forms)
Therapist feelings (during, before or after session)	• Therapist experiences anxiety before each session with a client • Therapist finds themselves experiencing anger during a session (either directed at the client or at a significant other in the client's life) • Therapist repeatedly experiences boredom with a client or finds their mind wandering during the sessions (Shepard & Morrow, 2003; Wiseman & Scott, 2003) • Attraction towards, or excessive admiration for a client • Therapist feels too comfortable in session or finds themselves looking forward to the session as one would when seeing a friend
Therapist thoughts	• Indifference to the client (*"I don't care about this client"*) • "Stuckness" (*"I don't have a clue where to go now or how to get therapy back on track"*) • Avoidance (*"I know I need to have a difficult conversation with the client but it's always the wrong time and I keep putting it off"*) • Over-responsibility (*"I have to get this client better", "No one else could help this client but me"*) • Self-criticism (*"Anyone else would be able to help this client more", "I'm such a useless therapist"*) • Self-justifying lack of progress or deviation from evidence-based approaches by minimising research evidence or thinking that principles of CBT don't apply (*"The evidence base doesn't apply to my clients/this client, etc."*)
Therapist physical responses	• Sick feeling in pit of stomach ahead of session • Tightness in shoulders or torso following session • Lack of physical sensation or emptiness in the body during session

(Continued)

TABLE 3.1 *(Continued)*

Marker domain	Example
Therapist behaviours	• Failing to agree clear goals with the client • Difficulty sticking to the agreed agenda (or not even agreeing an agenda) • Repeatedly doing little of therapeutic benefit within a session, just trying to "make it through" • Finding yourself lacking in creativity and doing very similar things with all your clients (e.g. *"Whatever the problem and formulation, increased behavioural activation is the answer!"*) • Deviating from evidence-based approaches rather than flexibly applying protocols using CBT principles • Moving from feeling irritated with a client (internal emotional cue) to actually displaying irritation through behaviours such as making critical comments or speaking in an angry or sharp tone of voice (*"What do you mean you haven't done the homework again?"*)
An identified rupture in the therapeutic relationship that has not been resolved in-session	• Client withdrawal (e.g. client is overly deferential or appeasing, client regularly engages in avoidant storytelling, minimal responses to questions) • Client confrontation (e.g. client complains about therapeutic activities, parameters of therapy or progress) See Eubanks, Muran and Safran (2015) for a fuller description of such observable ruptures and also resolution methods
Significant socio-cultural difference between therapist and client	• Client is from a different cultural background. This may include racial and ethnic differences, but the therapist should also be aware of other differences, such as age, religious beliefs and sexual identity (see Chapter 5 for more detail on socio-cultural factors)

PROCEDURAL GUIDANCE

How can therapists maximise their chances of noticing the markers indicating a need for self-supervision?

Most therapists are busy and at times can move from client to client without reflecting on the previous session or taking time to think about the next session and the potential stuck points that might arise. Each therapist needs to identify what works best for them in increasing their awareness of sources of information that indicate a need for reflection in self-supervision. A number of potential methods are detailed below:

• Take a few moments to become aware of thoughts and feelings ahead of, or following, each session. Some therapists might choose to use a more formal method, such as a brief mindfulness exercise (e.g. a three-minute breathing space).
• Use clinical measures at each session and review these in a spirit of curiosity and reflection. See Chapter 6 and Liness (2014).

- Use a post-session reflection form. For example:
  - Summarise session aims – did we achieve these?
  - Any unusual occurrences? Anything that surprised me?
  - Predominating therapist thoughts and feelings?
  - Did I follow the appropriate evidence-based protocol? If not, what thoughts or feelings caused me to change course or drift?
  - What were the main decision points during the session and what other options could I have considered?
  - What went well and what was my role in this?
  - What didn't go well and what was my role in this?
- Ask to see any clinical outcome data on your clients that your service may collect. Try to identify clients who did well and those who didn't. Can you identify any themes?
- Review any client feedback collected in your service using client experience or satisfaction questionnaires.
- Keep a reflective journal (Sutton et al., 2007).
- Develop your own mindfulness practice to increase awareness of your own thoughts, feelings and action tendencies within sessions.

ENGAGING IN SELF-SUPERVISION

Moving from an identified marker to a question or focus for planned self-supervision

During this stage, the therapist needs to move from the identification of a potential problem marker to the framing of this as a specific focus or question for self-supervision. Most importantly, the therapist needs to identify whether this problem is predominantly:

1. A problem with a specific client?
2. A wider problem with a type of difficulty, diagnosis or client?
3. A wider professional problem that is impacting on the wellbeing of the therapist and requires action? (See Chapter 10 for a full discussion on how to use reflection to maximise self-care).

These three categories are not necessarily exclusive, and in many instances a problem initially identified as a client–specific problem may come to be seen as representative of wider pattern or a need for specific self-care actions.

For example, a therapist (Angela) identifies a progress problem with a client who is experiencing significant social anxiety (Theo). The initial focus was the failure to achieve any meaningful change during the first seven sessions of CBT. During the self-supervision session it became apparent that while Theo is agreeable and motivated, this often manifests itself as an attempt to please Angela (for example, Theo neatly and perfectly completed the homework forms). It was hypothesised that both therapist and client are colluding in that Theo avoids entering any situations that actually evoke the key anxiogenic cognitions. This led to a plan to do things differently with Theo. It also led to the identification of a wider problem: that Angela allows therapy to become comfortable and does little to challenge or ensure meaningful exposure for her clients. This insight led to her identifying a need for self-supervision regarding her wider patterns and associated beliefs and behaviours.

Using self-supervision to combine clinical information and knowledge to move to a new understanding and plan

Client-focused self-supervision

The aim of client-focused self-supervision is to provide a structure to enhance the ability of the therapist to access and review relevant client information, identify knowledge and skills that might be applicable, develop a bridge between these two sources of knowledge and use this to come to a new understanding and plan for action.

This is similar to the process initially described by Bennett-Levy and Thwaites (2007) in their six-stage model for addressing therapeutic relationship difficulties, but it is equally applicable to other blockages in the therapeutic process (Bennett-Levy, Thwaites et al., 2009). The six-stage model is illustrated in Chapter 2, which should be read first. Table 3.2 shows how the model can be applied in self-supervision.

TABLE 3.2 *Procedural guidance for applying the six-stage model (Bennett-Levy & Thwaites, 2007) in self-supervision*

Stage and task	Key challenges and guidance for applying this within a self-supervision setting
Stage 1 Focus attention in order to identify the self-supervision question	• If I'm saying "*CBT isn't working*", what exactly do I mean by this? What isn't working and how can I formulate this using the principles of CBT? (Worrell, 2014) • Prepare a focused client-related question AS IF you were going to discuss the client in traditional supervision. • Make notes and record the question (don't try and do this in your head).
Stage 2 Reconstruct experientially	• Ensure you have identified a quiet time and space where you are unlikely to be disturbed. • Close your eyes and try to visualise the session, cue into sensory reminders, e.g. What did the room look like? What were they wearing? How was I feeling? • Replay the session, either from your perspective or try to imagine the session from the client's perspective. How might they have been feeling at the key points? • Use visual recordings as prompts if possible.

Stage and task	Key challenges and guidance for applying this within a self-supervision setting

Stage 3
Clarify experience (e.g. emotions, thoughts, bodily feelings)
	• Key into, and note down, your emotions, bodily feelings, thoughts and behaviours at that time (with particular note to any that you think might be contributing to the problem).
	• Try to put yourself into the client's shoes and remember their reactions in session. Note down what you think the client might be thinking and feeling.
	• Be curious, ask yourself questions:
	   ○ Do we have clear and agreed SMART goals?
	   ○ Do we have a clear shared formulation?
	   ○ What model are we using? If no evidence-based model is available, what CBT principles are guiding our treatment?

Stage 4 Establish a "best fit'" formulation of "stuckness" using relevant knowledge	• Try to formulate the therapy problem on paper. Draw out any maintaining processes or interactions. • Formulate and label the problem. • Identify any knowledge that you already have that might be applicable in this situation. • Use textbooks, articles or lecture notes, etc. if you identify a gap in your knowledge. • Answer "Can I understand and formulate this problem or do I need something additional from my supervisor?"
Stage 5 Plan and rehearse procedural skills	• Once the problem has been formulated, identify a range of potential solutions. Note each solution down. • Review the potential of each as a way forward and then decide on a final plan. • Identify potential barriers (e.g. therapist beliefs) and how you will work around these. • Practise saying the words, i.e. actually role-playing on your own. Use visual recordings if available.
Stage 6 Enact new strategy with client and review	• Review your self-supervision notes before the session. • Implement the plan. • Make notes directly after the session. Was your hypothesis confirmed? What went well? What could you have done differently? • Review in more detail during next self-supervision session.
Beyond Stage 6 Identify if this problem or "stuckness" is indicative of similar problems with other clients (Is there a pattern? How does the formulation of the "stuckness" manifest itself with other clients?). Are there any implications for my own self-care? What do I need to do to look after myself at this point?	• Search your memory for similar examples with other clients or any examples of experiencing the same thoughts or feelings with other clients – what happened in those scenarios? • Is there a more widely held or longer-term pattern or belief that you need to work on? • Make a note of key learning, try to draw up your own functional procedural rules using a "When… then…" format.

CLINICAL EXAMPLE
Anton, a newly qualified CBT therapist

Background

Anton has been accustomed to receiving high levels of supervision during training (often twice per week). While still receiving weekly supervision, he tends to rely on his current supervisor (Moira) to problem-solve for him, and habitually uses supervision as a means of troubleshooting or gaining reassurance at the expense of developing as a therapist, e.g. becoming more tolerant of ambiguity and uncertainty and/or developing confidence in his therapy-related knowledge and skills. Moira has observed that on many occasions when Anton presents with a problem or supervision question, it is not about him needing to be given more declarative knowledge (e.g. verbally by the supervisor, or directed to a book chapter), but about helping him to access his own knowledge and skills and apply these to what can seem like a new or different situation for Anton. Moira acknowledges that she has fallen into the reciprocal pattern of providing answers and solutions for Anton, but feels irritated and somewhat resentful post-supervision. Her attempts at eliciting the information and plans from Anton can at times work, but it feels as if there is no new learning, or transferring of knowledge and skills to other situations.

Aiming to increase clinical independence and self-reliance, Anton and Moira have agreed that Anton will work on developing and practising his self-supervision skills between supervision sessions.

Within self-supervision

During Anton's first self-supervision session, he identifies a problem with a client he is working with (Michael) who has panic disorder and who has been carrying out a range of behavioural experiments with little success. Although Michael has reported doing the behavioural experiment they agreed in therapy, he does not seem to be learning from them.

Stage 1: Rather than stating that "*CBT isn't working*" or jumping to his frequent conclusion "*I think the client may have an avoidant personality disorder*", Anton spends some time identifying a question for his self-supervision. After some reviewing of the session notes and measures he comes up with "*Why doesn't Michael learn, or change his beliefs following behavioural experiments?*"

Stage 2: Anton closes his eyes and tries to bring to mind the last session with Michael when they reviewed his behavioural experiment. Anton usually struggles to remember session content in detail, but finds that by reconstructing this in his mind's eye he can access more information, and can almost relive moments of the session.

Stage 3: Anton identifies that he feels slightly irritated and remembers snapping at Michael. He feels uncomfortable as he notices that he is having the thought "*I'm a bad therapist*" and recognises how anxious he felt in session. He also notices that their review of the behavioural experiment is quite vague. Neither of them can remember the exact thought they were testing out, nor any detailed predictions. Michael just says "*Nothing bad happened*".

Stage 4a and 4b: Anton starts to make links between his clarified understanding of the situation and declarative knowledge that he already possesses. He begins to remember some teaching on his course where his tutor emphasised the need to be specific about what was being tested in order to maximise learning (declarative knowledge). He also remembered a very successful treatment episode with a different client with social anxiety and he remembers just how specific they were during that process. He became aware of a mismatch between best practice and what he and Michael had been doing. He looked up his lecture notes to refresh his memory about how to maximise client learning from experiments. He decided to try to use a Behavioural Experiment Planning and Review sheet to increase the specificity of their work and make it easier for Michael to recognise and embed new learning. By this point Michael had successfully managed to create a "reflective bridge" between the current situation (Stage 4a) and his declarative knowledge (Stage 4b), leading to a new understanding and formulation of the current problem.

Step 5: Anton decided to practise filling in a Behavioural Experiment Planning sheet for one of their recent experiments and very soon realised how little information he had about the belief being tested and associated predictions. He then made a few notes and practised introducing the forms, especially thinking about how he might explain them to Michael to get them back on track.

Step 6: Anton made a note of some key learning for him (*"I have a tendency towards vagueness"*, *"I often avoid using written materials because I feel anxious that the client might not like them"*) and some potential procedural guidance he could use in future (e.g. *"When I notice myself making assumptions about how the client may respond to an intervention, then ask them and seek feedback"*, *"When the client does not seem to be learning despite engaging with behavioural experiments, then check if we are clear what is being tested or predicted"*).

Stage 6 of client-focused self-supervision often segues smoothly into the second main type of self-supervision: supervision focused not specifically on one client but on a wider pattern of which the therapist has become aware. This is described in more detail below.

Therapist development-focused self-supervision

Once the therapist has identified a wider pattern within their therapy, maybe through initially reflecting on an individual case, or from a review of self-supervision or supervision notes, the task is to identify the pattern more clearly and what is required to address it. Areas to address include:

1. Declarative knowledge that needs developing. For example, is there a new evidence-based, disorder-specific model I need to know about? Is there a specific intervention I need to read about? Do I need to learn about an aspect of the therapeutic relationship, such as the theory behind rupture-resolution? Or the latest thinking on how to use safety behaviours when working with anxiety disorders? Or is there a specific circumstance when I cannot access the knowledge I already have?

2. Procedural skills. For example, "Is there something that I struggle to do in therapy? What therapeutic furrows or ruts do I fall into? What do I avoid? Is there a gap between my knowledge of an intervention and my ability to use it flexibly and with artistry?" Identifying deficits or below-par performance can be challenge and there is a tendency for those performing worst to be least realistic about their performance (Sheldon, Dunning & Ames, 2015). To counteract this, focus on things that have gone less well in addition to those that have gone well, and use external feedback and ratings scales (see Chapter 6).
3. Unhelpful therapist beliefs. For example, What beliefs are playing a part in these repeated therapy patterns? In what situation are these likely to be triggered? What markers tell me that these beliefs have been activated? (See Chapter 4.)

Developing new declarative knowledge

Although a central task of supervision or self-supervision is often to provide a structure to help the therapist access already-held knowledge and apply this in a different scenario or setting, there will be many times when the novice therapist identifies a gap in their knowledge. One of the challenges to achieving this is being able to accurately gauge your own levels of knowledge or skill and, as referred to earlier, there is considerable evidence that poor performers are less likely to be able to accurately judge their own performance and potentially identify deficits (see Dunning, 2011, for a full examination of the Dunning–Kruger effect). One implication of this is that therapists would do well to access unambiguous objective or external feedback around performance or deficits, as discussed earlier.

Be specific about what you need to learn. Whittington (2014) discusses learning styles and methods for CBT therapists and we would advise that this becomes an integral part of self-supervision. Ask yourself: *"Given this need for new declarative knowledge, what would be the most effective way for me to learn this?"* Reading a specific chapter, journal article? Asking a colleague? Draw up a plan with attached time-scales and think of barriers to following through on plans, just as you would with a client.

Developing procedural skills

Similarly, for procedural skills, therapists need to be specific about what they need to learn.

*   Is it about learning a new skill "from scratch"? If so, what already-held skills could help?
*   Is it about a skill that has drifted away from best practice and that needs tweaking or returning to previous ways of doing things? (Waller, 2009)
*   Is it about improving the way in which you perform a specific aspect of therapy? Are there situations when you are less likely to follow best practice? Do you want to fine-tune your skills and identify more explicit or more nuanced procedural rules?

Once you have clarified your learning need, then consider how you might best learn it, for example watching a visual recording, shadowing a colleague, role-playing. How will you embed any new procedural skills? Can you make a note of these in a "when… then…" format? How will you remember to use these during the moments you most need to? Under what circumstances will you be most vulnerable to falling back into your old ways of doing things?

Unhelpful therapist beliefs

The first task during self-supervision that is focused on addressing unhelpful therapist beliefs is to try to put the belief into words, just as we would with a client. We may become aware of a feeling (e.g. anxiety) or a behaviour (e.g. avoidance of something) which we can use to identify a thought or belief. This may already be in the form of words (e.g. "*If my clients become distressed during sessions, I'm a bad person*") but often this can be an image ("*I get this picture of the client crying and they just don't stop and it never ends*"). We can use questionnaires to help us become aware of potential beliefs that might be acting as a barrier or limiting our effectiveness or development as a therapist (Haarhoff & Farrand, 2012). For example, to reflect on general therapist beliefs, a therapist could complete the Therapists' Schema Questionnaire (Leahy, 2001), or if the therapist hypothesises that they have a specific problematic belief (e.g. beliefs about self-compassion, difficulty tolerating uncertainty), then they could identify and complete a relevant validated questionnaire and use their self-supervision to plan how to move from an identified unhelpful belief to a plan to change this.

The same change processes apply for us as they would for a client. Our goal would be to aim for specificity and ideally to put the thought or belief in a form that can be addressed via a standard CBT method, such as a behavioural experiment, a pie chart, a thought diary, etc. (Haarhoff & Kazantzis, 2007). Whether the belief is about a specific client or is evoked by a wider range of circumstances, standard CBT can be used on ourselves – this is one of the advantages of the CBT model in that it has at its core the tenet that we are more similar to our clients than different, and the same maintenance and change processes apply to us. As Chapter 8 will discuss, there are additional benefits in practising CBT on ourselves in that we get a taste of the client experience and can use this to become more attuned, flexible and skilled therapists (Bennett-Levy et al., 2015).

Self-supervision: a caveat

Early proponents of self-supervision have suggested a developmental framework for supervision and within this they have identified self-supervision as a later stage when higher-order skills, judgements and motivations have been developed (Littrell, Lee-Borden & Lorenz, 1979). We would agree that novice therapists are less likely to possess these skills. Therapists also need to be taught the specific skills required for self-supervision rather than assuming they develop naturally. However, we would emphasise two points:

1. Self-supervision based on our working definition can be a valuable process for thera-
    pists at all stages of their career, given the correct training and supportive structures.
    The form and function of self-supervision will vary based on knowledge, skill and
    insight, but should not be reserved for experienced therapists alone.
2. Also, although we are clearly advocating the benefits of self-supervision as a reflec-
    tive structure for all therapists, whatever their stage of development, self-supervision
    should be used as an adjunct and not as a replacement to clinical supervision. There
    should be a clear route for questions and unresolved problems to be escalated to
    clinical supervision. In addition, the supervisory structures should not rely upon the
    self-report, awareness or insight of the supervisee alone; it should include objective
    inputs such as audio or visual recordings and an external perspective of an experienced
    clinician.

CONCLUSION

Within this chapter we have discussed the use of self-supervision across differing
therapeutic orientations and detailed CBT-specific procedural guidance for how
therapists can develop their own self-supervision practice. While we have made clear
distinctions between client and therapist development–focused supervision, in reality
there is often a considerable overlap.

This chapter provides a framework for both reflection and planning in order to
improve therapy delivery and develop therapeutic metacompetence. Self-supervision
needs to be seen as part of a wider process of developing self-sustainability as a therapist. Lowe (2000) supports this view, suggesting that clinical supervision should
"become a forum for facilitating expertise in self-supervision, with the traditional
role of the supervisor shifting from supervision of practice to supervision of supervision" (p. 512). Key to this is a shared supervisor and therapist vision of what such
self-sustainability might look like for an individual therapist, with "a conception of
self-supervision that becomes a vital part of the therapist's vision for his or her professional development, rather than being imposed in a top–down way (as yet another set
of competencies to be mastered)" (Lowe, 2000, p. 514).

While the concept of self-supervision is likely to have high face validity for most
therapists, to date there is limited research into the effectiveness of self-supervision
(although the evidence-base for traditional supervision is also fairly weak (Milne,
2009)). One of the few studies into self-supervision found little impact on the main
outcome of empathy, although, as the authors acknowledge, this was conducted
with novice therapists rather than more experienced therapists (Dennin & Ellis,
2003). We would hypothesise that it would be more effective with experienced
therapists, and also that it would have an impact beyond increasing therapeutic
empathy. One would expect many of the same benefits from traditional supervision, such as increased awareness of one's own thoughts, feelings and behaviours,
self- and observer-rated skill improvements, reduced burnout, etc. Further research
is required in this area and hopefully our operationalisation of self-supervision can
facilitate this.

TAKING IT FORWARD

What *declarative knowledge* have you learnt from reading this chapter?

- What has stood out for you in reading this chapter? How might you summarise it to a colleague?
- What are your thoughts or beliefs about self-supervision and its role in your development? Or your supervisees' development (if applicable)?

How might you develop your own self-supervision in order to develop and fine-tune your *procedural skills*?

- What would be the markers for you that you need in order to self-supervise on a specific focus? Can you think of a current or recent example?
- What gets in the way of you recognising a need for self-supervision?
- How can you make time for this?
  - o What unproductive tasks could you drop to find time for self-supervision?
  - o If you receive very regular supervision, could you negotiate using some of this time for self-supervision?
  - o Could you find a way to use the time before or after a session more productively? (A post-session reflective form only takes minutes to complete).

- Can you identify any therapy problems that you could have potentially solved yourself rather than taking them to supervision (if only you had a dedicated time slot and a self-supervision structure in place)?
- Think of one thing you could do to start to develop your own self-supervision?

Try to identify a structure that would work best for you to engage your *reflective system* within self-supervision?

- What are the conditions under which you would be best able to review your experience and bring to mind your bodily sensations, feelings, thoughts and behaviours? What would you need to put in place?
- How do you best reflect on, and bring together, clinical information about a client and your store of clinical knowledge and skills (from training, from reading and from your experience)? How do you make the bridge between the two?

SUGGESTED READING

Bennett-Levy, J., & Thwaites, R. (2007). Self and self-reflection in the therapeutic relationship: a conceptual map and practical strategies for the training, supervision and self-supervision of interpersonal skills. In P. Gilbert & R. Leahy (Eds.), *The therapeutic relationship in the cognitive behavioural therapies* (pp. 255–281). London: Routledge.

4

REFLECTING ON THE THERAPEUTIC RELATIONSHIP IN CBT

Beverly Haarhoff and Richard Thwaites

LEARNING AIMS

- To provide a rationale for the importance of reflecting on the therapeutic relationship in CBT
- To enhance therapist self-awareness regarding the possible impact of self- and therapist beliefs on the therapeutic relationship
- To present a number of conceptual models to structure therapist reflection on the therapeutic relationship
- To enable the development of procedural rules relating to the potential impact of both personal- and therapist-related beliefs on clinical practice
- To promote therapist self-understanding through reflection on the therapeutic relationship to improve overall competency and metacompetency in delivering CBT

INTRODUCTION

There is consensus that the quality of the therapeutic relationship is an important contributing factor to therapy outcomes in all recognised psychological therapies (Wampold, 2001). However, the emphasis on the shape, impact and use of the therapeutic relationship varies across therapy models. The cognitive behavioural perspective has been that the therapeutic relationship is important, but not in itself sufficient to bring about therapy change, whereas many other models, most notably those influenced by psychoanalysis, have positioned the therapeutic relationship at the very heart of therapy as the means through which psychological problems are understood and resolved. In contrast, the cognitive behavioural therapies have placed greater weight on the cognitive behavioural formulation of the genesis and maintenance of psychological problems and matched interventions. While this view remains pertinent, as we shall see over the course of this chapter, there have also been important shifts in CBT, which have meant that, in some instances, understanding and working directly with the therapeutic relationship has assumed a more central position in the formulation and treatment of the presenting problems. Many CBT therapists would now acknowledge that under some circumstances, the relationship is a key element in facilitating lasting changes. It is also important in managing interpersonal difficulties (e.g. Safran & Segal, 1990) which can often crop up in therapy with clients who have complex problems. Sharpening therapists' reflective skills is an important element in understanding the sometimes complicated, interpersonal transactions that can occur in therapy. The primary goals of this chapter are therefore to improve the focus and structure of CBT therapist reflection on their own beliefs and behaviours, and then to enable therapists' understanding of the possible impact of therapist beliefs and behaviours on the therapeutic relationship.

The chapter first summarises developments in contemporary CBT that have altered the way the therapeutic relationship is conceived in CBT. We make a distinction between seeing the therapeutic relationship as a "background" for interventions and as an "intervention". In this context we also describe what has come to be known as high and low intensity CBT models of therapy delivery in England, discussing the way in which the therapeutic relationship may be relevant to each of these groups. We then describe methods to enhance therapist self-awareness and understanding by introducing reflective methods to identify personal- and therapist-related beliefs and emotional schema.

Enhanced therapist self-awareness underpins the second part of the chapter, which looks at the therapeutic relationship in action. We show how therapists can use the CBT model to understand problems and stuck points in therapy, which can result from various combinations of therapist and client beliefs and behaviours. Beliefs and behaviours which, at best, maintain an unhelpful status quo and at worst, cause an irreparable therapeutic rupture. The psychodynamic concepts of transference and countertransference are briefly referenced as providing a background for some of the CBT approaches discussed. The following models are considered: the Therapeutic Belief System, client–therapist schema mismatch, the Cognitive-Interpersonal model and the Cognitive Therapy Interpersonal Process model. It is hoped that these models will enhance reflection in training, supervision and day-to-day clinical practice in both novice and experienced CBT practitioners.

CONTEMPORARY CBT AND THE ROLE OF THE THERAPEUTIC RELATIONSHIP

CBT continues to rapidly expand in a number of important ways: for example, offering treatment for increasingly complex diagnostic presentations where comorbidity, chronicity and interpersonal difficulties are prominent; incorporating new and adapted models such as Schema Focused Therapy (Young et al., 2003), Mindfulness-Based Cognitive Therapy (Segal, Williams & Teasdale, 2002) and compassion-focused models of CBT (Gilbert, 2009); and introducing new ways of delivering therapy and training therapists. The net result is that there is no longer a consistently unitary format for CBT delivery (Westbrook, Kennerley & Kirk, 2011). For clients presenting with complex and chronic problems, there has been a shift to longer-term therapy, with a greater focus on experiential learning within therapy, and the therapeutic relationship, where interpersonal factors with the potential to interfere with the progress of therapy may emerge. Here, implications for training have been to adapt traditional CBT interventions and introduce a greater focus on the interventions described above. The implementation of these strategies requires the simultaneous emotional, cognitive and physiological attunement of the therapist to his or her own processes and those of the client.

Low intensity CBT and the therapeutic relationship

On the other hand, the introduction of low intensity (LI) CBT models in England has led to a focus on structured, short-term interventions such as problem-solving and behavioural activation, delivered by Psychological Wellbeing Practitioners (PWPs) (see Chapter 9). PWPs are drawn from all walks of life and do not necessarily have a background in mental health. Training for these practitioners is circumscribed to the acquisition of a specific and limited number of skills needed to deliver short-term interventions, and the *content* of the manualised low intensity treatment protocols are considered to outweigh the personal contribution of the therapist (Bennett-Levy, Richards & Farrand, 2010). LI practitioners have a high client load, sometimes seeing over 40 clients per week. This can mean that time to process the interpersonal components of therapy may be limited, leading to increased stress and even burnout for these clinicians. Furthermore, as Chaddock (2013) has suggested, the therapeutic relationship may actually be even more important than in "traditional" CBT due to the low practitioner contact time:

> It is precisely because you will have limited contact with the client that interpersonal factors are so important. As a LICBT [low intensity practitioner] you have less time to elicit the information needed to understand the client's difficulty, to develop rapport and facilitate their initial engagement with the intervention materials, and to overcome any difficulties that arise. (Chaddock, 2013, p. 70)

This brings substantial challenges for those delivering low intensity interventions. Not only is there less contact time with the client, but also the high-volume model often means that there is less time available for reflection pre- or post-session. It can be harder to create the space to reflect on the therapeutic relationship and ask key questions, such as:

- "Is this relationship an effective vehicle for the delivery of effective low intensity interventions?"

- "Am I providing the most helpful combination of empathy, validation and support for new behaviours, thinking and learning to occur?"
- "If not, what might I need to do differently? Am I colluding with avoidance? Not recognising a client need for validation or recognition around their difficulties?"

Although, as yet, there has been no research into the effect of the role of the therapeutic relationship in low intensity working, Green et al. (2014) found that therapist effects accounted for around 9% of the variation in treatment outcomes for a sample of low intensity practitioners, a finding similar to studies investigating traditional therapies. While the study did not actually look at the impact of the therapeutic relationship, it did suggest that similar guided self-help interventions, provided to similar clients, were influenced by the low intensity practitioner who delivered them, pointing to a possible influence of interpersonal factors. The authors suggest that the most effective PWPs were able to resist therapeutic drift while delivering low intensity interventions in a flexible and individualised manner. To what extent that included the ability to rapidly develop and effectively maintain therapeutic relationships is a question for future studies. For the time being, though, there is consensus that practitioners assessing clients and delivering low intensity interventions need to be able to do so in the context of a therapeutic relationship, and potentially one that is developed more rapidly (and in different ways) than in traditional therapy (Chaddock, 2013; Farrand & Williams, 2010; IAPT, 2010).

For this reason, much of the content of this chapter is applicable to the delivery of low and high intensity therapies, although bearing in mind the specific challenges of time (lower contact times for low intensity interventions, often 20–30 minutes per contact) and the wider variety of delivery methods used in low intensity therapies (e.g. telephone contacts, email or SMS). Although low intensity interventions were not designed for complex clients or those with significant interpersonal problems, low intensity practitioners do sometimes end up seeing such clients and bring such clients to supervision. The reflective processes described in the models presented in this chapter can provide an equally valid framework for formulating the therapeutic relationship and reflecting on the practitioner's own contribution to the relationship. The difference is that the focus for low intensity practitioners is on developing and maintaining therapeutic relationships in the service of facilitating the successful use of low intensity interventions rather than using the relationship as the change method, which may occur more commonly in more intensive interventions.

In short, it is widely accepted that interpersonal factors in the context of high and low intensity therapy delivery are always important. It is difficult to engage in effective therapy unless the client feels safe and confident to talk about personal problems. In addition, because many of the problems brought to therapy have an interpersonal component (for example, social anxiety), similar interpersonal problems are likely to be activated in a therapy session. Therapists and clients will bring beliefs about themselves and others to the therapy relationship and this will affect the way therapy is done (for better or worse). It is therefore important that therapists recognise that beliefs about self and interpersonal relationships can lead to the therapist experiencing unexpected emotional and behavioural responses in any therapy situation, which can be detrimental to a productive and helpful therapeutic relationship.

THE THERAPEUTIC RELATIONSHIP IN CBT

To understand the way the therapeutic relationship is conceived in contemporary CBT it is useful to keep the following dual perspective in mind: (1) the therapeutic relationship as background for specific technical interventions, and (2) the therapeutic relationship as an intervention in itself (Persons, 1989; Safran & Segal, 1990).

The therapeutic relationship as background

Viewed as background, the therapist fosters a relationship of productive, helpful collaboration directed towards managing or resolving the client's presenting issues. The client should feel secure and confident that the therapist has their best interests at heart. To achieve this, it is recommended that qualities of warmth, empathy, genuineness, unconditional positive regard and professionalism are conveyed (Rogers, 1965). The client is encouraged to take an active role in the therapy and work towards becoming their own therapist. In this atmosphere of collaboration, guided discovery is a key CBT ingredient (Beck, 1995).

Viewing the therapeutic relationship in this way may be sufficient in straightforward, uncomplicated presentations, where the problem is clearly defined and interpersonal factors are not prominent. In the early days of CBT, Beck likened this type of relationship to that of a coach (Beck, 1976). As we have mentioned, viewing the therapeutic relationship as background (necessary but not sufficient) is still common in circumstances where the correct application of appropriate evidence-based treatment protocols are likely to be of greater importance than the interpersonal relational dimension (as mentioned above, this is particularly the case in the recently developed LI modes of CBT delivery). It should also be noted that this perspective remains, in many circumstances, appropriate to the skilful delivery of CBT.

The therapeutic relationship as an intervention

Using the therapeutic relationship as an intervention in itself to bring about change most typically comes into play when interpersonal factors are prominent and are interfering with the progress of therapy. This is particularly the case in complex presentations, such as clients with some form of personality problem that can impact on interpersonal engagement. In instances such as these, the therapeutic relationship can become a laboratory where the client can experiment (safely) with new ways of being in a relationship. Thinking about the therapeutic relationship in this way can be difficult for CBT practitioners used to seeing the relationship purely as background, and the influential psychodynamic constructs, transference, countertransference and resistance have often provided a conceptual springboard for CBT theory to evolve in this area (Leahy, 2001, 2007; Young et al., 2003). These concepts will be discussed in more detail later in the chapter.

This chapter focuses primarily on ways to enhance therapist reflection on using the therapeutic relationship as an intervention. It should be noted that this cannot be a hard-and-fast distinction, and as therapy progresses there will be often be a cross-over between these two modes of perceiving and working with the therapeutic relationship.

IMPROVING THERAPIST SELF-AWARENESS

Heightening the CBT therapist's self-understanding is an important first step in identifying and managing relevant interpersonal processes in therapy. To this end, the Therapist's Schema Questionnaire is introduced as a means to identify the CBT therapist's beliefs about themselves as therapists. We go on to recommend self-formulation as an additional mechanism for CBT therapists to increase awareness of their idiosyncratic underlying beliefs and compensatory maintaining behaviours. This section will conclude by emphasising the importance of therapists' awareness of their personal emotional schema that may impact on therapy in certain circum-stances. Therapists, like their clients, will bring beliefs about themselves and others to the therapeutic relationship. If the CBT therapist lacks self-awareness, these beliefs can become an obstacle to progress in therapy.

Identifying therapist's schema

A schema refers broadly to the mental structures that integrate and give meaning to events (Beck, Freeman, Davis & Associates, 2004). Schema can also be experienced holistically, as a combined bodily, emotional and cognitive experience (Bennett-Levy et al., 2015), and are not always problematic or negative. In CBT, however, schema are most often conceptualised as dysfunctional and are associated with various diag-nostic presentations. For example, overestimating personal vulnerability and external threat are common in individuals suffering from anxiety disorders (Beck, Emery & Greenberg, 1985). Individuals have schema about themselves, other people, the world, emotional expression, interpersonal relationships, and so on. Multiple and diverse factors are influential in the development of schema, for example, relationships with parents, developmental factors, life experience, and cultural influences. Schema are developed and elaborated throughout life. However, schema formed at an early developmental stage tend to be the most influential and least evaluated (by the person who has the schema). The concept of schema and core beliefs are sometimes used interchangeably in CBT and are conceived as pervasive, cross-situational, unconditional beliefs which exert a powerful influence over individuals, particularly in times of challenge and stress (Beck et al., 2004). Schema affect us all in different contexts of our lives and, as we shall see, therapists are not immune from the influence of the personal- or therapist-related schema. (For a detailed account of Schema Focused Therapy, see Young et al., 2003.) Young and his associates have also developed a number of inventories aimed at identifying what Young has called Early Maladaptive Schema (EMS), associated compensatory behaviours, underlying assumptions and early relevant developmental experiences with parents or other significant adults (Young, 1995; Young & Brown, 1990; Young & Rygh, 1994).

Therapist schema

Influenced by Young's work, Leahy (2001) introduced the concept of therapist schema (TS). TS are beliefs, held by the therapist, which relate specifically to the way the therapist perceives him or herself in the therapeutic context (beliefs about self-as-therapist, beliefs about clients and the course of therapy). TS are described as less pervasive and unconditional than EMS, and are triggered in certain therapy-related contexts. Although dysfunctional to varying degrees within the therapeutic context, they do not necessarily signal early developmental attachment issues or mental health problems. Factors influencing TS are more present-focused and include training experiences, supervision, peer group, psychotherapy model and formative experiences with clients. Some examples of TS identified by Leahy are: demanding standards (a perfectionistic approach to the client's performance in therapy, usually involving a high expectation of client improvement and compliant therapy attendance, completion of homework, etc.), abandonment (concern about being abandoned by the client), need for approval (people pleasing), excessive self-sacrifice (the inability to set boundaries and act in an appropriately assertive way with clients), and special superior person (an over-inflated or grandiose view of one's skill as a therapist). Many of the same maintenance factors which apply to self-schema also maintain TS. Chapter 10 provides an example of the development and maintenance of therapist beliefs that can lead to burnout.

The Therapist's Schema Questionnaire

The Therapist's Schema Questionnaire (TSQ) lists 46 assumptions underlying 14 of the most common therapist schema (Leahy, 2001). The TSQ is scored by noting the degree of endorsement, on a Likert scale ranging from 1–6 (where 1 represents very untrue and 6 very true). An endorsement above 5 of any of the listed assumptions could signify the presence of a related therapist schema. Table 4.1 includes a list of therapist schema and associated underlying assumptions.

TABLE 4.1   *Therapist schema and assumptions (adapted from Leahy, 2001, p. 256)*

Schema	Assumptions
Demanding standards	I have to cure all my clients. I must always meet the highest standards. My clients should do an excellent job. We should never waste time.
Special superior person	I am entitled to be successful. My clients should appreciate what I do for them. I shouldn't feel bored when doing therapy. Clients try to humiliate me.
Rejection sensitive	Conflicts are upsetting. I shouldn't raise issues that will bother the client.
Abandonment	If my client is bothered by therapy they might leave. It is upsetting when clients terminate. I might end up with no clients.
Autonomy	I feel controlled by the client. My movements, feelings or what I say are limited. I should be able to do what I wish. I wonder whether I will lose myself in the relationship.
Control	I have to control my surroundings or the people around me.
Judgemental	Some people are basically bad people. People should be punished if they do wrong things.
Persecution	I often feel provoked. The client is trying to get me. I have to guard against being taken advantage of or hurt. You usually can't trust people.
Need for approval	I want to be liked by the client. If the client isn't happy with me, then it means I'm doing something wrong.
Need to like others	It's important that I like the client. It bothers me if I don't like the client. We should get along – almost like friends.
Withholding	I want to withhold my thoughts and feelings from the client. I don't want to give them what they want. I feel I am withdrawing emotionally during the session.
Helplessness	I feel I don't know what to do. I fear I will make mistakes. I wonder if I am really competent. Sometimes I feel like giving up.
Goal inhibition	The client is blocking me from achieving my goals. I feel like I'm wasting time. I should be able to achieve my goals in session without the client's interference.
Self-sacrifice	I should meet all my client's needs. I should make them feel better. The client's needs often take precedence over my needs. I sometimes believe I would do almost anything to meet their needs.
Emotional inhibition	I feel frustrated when I'm with this client because I can't express the way I really feel. I find it hard to suppress my feelings. I can't be myself.

The TSQ can be used in training or supervision in a number of ways to increase self-understanding regarding the therapist's contribution to difficulties in the therapeutic relationship.

The TSQ as a screening device in training and supervision

Used in supervision or training, responses to the TSQ can highlight significant TS or combinations of TS which may be problematic to therapy, or to the therapist's professional development in general. Once identified, TS can be discussed and either normalised or challenged. Endorsement of a large number of TS could signal that a trainee may be suffering from difficulties with depression, be in an unsupportive professional environment, or may have significant interpersonal difficulties (Haarhoff, 2006). Conversely, the reverse might indicate that the trainee was not experiencing challenge, could possibly lack personal insight, or might be somewhat complacent about their performance as a therapist. Caution regarding the interpretation of such a measure should *always* be exercised. However, the TSQ can be used as a means to initiate discussion and reflection on the impact of TS on the trainee.

Identifying general themes relevant to stage of training

When particular TS are prominent in a group, they can be made part of a group or class reflective discussion. Research has indicated that demanding standards, excessive self-sacrifice and special superior person are prominent in trainees (Haarhoff, 2006; Young, et al., 2003). In addition, Leahy (2001) suggests that demanding standards is a commonly held schema in therapists drawn to the CBT model, bringing with it high expectations for the success of the model, a determination to stick to a rigid structure and impatience with clients who do not cooperate and "get it right". Unrealistic expectations and the importance of tolerating ambiguity and uncertainty can be fruitfully discussed in relation to this therapist schema (Leahy, 2007). TS such as these can be named and normalised as typical of various stages of professional development, and strategies such as behavioural experiments can be introduced as a way of testing unhelpful assumptions associated with these schema. Table 4.2 illustrates the cognitive profiles that are consistent with the three most common therapist schema observed in trainees.

TABLE 4.2 *Cognitive profiles: demanding standards, special superior person and excessive self-sacrifice (adapted from Haarhoff & Kazantzis, 2007)*

	Demanding standards	Special superior person	Excessive self-sacrifice
Triggers in therapy	Homework non-compliance	Client's failure to improve in therapy	Perceived demands or requests by clients Perceived client vulnerability Need to be liked
Therapist beliefs about self	Incompetent, worthless, accountable, responsible	Special, unique, superior	Unworthy, not good enough
Therapist beliefs about client	Non-compliant, irresponsible, lazy, unmotivated	Inferior or superior	Vulnerable, needy
Therapist beliefs about CBT	Thing should go according to plan, CBT should work	This is an opportunity to shine	CBT is difficult, I will not succeed

	Demanding standards	Special superior person	Excessive self-sacrifice
Unhelpful strategies	Making too many demands on the client, technique-driven, overemphasis on structure, demanding, over-controlling, intolerant, refuse to see clients perceived as too difficult	When things become difficult, devalue and blame the client, lose interest, become bored, neglect routine, empathy failure, superficial approach to CBT	Lack of boundaries, overextending the therapy hour, reducing fees, tolerating missed appointments, avoiding issues and strategies perceived to be upsetting to the client
Healthy alternative (post-SR)	Practise decreasing control and increasing collaboration and client autonomy	Practise empathy	Challenge assumptions about perceived difficulties and client vulnerability

In addition to completing the TSQ, it can be useful for trainees to complete and reflect on the inventories developed by Young and his associates which identify EMS (Young, 1995; Young & Brown, 1990; Young & Rygh, 1993). Although differentiated from therapist schema, EMS can overlap and influence TS.

Self-formulation

An individualised CBT case formulation integrates cross-situational repeating themes encapsulated in core beliefs, underlying assumptions and resulting compensatory behaviours. At times the self-formulation would include significant developmental or historical information which may have led to experiences, and perceptions of self, underpinning prominent underlying assumptions and core beliefs (Beck, 1995). The CBT formulation model is a structural model, and three levels of increasing complexity are identified. The first level, often described as *situational*, describes the presenting problem functionally, using methods such as the five-part model (Padesky & Mooney, 1990) or thought record. A situational formulation aims primarily to promote an understanding of the problem by helping the client see patterns and cycles that maintain the status quo. The second level, whereby cross-situational conditional underlying assumptions and compensatory behaviours are identified, provides an explanation for the maintenance of an identified problem. Finally, the third, deepest level is that of underlying schema or core beliefs. At this level relevant developmental data are included to offer a longitudinal perspective to facilitate understanding of the origin of underlying beliefs (Kuyken, Padesky & Dudley, 2009).

When confronted with problems in therapy, for example a client's non-compliance with homework tasks, therapist and client understanding is dependent on a sound working cognitive formulation of the client's presenting issues. However, it is also very useful for the therapist to reflect on how therapist beliefs and reactions may also be playing a role in any therapy-interfering behaviour. This can be achieved through self-reflection in supervision or self-supervision using the different levels of case formulation described above. The three case examples that follow illustrate how each level of case formulation can be used to illuminate the "problems in therapy" identified by the therapist. In each of the examples the therapist identified the client as the obstacle to progress. However, unpacking the situation using the different levels of CBT formulation showed that the therapist's beliefs were also significantly contributing to the situation.

Case example one

Shanti reported difficulties in getting an elderly depressed client to complete a thought record for homework, attributing the difficulty to her client, whom she described as "overwhelmed with depression and unable to cope with the assigned task". Reflecting on her therapy tape in supervision, Shanti noted that she had rushed through the rationale and explanation regarding the homework assignment, present-ing the task in a flippant and self-depreciating manner. Shanti and her supervisor collaboratively identified the possibility of a potential therapist contribution to the problem of non-compliance, and it was proposed that she explore the problem using a five-part model (Padesky & Mooney, 1990).

> Situation: *Assigning homework with an elderly client.*
>
> Emotions: *Anxiety and frustration (intensity 50%)*
>
> Thoughts: *"I don't like the word 'homework' – it makes me feel like a teacher", "I don't want to be mean and put pressure on her", "She is older than me; it's uncomfortable telling her what to do", "I am no good at setting homework."*
>
> Behaviour: *I rushed and trivialised the setting up of the homework task with the client.*
>
> Physical impact: *Slight increase in heart rate.*

Recognising this as a pattern in other situations and reflecting on her background, Shanti concluded that cultural factors had played a part, describing the way in which her Indian family of origin had always emphasised respect for elders. She noted that at home there were rules that prevented the expression of opinions contrary to those of her elders under any circumstances. She identified a personal assumption "*It is improper and disrespectful to tell your elders what to do*". Her day-to-day clinical experience was mainly with children and adolescents and the problem identified in supervision did not at first manifest in that situation. However, on further reflection Shanti concluded that similar culturally generated schema prevented her from being appropriately assertive with the parents of the children with whom she habitually worked. She reported that her "rational self" did not feel comfortable with what she described as "being a complete pushover" and that she would like to work at challenging this belief in the workplace at least. Completing a thought record and reviewing factual supporting and disconfirming evidence relating to the hot thought, she arrived at a more balanced perspective: "*I can check out more clearly what she considers overwhelming and engage her in designing the homework so it is not too difficult*" and "*I do have some difficulties in assigning homework, but if I pace the session better there is a chance that the resultant homework will be more understandable to the client and they will complete it*".

Her cognitive shift facilitated an action plan to practise taking more time to design and assign homework with her clients, offering clearer explanations, allowing time for practice and eliciting the client's views as to the utility and doability of the task. Through increased collaboration and discussion she came to understand that her client had arthritic fingers, making writing difficult (the real reason for apparent non-compliance). Shanti constructed a computerised template for the client, enabling her to comfortably complete her homework. The result was successful homework completion and improved mood for the client, and greater confidence and competence in Shanti.

Case example two

There may be indications that a deeper, more complex level of self-formulation may be necessary. In the previous example Shanti experienced a relatively mild emotional reaction. Thus she was able to challenge her belief with relative ease. In the case of Helen, a more intense emotional reaction, rated 80% anxious, was experienced when she contemplated setting an exposure homework task for a client she described as having vulnerability and dependency schema. Helen characterised her client as having a long psychiatric history and being extremely disabled by her symptoms. She was reluctant to collaboratively design an appropriate behavioural experiment involving an exposure exercise to target the social avoidance of the client. After completing a thought record in supervision, her thoughts were: "*It won't work*", "*I haven't assigned a behavioural experiment before*" and "*I will look silly*" (hot thought). Using the downward arrow technique (Greenberger & Padesky, 1995) to elicit the meaning behind the thought, the following pervasive underlying assumptions and beliefs and compensatory behaviours relevant to the therapy process emerged:

Assumption: *If I try something new, then I should always get it right*

Rules: *Always prepare for every eventuality*

Behaviour: *Constant reassurance-seeking from supervisor; avoidance of risk-taking or trying something new in therapy.*

Having previously completed the TSQ, Helen was aware that she had demanding standards as a therapist schema, manifesting as a need to "get it right" and a low tolerance of any degree of ambiguity. Reflection on her thought record led to a useful discussion in supervision concerning the advantages and disadvantages of holding these beliefs. As a result, Helen planned a behavioural experiment to test out a more optimistic view of her client's resilience, taking the risk of assigning homework and tolerating the uncertainty of the outcome. After completing the experiment, she was greatly surprised by the client completing her homework. Helen's increased self-awareness of her underlying therapist beliefs resulted in her gradually decreasing her reassurance-seeking and tolerating a greater degree of ambiguity in therapy. She resolved to continue to allow herself and her clients the opportunity to learn from mistakes.

Case example three

It is useful to distinguish between personal- and therapist-self-schema (Bennett-Levy, 2006). To function optimally, therapist self-understanding should incorporate knowledge of both types of schema and their interaction in the different components of therapy delivery. In addition to acknowledging therapist schema common to many trainees, a supervisor should assist trainee reflection on idiosyncratic beliefs and behaviours likely to be triggered by particular clients (see Chapter 2 for further details). The following example demonstrates such an instance.

Mike's client was socially anxious. To combat the client's avoidance, Mike was using activity scheduling as an intervention and the client had scheduled, and engaged in, a number of healthy activities, such as healthy eating (thinking about his diet and making salads) and brain-gym (doing crossword puzzles). However, the client continued to avoid most social and occupational situations and, consequently, his limited and boring lifestyle continued. He remained frustrated by his empty lifestyle and paralysed by his core beliefs, "*I am different and defective*" and "*Others are critical, cruel and rejecting*". He had a history of being severely bullied at school. There was a strong therapeutic alliance, and the client was attending sessions and compliant with the homework. The low-risk activities received a great deal of praise from Mike, who labelled them as accomplishments. The client disagreed, arguing that brain gym, healthy eating and writing were not challenging and therefore did not constitute much of an achievement. Mike responded to the client's self-reflection with more reassurance and praise. During discussion in supervision, the supervisor drew attention to the lack of progress and queried whether these behaviours might be more usefully conceptualised as avoidance strategies (pointing out that the client had already recognised this). Acknowledging the progress Mike had made in developing a strong therapeutic alliance, the supervisor suggested that exploring the client's perception of challenge might prove beneficial, and that scheduling more challenging activities could be collaboratively undertaken. Uncharacteristically, Mike became quite defensive, agitated and irritated with this suggestion. For homework, the supervisor suggested that Mike reflect on his beliefs about himself and others and consider what compensatory behaviours might logically result. At the next supervision session Mike presented the following set of beliefs and associated behaviours:

Core beliefs: *"I am different and possibly defective", "Others are critical and rejecting."*

Compensatory behaviour: *Avoidance of situations where I can be judged or rejected.*

On reflection, Mike noted the similarity between his personal beliefs about self and others and those of his client, noting that he too had been bullied at school. He recognised the possibility that he may be over-identifying with the client's distress and colluding with the client's view of others. He was able to reflect that he may have become over-protective of the client's perceived vulnerability, thus unwittingly supporting his "keep safe at all costs" behaviours. He resolved to trust the strength of the therapeutic alliance and allow the client to take some risks.

These examples illustrate the benefits of therapist reflection on the different levels of self-formulation in the context of perceived difficulties in therapy. It should be noted that it is not always necessary to uncover the deepest levels of thought. The degree of emotion or upset experienced by the trainee/supervisee should be the guide (the more intense the emotional reaction, the more likely that core belief or schema is being activated).

Identifying emotional schema

Leahy (2007) has observed that therapists and clients have schema about the expression of emotion that is derived from the way in which our emotions are validated or devalued by significant others. Clients who have long-standing difficulties in the interpersonal domain often have unhelpful negative emotional schema. Some examples of beliefs about emotional expression are: that one should always be rational and that emotions are unacceptable; that emotions should be eliminated; that emotions are uncontrollable, intolerable, shameful and will last a long time.

Unidentified emotional schema for therapists, as with clients, can hinder or impede therapy and Leahy suggests that there is a possibility that CBT may even attract practitioners who have emotional schema which make them uncomfortable with emotional expression (for example, individuals who value the cool-headed rational approach and feel uncomfortable with what they might regard as more "touchy-feely therapies") (Leahy, 2007). Others may have the misguided and simplistic view that negative emotions should be eliminated, that CBT is all about changing negative cognitions so that happy, rational thoughts and good feelings can prevail. It is important, therefore, that therapists reflect on personal emotional schema by asking questions such as:

- How comfortable am I with my emotions?
- Am I more comfortable with some emotions than others?
- Am I irritated or frightened by some emotions?
- How did my family of origin view the expression of emotion?

Cultural factors can also come into play regarding emotional expression, such as the stereotypical English belief in maintaining a "stiff upper lip", which can influence the expression of emotion in therapists in the same way as it does in clients.

The whole point about the CBT therapist becoming aware of therapist beliefs, and more generalised beliefs about themselves, is to be able to apply this increased self-understanding to the interactive context of the therapeutic relationship. The second part of the chapter therefore addresses the therapeutic relationship *per se*, and describes a number of models that can assist the CBT therapist's reflection on the interaction between therapist and client.

THERAPIST REFLECTION 'ON' AND 'IN' THE THERAPEUTIC RELATIONSHIP

Transference and countertransference and CBT

While most CBT therapists will be reluctant to import the unmodified con-structs of transference and countertransference into CBT, some therapists who work with, and write about, the treatment of complex problems reference these constructs as providing a useful theoretical framework for understanding the therapeutic relationship with clients who have rigid and problematic interper-sonal styles that are likely to trigger unhelpful responses from a therapist who lacks self-awareness (Arntz & Van Genderen, 2009; Gilbert & Leahy, 2007; Young et al., 2003). When thinking about these constructs we need to bear in mind that CBT is based on a set of principles that diverge markedly from other modalities. For example, sessions are structured and therapist and client work collaboratively, through a shared formulation, to understand the problems. Guided discovery, through the use of Socratic questioning, is fostered. The CBT model is made explicit and clear rationales for treatment interventions are provided. The client is an active participant in the treatment process and encouraged to work towards becoming his or her own therapist (Beck, 1995). Similarly, if therapeutic relation-ship factors are prominent, the expectation is that these factors will be clarified and interrogated in the same manner as other unhelpful patterns of thinking, feeling and behaving (Layden et al., 1993; Rudd & Joiner, 1997). A clear CBT assumption is that these processes are accessible and can be brought into pre-sent conscious experience. Understanding transference, countertransference and resistance in CBT follows these principles (making the process explicit). Table 4.3 shows how CBT interpretations of these processes differ from more traditional psychodynamic conceptions.

A CBT definition of countertransference, which emphasises the CBT perspective, is: "the totality of the therapist's responses to the client, including automatic thoughts, underlying beliefs or schema, emotions, actions and intensions" (Layden et al., 1993, p. 117). The social cognitive model, which postulates that mental representations of significant others exist in memory, and that such representations can be triggered by relevant cues in any context, including therapy, leading individuals to view *new* others through the lens of existing significant others (Miranda & Andersen, 2007, p. 165), provides theoretical and empirical support for the basic tenets of transference and countertransference. In a nutshell, countertransference conveys the view that in some interpersonal transactions with particular clients, a therapist may have a set of emotions and cognitions unexpectedly triggered and that this reaction can be related to the therapist's own historical and developmental experience. Leahy is emphatic that recognising the existence of countertransference is important and that failure to do so can lead to serious therapy problems, such as ambivalence about using certain techniques and strategies, fearing that the client will be upset (see the example of Helen on page 65), feeling undermined and insecure when working with clients

TABLE 4.3 *Differences between psychodynamic and CBT approaches to transference and countertransference*

Psychodynamic	CBT
Operation of unconscious processes.	Rejection of unconscious processes. The nuances of the therapeutic relationship, although subtle, can be brought to self-awareness (cognition is knowable and accessible through identifying cognitive processes).
Early developmental timeframe.	Present-centred timeframe (links to the past acknowledged but worked through in the here and now).
The client is perceived as passive, under the control of unconscious forces. This can result in a tendency to pathologise the client.	The client is perceived as an active participant. Attempts to resolve relationship difficulties are done in the spirit of collaborative empiricism.
The influence of the unconscious and motivational drives is emphasised.	The influence of cognitive processes is emphasised.
Implied inaccessibility of unconscious processes which can only be accessed indirectly.	These processes are operationalised as underlying beliefs, emotions and physiological reactions resulting in a variety of compensatory behaviours, including avoidance. These processes can be brought into awareness using relatively straightforward interventions. The focus is on activating, articulating, restructuring and integrating these processes.

who behave in an entitled manner, and failing to set limits or enforce appropriate boundaries. He goes on to propose the following guidelines to assist CBT therapists in understanding their countertransference:

- Acknowledge and accept that it exists
- Examine the kinds of problems and the kind of clients which trigger strong therapist feelings (for example, angry or needy clients)
- Notice feelings of boredom and other emotional and physiological reactions
- Question your reaction when clients feel like old friends and therapy seems "easy"
- Acknowledge typical self-schema
- Recognise and try to make connections between the therapist's own repeating interpersonal conflicts with family members, friends or colleagues and the therapist's reactions to particular clients. In other words, be conscientious about noticing your reactions in and after therapy sessions, noticing whether you have cognitive, emotional or physiological responses. (Leahy, 2001, pp. 242–243)

The remainder of the chapter will present a number of conceptual models, some of which reference a version of transference and countertransference that is compatible with CBT. However, the Cognitive-Interpersonal model (Safran & Segal, 1990) and the Interpersonal Process model (Armstrong, Barton, Twaddle, Thwaites & Platz, 2007) are uniquely CBT approaches. All of these models have some degree of conceptual overlap and the reader is invited to consider which model fits best with individual requirements. It should also be noted that it is beyond the scope of this chapter to fully describe each of these models. The aim is to provide the reader with a smorgasbord taster to encourage further engagement with the suggested readings at the end of the chapter.

The Therapeutic Belief System

The Therapeutic Belief System (TBS) is proposed as a CBT conceptual framework to assist therapists and clients to collaboratively make sense of relationship problems occurring in therapy (Rudd & Joiner, 1997). The TBS is an interactive system that identifies common therapist and client beliefs about themselves (as client and therapist), each other (client beliefs about the therapist and therapist beliefs about the client), and the course of therapy, the emotions triggered by these beliefs, and typical behavioural responses from each party.

For example, the therapist may see themselves as either a victim (*my clients are overwhelming me*), a collaborator (*we are working constructively together*) or a saviour (*only I can help this client*); the client as a hostile aggressor (*this client is undermining me*), a helpless victim (*this client is so vulnerable and helpless*), or a collaborator (*we can work together*); and therapy as hopeless (*therapy is a waste of time*), as maintaining the status quo (*nothing will change*), or as productive (*I feel optimistic about the outcome*). Each of these beliefs will result in a different emotional and behavioural reaction from the therapist. For instance, perceiving the client as a helpless victim might lead to a depressed or anxious response in the therapist, resulting in over-cautious or excessively nurturing behaviour that could result in avoiding appropriate treatment interventions because of beliefs about the client's vulnerability. The same patterns occur as a result of client perceptions regarding themselves, the therapist and the course of therapy. For example, the client can perceive the therapist as a rescuer, persecutor or helpful collaborator.

The interactive components of the therapeutic relationship are described as operating overtly (automatic thoughts, emotions and behaviours) and covertly (underlying assumptions and core beliefs). Conceptual taxonomies such as the TBS provide clinicians with a useful CBT structure to reflect on their own responses within the therapeutic relationship. A model such as this helps the clinician develop the awareness that a strongly felt emotional response often has an underlying cognition and will frequently result in a compensatory behaviour if it is not observed and identified through reflection.

Simplified visual models such as the TBS provide visual models for reflective discussion between therapist and client. Individuals can readily identify with descriptors such as *rescuer, persecutor* and *victim*. This can also facilitate discussion in supervision that can deepen when more idiosyncratic beliefs and behaviours are uncovered.

Client–therapist schema mismatch

It has been observed that particular combinations of client and therapist schema, if unacknowledged, can interfere with therapy in a number of important ways, depending on the way in which the schema processes of avoidance (avoiding situations where the schema can be activated), surrender (accepting the implications of the schema completely "as if" it were true), or overcompensation (behaving in a way completely opposite to the schema) are activated. A number of these therapist/client schema-related interactions, which can have a negative impact on the therapeutic relationship, have been identified (a detailed account with clinical examples can be found in Young et al., 2003, pp. 186–198).

For example, *Schema overlapping* is where the therapist and client both have the same schema. "Personal vulnerability" is an example of this type of mismatch. The example of Mike on page 66 shows how over-identification with client schema can result in a loss of objectivity. Another example, shown in Table 4.4, is *schema clashing*, which describes therapist and client schema that are diametrically opposed, in this instance a client with abandonment schema and a therapist who has schema relating to autonomy and control.

TABLE 4.4 *Therapist and client schema clash (adapted from Leahy, 2007)*

	Client: Abandonment schema	Therapist: Autonomy and control
Beliefs	Others will not be available to me or support me. Others will abandon me.	I feel controlled by the client, I will lose myself in the relationship. I have to control my surroundings.
Behaviours in therapy	Contacts the therapist frequently between sessions, has difficulty with the agenda, wants to talk about others.	Refuses to communicate between sessions, emphasises the importance of boundaries, rigidly controls the session, sticking doggedly to an imposed session structure.
Resulting client & therapist experience	"I can't count on my therapist." "I will be abandoned if I don't do therapy in the right way." "My therapist does not understand how hard it is for me."	Frustration and irritation. Highly anxious and worried about personal boundaries being violated.

Cognitive-Interpersonal model

In 1990, Jeremy Safran and Zindel Segal published the ground-breaking book entitled *Interpersonal Process in Cognitive Therapy*, which described, for the first time, a sophisticated and CBT-specific conceptualisation of the therapeutic relationship and the processes involved in building, maintaining and repairing such relationships (Safran & Segal, 1990). This has been developed into a treatment approach in itself (Eubanks, Muran & Safran, 2015; Safran & Muran, 2000), but many of the principles remain consistent with CBT and bring a useful perspective to the understanding of the therapeutic alliance within CBT.

The model provides guidance for clinicians to help them to recognise the early signs of a rupture in the therapeutic alliance and then, through exploration, uses these signs of rupture to recognise the client's interpersonal patterns and underlying feelings and thoughts, thus leading to the potential for new ways of behaving and new learning. Alliance ruptures are defined as "a deterioration in the alliance, manifested by a *lack of collaboration* between patient and therapist on tasks or goals, or a strain in the emotional bond" (Eubanks et al., 2015, p. 2) (note that the rupture is related to the lack of *collaboration*, not a lack of agreement). They have subdivided ruptures into two main categories: *withdrawal ruptures* and *confrontation ruptures*, and below we provide examples of these taken from their coding manual (Eubanks et al., 2015).

Withdrawal ruptures represent a moving *away from* the therapist or therapy process. This would include:

- avoiding answering or providing minimal responses to questions
- using abstract or vague language to avoid discussion of more meaningful thoughts or feelings
- shifting topic or switching into storytelling mode
- becoming overly compliant or deferential to appease the therapist
- showing a mismatch between content and affect (e.g. smiling or laughing when discussing something distressing).

Confrontation ruptures involve the client moving *against* the therapist or the therapy. Examples may include:

- expressing negative feelings about the therapist
- rejecting or dismissing interventions
- complaining about the activities, parameters or progress of therapy.

A model for the resolution of ruptures has been developed (e.g. Katzow & Safran, 2007; Safran & Muran, 2000) and reflection-in-action (Schön, 1983) on the part of the therapist is central to each stage of the process. Self-reflection allows the therapist to step back and observe their internal responses, which then help them to provide the client with the most therapeutic response to the client's interpersonal behaviour, rather than an automatic response. This explains the importance that Safran and colleagues place upon the therapist being able to observe their own thoughts, feelings and tendencies to act *while* actively participating in the interaction. Without reflection in the moment, the therapist is likely to be hooked into responding in a way that may be less therapeutic or constructive. For example, a client may tend to avoid feelings of vulnerability by starting to tell long and rambling stories when they start to feel uncomfortable or vulnerable. This may have the effect of distancing others and preventing genuine closeness. Without the therapist being able to step back and reflect upon their own thoughts and feelings in the moment, they might replicate the usual responses to this behaviour and become critical of the client or perhaps appear dismissive or disinterested.

Katzow and Safran (2007) have defined the five stages as:

1. The occurrence of a potential rupture marker.
2. The therapist recognises, steps back from and draws attention to a potential marker of a rupture in the therapeutic relationship.
3. The therapist tentatively and skilfully (with client consent) explores the client's experience of the rupture and the events leading up to it using their standard CBT and interpersonal skills.
4. The therapist uses their interpersonal skills to help the client to stay in the moment, with any difficult feelings (e.g. vulnerability, sadness).
5. Facilitating the client in accessing and expressing underlying thoughts, feelings or needs.

This model provides a framework for identifying potential alliance ruptures and using these in the service of therapeutic progress, rather than ignoring them or acting into them, which could result, at best, in the maintenance of interpersonal schema and, at worst, in client disengagement and drop out.

Reflection during and after sessions is required to be able to avoid being hooked into interpersonal cycles and many of the chapters in this book provide suggestions on how to improve this reflective ability moment-to-moment, whether in supervision (see Chapter 2), self-supervision (see Chapter 3) or by increasing awareness of one's own thoughts and feelings in a wider range of contexts by taking part in an SP/SR programme (see Chapter 8).

The Cognitive Therapy Interpersonal Process model

The Cognitive Therapy Interpersonal Process (CTIP) model in CBT is defined as "the relationship between two people in different therapeutic roles that unfolds across a course of treatment as they work towards the amelioration of the patient's difficulties" (Armstrong et al., 2007). The therapeutic alliance is a product of the interpersonal process, and both the *nature* (is the relationship one that is supportive, befriending, meeting the therapist's needs or appropriately therapeutic?) and the *strength* of the relationship, described as the degree of "us-ness", is considered.

There are three main aspects of this model:

1. *Client and therapist perspectives*: "How I represent myself in the relationship" (self), "How I represent you in the relationship" (other) and "How I represent what we are together" (us).
2. *Therapeutic domains*: Problems, goals and tasks. These are often considered to be more relevant to the client, but in reality often involve the therapist's perception concerning what these problems should be.
3. *Similar and discrepant (different) perspectives regarding problems, goals and tasks* (see Table 4.5). It should be noted that similar is not always good, and discrepant is not always bad. These perspectives will shift according to the focus of the therapeutic work.

TABLE 4.5 *Helpful and unhelpful consequences of similarities and differences between therapist and client (adapted from Armstrong et al., 2007)*

	Similarities	Discrepancies (if tolerated and open to learning)
Helpful	Agreement about the content of problems, goals, tasks and client feeling creates a clear therapeutic focus and purpose. It helps both parties to make the therapy manageable and maintain empathy for the client's predicament and aspirations.	At the start of addressing a difficulty it can be helpful if the parties have different ways of understanding the problems. Different knowledge, questions, beliefs and hypotheses provide the setting conditions for new learning.
Unhelpful	Parties that are over-matched in their knowledge, questions, beliefs and hypotheses can limit new information and compromise learning.	Discrepant views about the current problems, goals, tasks and client feeling can create confusion, frustration and miscommunication. Empathy can be strained.

Process problems, such as non- or partial-engagement, mistrust, weak alliance, miscommunication, non-compliance, "stuckness", rupture, complaint or dropout, are all the product of discrepancies in perspective, where agreement is needed, or of "over-matched" ways of understanding, where difference is needed. Process problems can come from either part of the therapeutic dyad. The model described above offers a way forward in terms of framing a reflective discussion regarding similarities or discrepancies.

For example, Kim, a CBT trainee therapist, reported that one of her clients, Janine, had left a therapy session extremely angry and tearful, threatening to self-harm and unable to say what the issue was. Kim was extremely upset and found it difficult to understand what had provoked the outburst. Reflecting on the Interpersonal Process model described above, she fruitfully explored unhelpful discrepancies between therapist and client perspectives, which were occurring in all three domains. She was able to share the model with the client and collaboratively and explicitly negotiate a way forward, where a more collaborative alignment of the three domains could be achieved. The discrepancies are illustrated in Table 4.6.

It should also be noted that in this example Kim's therapist schema regarding her need to maintain autonomy had been activated by this particular client, who had a very strong schema relating to abandonment. Prior to embarking on training as a CBT therapist Kim's background clinical experience had been in a secure forensic unit providing psychiatric care. Clearly this work had required that she maintain great vigilance concerning personal boundaries and this background experience underpinned her high need to maintain autonomy in the therapeutic relationship. Working with Janine, a client diagnosed with borderline personality disorder traits and high needs regarding attachment, validation and emotional containment, had resulted in a clash of schema, as described in the previous section (see Table 4.4). The schema clash exacerbated the domain discrepancies between therapist and client. Reflecting on the therapeutic relationship using both of these conceptual frameworks in supervision proved very helpful to the trainee and her client.

TABLE 4.6 *Discrepancies between therapist and client identification of problems, tasks and goals*

Therapeutic domains	Therapist perspective: Kim	Client perspective: Janine
Problems	• Depression • Interpersonal relationships • Emotional dysregulation	• Her weight • Others not coming up to scratch and meeting Janine's needs
Tasks	• Adherence to CBT depression protocol, emphasising behavioural activation in the first instance	• To be able to tell the therapist about all her problems • To complain about her partner and family
Goals	• To help Janine manage her depressive symptoms • To stick closely to the agenda (the therapist's) • To meet my learning needs as a trainee CBT therapist • To maintain clear boundaries	• To be listened to • To be "fixed" • To find a "mother" figure

CONCLUSION

There is widespread consensus that managing and working successfully with the therapeutic relationship is relevant to successful therapy outcome, especially with complex clients. An important part of achieving this goal requires therapists to reflect on their own psychological processes as well as the interaction between therapist and client responses (cognitive, emotional and behavioural). In order to help CBT therapists decode their personal and often unexpected emotional reactions in therapy, this chapter introduced a number of models that can be used to structure therapist reflection and facilitate greater understanding of interpersonal transactions in therapy.

TAKING IT FORWARD

What *declarative knowledge* have you gained from reading this chapter?

• Did any of the conceptual models presented in the chapter seem particularly relevant to you?
• How might you go about increasing your knowledge in this area?

What *procedural rules* for understanding and working with the therapeutic relationship can you start to develop after completing the exercises below?

• Think of a client with whom you are experiencing difficulties. Take a moment to experience any thoughts, emotions and bodily sensations.
• What sort of behaviour might result?

- What do these thoughts mean about you as therapist?
- What are your beliefs about the course of therapy for this client?
- Could you use any of the models described in this chapter to make sense of this difficulty? Reflecting on this exercise, can you think of any procedural rules you might apply if this situation were to reoccur?

Focusing on the way in which you experience emotions:

- How were emotions expressed by significant others in your childhood?
- How do you think this may have impacted on the way you characteristically express emotions?
- What are your beliefs about the expression of emotion?
- Do you think your beliefs about emotional expression have any impact on your work with your clients?
- On the basis of this self-reflection, are there any procedural ("when… then…") rules you could develop regarding your beliefs about how you should manage and/or express your emotions?

What strategies are you going to put in place to facilitate the engagement of your *reflective system*?

- What specific actions could you take to increase your reflection on the therapeutic relationship?

SUGGESTED READING

Gilbert, P., & Leahy, R. L. (Eds.). (2007). *The therapeutic relationship in the cognitive behavioural psychotherapies*. London: Routledge.

Safran, J. D., & Segal, Z. V. (1990). *Interpersonal process in cognitive therapy*. New York: Basic Books.

5

REFLECTING ON OUR SOCIO-CULTURAL BACKGROUND:

Becoming More Culturally Sensitive and Effective CBT Therapists

Beverly Haarhoff and Richard Thwaites

LEARNING AIMS

- To develop declarative knowledge regarding the interface between socio-cultural factors and CBT
- To expand our self-awareness of diverse and idiosyncratic cultural influences
- To introduce reflective tools to advance CBT therapists' awareness of the personal and professional impact of socio-cultural factors
- To highlight the importance of identifying the subtler forms of personal bias residing in tacit, unchallenged assumptions and beliefs regarding culture

INTRODUCTION

Understanding the influence of culture and diversity on the effective delivery of CBT is a complex task and the goals for this chapter are modest. They are confined to examining the part that reflection can play in increasing CBT therapists' awareness of culture and its impact on therapy. The ability to self-reflect is a key element of this process and is widely considered to be the starting point for the development of cultural competency (Sue, D.W. & Sue, 2008). Our aims are to outline some of the cultural challenges facing CBT therapists and to give CBT therapists the tools to facilitate structured self-reflection on the impact of culture for both therapist and client, with a particular emphasis on identifying therapist bias.

Many authors have commented that the concept of culture is difficult to capture in a single definition. Any definition that has relevance to psychological therapies is more usefully considered in the context of five influential multicultural themes. These themes are identified as (1) cultural universality versus cultural relativism, (2) the emotional consequences of "race", (3) the inclusive or exclusive nature of multiculturalism, (4) the socio-political nature of psychological therapies, and (5) considerations of what constitutes cultural competence (Sue, D.W. & Sue, 2008).

The chapter is structured in the following way. First, to provide context, each of the cultural themes listed above will be briefly discussed. Consensus dictates that the first step towards understanding and working constructively with cultural diversity is therapist self-understanding regarding the personal impact of their culture or "bringing into awareness one's assumptions, biases, thoughts and feelings regarding oneself and others … as self awareness increases, acceptance of others increases" (Spieght, Myers, Cox & Highlen, 1991, p. 33).

The remainder of the chapter therefore focuses on developing reflective skills to facilitate and support CBT therapists' self-awareness of the personal and professional implications of culture and, in addition, to identify culturally engendered personal bias. We recognise that personal bias moves well beyond obvious prejudice and can be embedded in subtle, taken-for-granted assumptions that influence, and even undermine, therapy with individuals whose cultures differ from that of the therapist. The chapter therefore explores some of the dimensions of culture considered relevant to mental health, particularly contextualising some of the tensions and contradictions in the application of Western models of psychological practice, such as CBT, to diverse groups of people unfamiliar with the Anglo/Eurocentric worldview and stance. CBT therapists are then invited to reflect on their personal cultural influences, using what has come to be known as the ADDRESSING acronym, which points to nine cultural influences that affect everyone, to build up a personal cultural profile (Hays, 2013).

Thinking about the influences of culture is often framed in terms of deficits and restrictions. However, in this chapter we emphasise the importance of identifying cultural strengths in order to build resilience, where appropriate. Heightening cultural awareness and integrating this awareness in a useful and therapeutic manner is a delicate balance and the reader is reminded that the relative importance of culture is variable. Some individuals experience it as "…rather like the air that surrounds us. It is vital, but we remain unaware of it" (Papworth, 2013, p. 256), whereas for others it is an important component of their existence. The relative significance of culture is often linked to the degree to which groups experience their culture as challenged or disregarded in contrast to individuals who experience their culture as "the way things are".

MULTICULTURAL THEMES

Discussing cultural diversity can be difficult. It can provoke a variety of reactions, for example, avoiding the topic completely (pretending it does not exist) or becoming very emotional and/or defensive about the subject. The five themes summarised below attempt to capture some of these contradictions. As a first reflective step, the reader may like to consider where they personally stand regarding these themes, and to notice if they experience a personal emotional response to any of them. The reader can also consider whether this emotional response is likely to influence the delivery of CBT in therapy contexts triggering unexamined cultural beliefs or assumptions. It should be noted that these arguments are complex and nuanced, and we have presented an abbreviated version of the main points (see Sue, D.W. & Sue, 2008).

Cultural universality versus cultural relativism

The universalistic perspective emphasises that which is common to all human beings. For example, in the mental health field it would be argued that particular types of disorder (e.g. schizophrenia or depression) occur in all cultural groups in the same proportions – we all pass through the same developmental milestones etc. The end point to this perspective is that we need to discover the "best" intervention/treatment and apply this with maximum skill and competence. "One size fits all" but this needs to be the best size! The universalistic perspective reflects what is generally considered to be the "dominant" cultural norm in the West (Anglo/American/Eurocentric). The universalistic perspective, it is argued, is supported by hard facts and empirical science (evidence-based practice). The relativist position, in contrast, gives greater weight to differences between cultural groups. It is pointed out that therapies and treatments developed in the West are culture-specific to the dominant society and are not necessarily an optimum approach for all (Sue, D.W. & Sue, 2008).

The emotional consequences of "race"

Most people will recognise that "race" is very often a highly emotive topic. Again, there can be a simplistic division between those who believe that there is no such thing as "race" and other groups who place enormous significance and investment in either their own identification with "race" or the exclusion of those belonging to another "race". Discussions about race can provoke a whole range of emotions (pride, guilt, defensiveness, suspicion, fear etc.).

The inclusive or exclusive nature of multiculturalism

The first two themes have led to debates concerning the ways in which cultural influence should be described and addressed, with some authors broadening traditional definitions of culture to include factors such as gender, sexual orientation, age and disability (Hays, 2013). These authors argue that each of these categories brings particular cultural ideas, advantages, or constraints that warrant consideration in the context of mental health. Authors concerned with the impact of more visible cultural differences consider this broadening of the definition to dilute and obscure what is perceived to be the important cultural implications of belonging to a minority cultural group, which is almost always associated with ethnic identity ("race"), and that this "race" is more often than not "non-European" in origin (Levinson, 2012).

The socio-political nature of the psychological therapies

The psychological therapies that originated and developed in the West consider the scientific method to be pre-eminent. However, it is important to note that psychological research has focused almost exclusively on people identified as Anglo/ American. This group, identified as "WEIRD" (Western, Educated, Industrialised, Rich and Democratic), constitute 12% of the world's population but represent 95% of participants in behavioural and psychological studies (Henrich, Heine & Norenzayan, 2010). This certainly cannot be considered a representative sample of the world's population. Many individuals from racial and ethnic minorities, along with some women, gay, lesbian and other groups identifying as minorities, believe that the psychological practice developed from this "research" does not reflect their needs. Some members of these groups express the view that, in some instances, the "evidence-based" psychological therapies are experienced as being "imposed" from a more powerful "establishment". Taking CBT as an example of Western psychological therapy, there is generally a focus on individual personal change rooted in the idea of personal responsibility. It has been argued that rational and objective verbal discourse are emphasised, and that the model is largely (at least initially) present focused, and can be seen to neglect the past. Spirituality, myth and metaphor can also be perceived to take a back seat. This is an over-generalised picture and contemporary CBT is more nuanced in the factors that are given consideration, and many contemporary authors have highlighted the therapeutic utility of metaphor and myth (Blenkiron, 2010; Stott, Mansell, Salkovskis, Lavender & Cartwright-Hatton, 2010), the importance of early childhood experiences (Young et al., 2003) and experiential, emotion-focused interventions (Beck, 2011). In contrast, again from a somewhat generalised perspective, non-Western cultures tend towards a greater emphasis on communal and family experience, valuing interdependence. Acceptance over change is often promoted and links to the past are important, particularly for cultures with little recorded history, such as First Nation people (e.g. Māori, Australian Aboriginal people and Native Americans). Spirituality, myth and folklore are emphasised, and communication styles – for example, little eye contact, indirect answers to questions and expectation of clear direction from professionals – are also different and can be interpreted as being rude, passive and lacking in personal responsibility, when these interactions may mean the exact opposite (Hays, 2013).

Cultural competence

The themes briefly discussed above have influenced various conceptualisations of cultural competence. Since the Second World War, 50 million refugees have been forced to flee their homes, through conflict, persecution and scarcity (Guterres, 2013). Many of these population groups, be they economic migrants, asylum seekers or refugees, have their origin in non-Western countries. This has meant that in certain urban areas (usually Western) the original inhabitants may feel challenged by different customs and behaviours. This has, on some occasions, led to migrants feeling unwelcome or excluded from mainstream society. As population diversity in the West increases, there is a growing awareness that mainstream psychotherapeutic resources may not be adequately meeting the varied and complex psychological needs of immigrants, refugees, and individuals belonging to ethnic and cultural minorities (Fernando, 2003). Statistics frequently appear to confirm this fact, with individuals from some of these groups often being over-represented in a variety of negative social indicators, such as drug and alcohol abuse, unemployment and poor physical and mental health (Levinson, 2012). This disadvantage is often blamed on racial discrimination and other negative factors associated with immigration and other marginalised groups in the host country. However, to date there remains a lack of research regarding the effectiveness of recognised evidenced-based therapies, such as CBT, with these disadvantaged groups (Smith, 2008).

Discrimination, prejudice and oppression are challenged and deemed unacceptable within mainstream psychological therapies, and the consideration of how multicultural and bicultural factors ought to be addressed in contemporary psychology is increasingly seen as a priority, so much so, that multi-cultural therapy (MCT) has been considered a Fourth Force in psychology, coming after the established psychoanalytic, humanistic and cognitive-behavioural psychological therapies (Pedersen, 1990). Questions are asked as to the utility and effectiveness of psychological therapies such as CBT for individuals residing in the West who do not conform to Western norms, and also the degree to which the principles and practice of CBT are transferable to individuals in other continents, such as South East Asia, India, Africa and South America. As a result of these factors, mental health services in most Western countries are attempting to find ways to adapt to and accommodate the varied needs of diverse populations, and there are increasing calls for cultural competency in mental health practitioners. In fact, many professional codes of ethics list this as a core competency (British Association of Counselling and Psychotherapy, 2007; New Zealand Psychologists' Board, 2014). However, it is as well to hold a tandem view of how cultural incompetence looks. Sue, D.W. and Sue (2008, p. 35) propose the following as indications of incompetence:

- Insensitivity to the needs of culturally diverse clients, showing little understanding of personal biases and prejudice.
- Minority groups that include individuals of differing sexual orientation complain that they feel intimidated or harassed.
- Discriminatory mental health practices such as over-diagnosis of certain groups, for example, in terms of "dangerousness".

- Mental health training programmes which continue to ignore the implications of ethnicity, gender and sexual orientation.
- In addition Sue (2010) highlights the importance of developing awareness regarding what is termed 'microaggressions'. Microaggressions are described as "brief everyday slights, indignities and denigrating messages sent out to marginalized people" (e.g. females, individuals from an ethnic minority background, LGBT groups, etc.). Microaggressions signify unconscious bias articulated by individuals who see themselves as fair-minded and unprejudiced. Some examples of microaggressions are complimenting a Chinese woman on her "excellent English" when she has been born and raised in the UK, or holding tightly to a handbag when passing a black man. The net result of repeated microaggressions is individuals from minority groups can feel marginalised, excluded, abnormal and as if they are second-class citizens. CBT therapists can guard against mcroaggressions by being constantly vigilant, open and non-defensive, becoming an "ally" to marginalised individuals.

A FRAMEWORK FOR UNDERSTANDING THE INFLUENCE OF CULTURE

An alternative to a confining definition of culture can be found in a tripartite model comprising three concentric circles that encapsulate all the features that contribute to our experience of culture. At the core, we are wholly unique and individual: this circle includes our genetic constitution and pre-birth experience. The next circle contains that which we experience as a consequence of being part of a group: it includes aspects such as sexual orientation, generational influences, religion, ethnic identity, geographic location, and marital status. The large enclosing circle is universal and contains that which makes us human: our biological similarity, self-awareness and ability to use symbols (Sue, D.W. & Sue, 2008). When conceptualising the impact of culture, it is useful to consider the themes discussed above and to use this model, showing the intersection between human universality, individual uniqueness and cultural specificity, as contributing to each individual's worldview (Cox, 1982).

TOOLS TO SUPPORT CBT THERAPIST REFLECTION ON PERSONAL CULTURAL BIAS

Despite the fact that, up until recently, few CBT textbooks have referenced culture (Hays, 2006), CBT and Multi Cultural Therapy (MCT) share a number of underlying principles, such as a strong orientation towards empiricism, a transparent and collaborative approach regarding sharing information with the client, a recognition of the importance of integrating idiosyncratic client phenomenology into the formulation of presenting problems, a belief in client empowerment, and an increasing focus on developing resilience through identifying strengths (Hays, 2006; Kuyken et al., 2009). There is also growing evidence that CBT (adapted and tweaked) can be effective for groups belonging to non-Western cultures (Bennett, Flett & Babbage, 2007; El-Leithy, 2014).

To reiterate, developing cultural competence depends on increased cultural self-awareness on the part of the individual CBT therapist (Hays, 2009). Confronting personal bias can be difficult for CBT therapists, who are usually predominantly representative of the dominant culture (American Psychological Association, 2005; New Zealand Psychologists' Board, 2014) and generally perceive themselves to be culturally neutral, largely benign and without bias. Cultural bias is often seen as holding negative beliefs or prejudicial attitudes to different cultures, attitudes most therapists work hard to avoid. It is, however, more difficult to identify and explore differences in core values, which can be subtle and reflect a perception that Western values and ideals are more advanced, scientific, more "the way things should be", and are generally consistent with the attainment of optimum wellbeing. Another salient factor is that when asked directly about the influence of culture, this group will often respond that they have no culture. It is indicative of the perception that the way they are is "just normal", as illustrated by the following self-reflective comments made by a group of CBT trainees:

> *"I was raised European with little cultural influence."*

> *"I have stronger cultural perspectives than I knew – I didn't think I had any."*

> *"I now realise my culture influences my life more than I thought."*

Using the ADDRESSING categories to uncover personal bias

As previously mentioned, the acronym ADDRESSING is proposed as a convenient and inclusive mnemonic to encapsulate a number of culturally influential factors beyond visible racial ethnic minority groups (Hays, 2013), for example: age and generational factors, developmental disabilities, disabilities acquired later in life, religious and spiritual orientation, ethnic and racial identity, socio-economic status, sexual orientation, Indigenous heritage, national origin and gender. Each of these factors influences the way we see ourselves and the way others see and respond to us. Reflecting on these categories, and building up an individualised ADDRESSING profile can help CBT therapists deepen their understanding of the influences of their culture. The different facets of each of the ADDRESSING categories are summarised below. Each of these categories warrants a discussion beyond the scope of this chapter and the reader is encouraged to enlarge on some of the ideas presented here to move from declarative understanding to an operationalisation of the procedural implications of each category, building personal and professional "when… then…" rules or guidelines.

Age and generational differences

Different generations are subject to particular environmental and socio-political experiences that shape values, perceptions and expectations. Western generational cohorts have been named: the Great Generation, Baby Boomers, Generation Jones and

Generations X and Y (Carlson, 2008; Ulrich & Harris, 2003). The Great Generation, born between 1928 and 1945, experienced the Second World War and the potential of nuclear power as an agent of total destruction. Growing up with a large degree of uncertainty, this generation is often characterised as conservative, valuing security. In contrast, the Baby Boomers, born between 1946 and 1965 in the West, experienced post-war economic growth and prosperity, benefitted from free tertiary education, cheap housing, the birth control pill and generally socially supportive political systems. This generation is often referred to as the "me" generation, but it was also instrumental in initiating and supporting significant social change, such as the anti-apartheid movement, the sexual revolution and feminism. This generation tends to be influenced by a "universalistic view of culture", wanting to believe that everyone is equal, the "same under the skin" and that "race" neither exists nor matters.

Clearly over-generalisations abound when entire generations are endowed with certain characteristics. However, self-reflection regarding one's personal generational cohort can be revealing. Age also influences the ways in which individuals are perceived and treated. Elderly people can be respected and deferred to in some cultures, or disregarded in others. Children and young people also evoke varied responses and modes of discipline in different cultures.

Developmental disabilities

Some individuals born with genetic or birth-related conditions, such as achondroplesia (dwarfism), cerebral palsy and deafness, express the view that they represent a particular cultural identity or perspective and espouse a view that, in many instances, they can feel excluded, ridiculed or not taken seriously by mainstream society. Individuals experiencing these conditions find certain forms of language describing these conditions as derogatory, for example, many take issue with being labelled "disabled". Some such groups have developed their own preferred descriptor. For example, some individuals with dwarfism prefer "Little People" or "LP" (Little People UK, 2015).

Disabilities acquired later in life

These can include chronic physical or mental health conditions that may or may not have a genetic component. Disability can also be caused through accident. Individuals in these groups can experience similar difficulties to those described in the previous category. They may, in some instances, feel stigmatised and judged. There can also be a "before" and "after" experience requiring adjustment and reorientation.

Religious and spiritual influences

Religious and spiritual identities are very influential in some cultures and it is important to recognise that "spirituality is often the language of culturally diverse people" (Brinson & Cervantes, 2003, p. 124). Many of these individuals may have a fatalist view of adversity, accepting mental health problems as "the will of God".

This may contradict some CBT therapists' standpoints, which might prioritise self-efficacy. In contrast to the spiritual perspective, the Western scientist-practitioner is often assumed to be agnostic or atheist, and to view this belief system as more rational or healthy. This is of course a very generalised perspective and CBT practitioners obviously subscribe to a range of spiritual and religious views. However, those clients with a more fundamentalist religious outlook may assume that psychological practitioners will espouse non-religious views and that these will be disrespectful. Attitudes to sexuality, marriage, gender, independence, autonomy, education, clothing, food and child-rearing practices are just some of the areas impacted by religious and spiritual beliefs. The experiences of belonging or feeling alienated and different are also important. Prejudice, trivialisation of values and practices, and persecution can result from religious views.

Ethnic and racial identity

This is probably the influence that most individuals notice or attend to. As mentioned previously, some authors worry that broadened conceptualisations of culture, as depicted by the ADDRESSING model, obscure the socio-political relevance of race and ethnicity for some groups, particularly those who identify as being from a minority, disadvantaged background (Levinson, 2012). Ethnic minorities may experience varying degrees of acceptance, with some groups finding it easier to blend in with the dominant culture than others.

Socio-economic status

Socio-economic position, which is determined by factors such as income, occupation, education and class, is influential in how groups within populations experience the world. Higher socio-economic status is generally associated with dominance and power. Historically, in countries such as Britain, social class has played an important role in controlling access to power and economic resources, and limiting social mobility (Cannadine, 2000). Since the mid-twentieth century, however, it has been suggested that the existence of a restricting class structure has been challenged socially, politically and educationally, as encapsulated by Tony Blair's "the class war is over" statement in 1997 (Marsden, 1999). Most people in Britain would now define themselves as middle-class, although seven socio-economic classes have now been identified (Savage et al., 2013). Statistics tell a different story, with recent data confirming Britain as having one of the lowest rates of social mobility in the developed world, with indications that this situation is likely to worsen (Harrison, 2013). Different theories are proposed to account for this situation, with some prominent commentators coming down on the continued influence of class on the distribution of wealth and power (Erikson & Goldthorpe, 2010). As the more obvious manifestations of the class struggle have been obscured, it has been observed that there is a disconnect between the economically advantaged and disadvantaged, with privileged groups having no knowledge of the implications of experiencing poverty and unemployment

(Standing, 2011). Other Western democracies, such as the USA, Australia and New Zealand, show similar mobility trends but often delude themselves that they are egalitarian societies. In reality, however, the dominant group (Anglo/European) are carrying what has been called "the invisible knapsack of privilege" (McIntosh, 1998). Privileges can be very subtle, for example, being able to behave in all kinds of negative ways without your behaviour being attributed to your ethnic background, having your history and culture continually validated by all forms of media, and so on (McIntosh, 1998).

Sexual orientation

Although there has been progress towards a greater acceptance of individuals identifying as lesbian, gay, bisexual, transgendered or queer/questioning (LGBTQ) in the West, individuals within these groups continue to report experiencing prejudice, stereotyping and minority status in many social and legal instances. What is termed disparagement humour is still common in some media, and hate crimes continue to be committed (British Psychological Society, 2012a). This is also a complicated area for therapists to negotiate in cultural groups that do not accept that alternatives to heterosexual expression of sexuality are acceptable.

Indigenous heritage

Indigenous groups are those groups identifying as First Nation or original inhabitants. These groups, once the majority, have suffered historically through the colonisation process (Fanon, 1969). Populations have generally been reduced and many Indigenous individuals experience marginalisation in their own land (King, 2003). These groups are exposed to similar problems experienced by other minority groups and have additional concerns about the loss of their land and right to natural resources. Many individuals identifying as Indigenous also have strong links to the dominant culture through marriage and the degree to which they experience the impact of Indigenous heritage can vary greatly.

National origin

National origin refers to the individual's country of birth. The importance of national origin can shift and change, particularly in settler countries such as America. For example, Irish and Italian immigrants to the USA were originally perceived as minority groups, although they are now established over several generations and are considered wholly American. These individuals are no longer referred to as either Irish or Italian Americans. In contrast, Nigerians, Congolese and other African ethnic groups transported to America as slaves, at the same time or earlier, are still referred to as Black Americans rather than Americans. This is perceived as exclusionary to individuals of African descent who have resided in the USA for generations and experience themselves as being wholly American (Walker, 2014).

Gender

Cultural stereotypes affect both men and women. Men are generally recognised as dominant in most economic, political and societal institutions. As with sexuality, several waves of feminism have occurred in the West and the status of women has, on the whole, been positively affected. However, many women still experience themselves as having unequal or lesser status than men, as evidenced by income and power differentials. Domestic and many other forms of violence also continue to be predominantly directed towards women. Women from non-dominant religious and cultural groups are often more visible in terms of externalised signs of culture, such as dress, and may experience additional prejudice because of this. For example, women wearing a headscarf, hijab or burka can be harassed. Individuals identifying as transgendered continue to suffer minority status and abuse, and have high rates of mental health concerns, particularly anxiety disorders, depression, eating disorders, self-harm and suicide attempts. These problems are often related to a perception of prejudice and sometimes to "well-meaning" efforts to change the individual's pre-ferred orientation (British Psychological Society, 2012a). There can also be practical issues to confront, for example, using gender-specific public toilets or men who chose to identify as female having to go to a male prison.

Gender definition is a complex and changing area of discourse as binary gender categorisations are challenged. This is a field where CBT therapists may have lit-tle factual information and self-reflection regarding personal attitudes, biases, social, religious and historical influences is of particular importance. Recognising ignorance and bias in this area is crucial as some interventions are extreme (e.g. surgical gender reassignment) and are reliant on psychological assessment and support.

Additional points to consider in conjunction with the ADDRESSING categories

- The effect and **implications of overlap** between categories from both a personal and client perspective (for example, an individual can be elderly, belong to an ethnic minority group and have a minority sexual orientation).
- **The importance of language**. Terminology is both culturally- and time-dependent, and changes rapidly. There can also be a disconnection between the preferred language of those individuals identifying with particular groupings and that of the therapist. This is particularly evident in the gender and sexual orientation categories (World Professional Association for Transgendered Health (WPATH), 2001). It is important therefore to reflect on the appropriate use of one's own cultural language.

Reflecting on and developing a personal cultural profile

To deepen cultural self-awareness, CBT therapists can complete a personal cultural profile or sketch based on the individually relevant ADDRESSING categories (see Table 5.1). After developing a personal cultural profile, consider the questions below.

TABLE 5.1 *ADDRESSING cultural influences (adapted from Hays, 2013, p. 15)*

Cultural influences
Age and generational influences
Developmental and other disabilities
Religion and spirituality
Ethnic and racial identity
Socio-economic status
Sexual orientation
Indigenous heritage
National origin
Gender

When addressing these questions, it is useful to keep in mind that there are no straightforward answers, and there will always be ambiguity and uncertainty in these areas. What is important is that therapists reflect on their point of view.

- Which of the categories associate you with either the dominant or non-dominant group? What do you make of this? How does this impact on your work as a therapist?
- Consider your "knapsack of privilege" in conjunction with the ADDRESSING categories. This can be applied from both perspectives, therapists who have an "invisible knapsack" and those who believe they do not.
- What is the intersection between your cultural profile and that of your clients? Similar or different? What are some of the implications of this intersection? For example, a therapist with an Anglo/European background delivering therapy to an Indigenous or ethnic community. Some mental health services try to "match" client and therapist in terms of cultural dimensions, for example in New Zealand in the mid-1990s there was considerable debate concerning the importance of matching client/therapist gender. This particular debate is now almost non-existent. There remains concern regarding Indigenous clients who are often asked whether they want to see a Maori therapist or not. What do you think about this type of debate? What are the advantages, disadvantages and difficulties in these debates?
- Are there any particular clients whose ADDRESSING profiles differ markedly from your own? Reflect on your therapy-related assumptions and behaviours which may have resulted from this difference. For example, an older therapist nearing retirement working with adolescents, a heterosexual therapist working with transgendered, gay or lesbian clients, or an agnostic therapist seeing clients with fundamentalist religious beliefs.
- How has your cultural profile affected your attitude to your training or clinical practice? For example, some cultural groups have an extremely respectful attitude regarding their supervisors or trainers and might be inclined to accept all statements from

authority figures without question, expect categorical answers and become distressed when faced with a more guided CBT approach. This can be a challenge for a supervisor used to a more informal and independent style and can upset students who want more authoritative direction.

- How can you gain more declarative knowledge in those areas where you have identified gaps?
- Is there anything that you would like to do differently or change?

Below are a number of case examples drawn from a group of novice CBT practitioners using the ADDRESSING model (Table 5.1) to reflect on the interface between aspects of their personal cultural profiles and their current CBT practice.

Tuiara's national identity is as a New Zealander, although her ethnic identity is Cook Islander (Pacific Island). Reflecting on her profile, she considered the following as a major challenge in her CBT practice and reflected:

> "I strongly feel that my cultural values influence the way I think and practise. There are two major cultural values that I always find challenging when it comes to being a therapist or having a leadership role (taking into account my age) – and that is Respect and Submission. Culturally, the qualification/achievement that you have doesn't necessarily give you authority/right to provide advice – but what is culturally appropriate is that when you are dealing with people (in general), you need to give 100% respect and submission to those older than yourself. I am seeing an older client at the moment, and I am finding it challenging when I am giving advice as a therapist having that 'I also need to submit' mentality, in the background, because of my age."

Tuiara experienced similar difficulties with another client, an adolescent boy with learning difficulties who was experiencing symptoms of social anxiety. The client reported being verbally and emotionally harassed and belittled by his Cook Island parents, who believed this approach would motivate change. The parents were older than the therapist and therefore she thought that they could not be approached and apprised of the fact that their response to their son's symptoms was compounding the problem. Tuiara had to enlist the aid of the community minister. He was able to use his authority to instruct the parents to desist. This was done in a fairly authoritarian manner but had a positive effect.

   This example illustrates a myriad of problems that can occur at the interface between cultures, such as the age of the therapist, child-rearing practices, and the principles of CBT (collaboration and assertiveness). In this case, the therapist was an ethnic match, however her socio-economic status and tertiary education at a Western university meant some of her cultural values had been challenged. As an enthusiastic novice CBT therapist she had to find ways of negotiating this impasse, which may have been almost impossible for someone with no knowledge of the culture.

   In contrast to Tuiara's experience, Tatjana, a Serbian from the former Yugoslavia, identified the opposite experience. She stated that in her Serbian culture: "*as a professional you had better know what you are doing*". This generated anxiety during her clinical placement year as she felt she should be showing and delivering expertise far beyond what she could realistically expect to know at her level of experience.

A number of therapists in the group identified as having British cultural roots and unanimously agreed that they had never considered their culture as an influence. After completing the ADDRESSING table, they all agreed that maxims such as "having a stiff upper lip", "keeping up with the Joneses", and having to make things work and be perceived as a success, were all strongly-held, culturally-derived views which played an important part in both their professional and personal lives. For example:

"Keeping a stiff upper lip limits my emotional reactions which is not good personally."

"My beliefs regarding independence, strength and resilience aren't always healthy."

"Perfectionism and performance anxiety are evident in my European upper middle-class upbringing where the individual must make her mark/make it happen/do it excellently. This driver is hard to unpack after 54 years."

Constructing a "cultural" genogram

In addition to building a cultural profile, cultural self-awareness can be enhanced by constructing a personal genogram, noting helpful and unhelpful cultural messages conveyed by various family members, and asking oneself how influential these family influences have been (Brinson & Cervantes, 2003). Reflecting on early educational experiences can also be an illuminating influence. Prejudice and bias can be instilled by these experiences, quite often by the omission of facts rather than blatant misrepresentation. For example, in the recent past, in settler countries such as South Africa, Australia and New Zealand, European history was privileged over the history of the Indigenous population. Educational experiences such as these can lead to knowledge gaps, which, at worst, can engender assumptions of superiority or inferiority, in both dominant and non-dominant groups.

Using reflection to identify and integrate cultural strengths

CBT is often referred to as a short-term, problem-focused therapy and therapists are well schooled in the importance of eliciting and prioritising clients' presenting problems. Clients also expect to talk about their problems, after all this is the primary reason for embarking on psychological therapy. However, contemporary approaches to CBT increasingly emphasise the importance of adopting a strengths-based approach to tackle presenting problems and build resilience, and the idea that it is more fruitful to develop a New Way of Being, as opposed to challenging and dismantling Old Ways of Being, is taking root (Bennett-Levy et al., 2015; Kuyken et al., 2009; Mooney & Padesky, 2000).

However, being modest, self-critical and distancing oneself from "blowing one's own trumpet" or boasting is a stance shared by many cultures, although it is probably more prominent in older generations. Many cultures overtly embrace the idea that self-criticism and receiving criticism from others is character building and prevents complacency and sloth. This can be particularly true in Asian cultures. Nations such as Australia and New Zealand take pride in egalitarianism and sometimes equate an individual's awareness of their strengths as "being a tall poppy", and work together to cut such individuals down. However, the quest for a more affirmative view of self has, since the mid-1960s, been increasingly emphasised in Western countries through Positive Psychology and Self-Actualisation movements (Seligman, 2002). The Baby Boomers were referred to as the "me" generation, and Generation Y is called the "me me" generation or the narcissistic generation.

Despite this move towards embracing positive self-affirmation, clinical experience suggests that when invited to identify their strengths, both clients and therapists often express anxiety and embarrassment, claiming that the task is difficult and that they are drawing a blank. It is now recommended that identifying strengths becomes a routine part of clinical assessment and case formulation (Kuyken et al., 2009). In parallel, identifying cultural strengths as a cultural resource that can build resilience and be built into some treatment interventions is also recommended (Hays, 2009). An important goal in expanding therapist self-reflective capacity is that the attendant increase in self-awareness transfers to clinical practice. To facilitate awareness, CBT therapists can reflect on their cultural strengths. Thinking about what you do well can be a good start. As far as cultural strengths are concerned, personal, interpersonal and environment supports often yield interesting information. Personal supports can be cultural identity, spiritual faith, creative ability, language and helpful culturally-specific beliefs. Interpersonal support can include extended family, traditional celebrations, and political and social action groups. Environmental supports can be found in food, nature and creative arts (Hays, 2009).

ADDITIONAL AVENUES FOR THERAPIST SELF-REFLECTION

There are many pathways leading to increased socio-cultural awareness. At the most obvious level, simply paying attention to the cultural diversity present in your social group, place of residence, work situation, town and country can be very informative. Participating in cultural or religious festivals outside your own can be an interesting and enlightening experience. Western festivals such as Christmas and Easter are widely celebrated in the West and beyond. Take opportunities to attend other major cultural festivals, such as Chinese New Year, Diwali and Eid. Visiting ethnic markets, eating different food, going to films from unfamiliar countries, exposing oneself to different forms of literature and generally adopting an attitude of openness and respectful curiosity can expand cultural awareness. At a deeper level, finding out about the experiences of individuals belonging to non-dominant groups is important. Individuals belonging to these groups are often more than willing to talk about their experience, as their experience is all to often that of marginalisation. Reflecting on your reactions to experiences such as these and identifying preconceptions and/or predictions about the nature of these experiences can be a useful exercise and will go some way towards enabling the therapist's development of what Hays (2009) calls "cultural schema". Hays (2009) emphasises that it is not up to clients to explain their culture to the therapist; it is the therapist's responsibility to do their own research and ask the client only questions that are relevant to the client's unique experience of culture in the therapeutic context.

PROCEDURAL GUIDELINES FOR DEVELOPING CULTURAL SELF-AWARENESS

- Develop the ability to actively self-monitor in therapy situations where cultural difference is apparent and attend to your cultural assumptions and biases. Remember that bias can be positive (halo effect) and negative. Notice your emotional responses.
- Be vigilant about possible cultural blind spots you may have identified when doing some of the exercises suggested in this chapter. In addition, ask others for feedback and listen to the feedback you get.
- Actively seek out cultural advice and consultation from relevant cultural representatives, when appropriate.
- When working with interpreters, reflect on the additional layer of potential socio-cultural difference and the potential for unhelpful interactions.
- Make a regular and consistent time for reflection on cultural concerns, and do not assume that just because you do not experience yourself as a biased person that you have no bias.
- Brinson and Cervantes (2003) recommend that therapists pay particular attention to their personal beliefs regarding religion and spirituality and think about how these personal beliefs might impact on professional practice. As previously mentioned, a spiritual outlook can often be given greater emphasis in some cultures.

CONCLUSION

Delivering CBT in a culturally sensitive and aware manner can be a complicated enterprise and it is important to recognise that the impact of culture is always an idiosyncratic experience and can differ in felt intensity. Understanding and integrating client and therapist socio-cultural influences is a task to be approached with honesty, sensitivity, respect and curiosity. Recognising that these factors exist, are important, and that we as therapists are often unaware of our own cultural influences, let alone those of our clients, should always be kept in mind. The task of increasing cultural competence is ongoing and must always begin with the therapist's personal exploration of the impact of cultural influences on their beliefs, assumptions and resulting behaviours. This chapter has concentrated on developing self-understanding through reflection as a first step, noting that "a culturally responsive approach to CBT begins long before the start of therapeutic work with clients. It begins with the therapist's attention to those areas where they may hold biases because of inexperience or knowledge gaps" (Hays, 2006, p. 8). It is only through disciplined self-reflection that this process can begin.

TAKING IT FORWARD

What *declarative knowledge* have you gained from reading this chapter?

- Identify one important fact you have learned
- How will you utilise this knowledge?
- How would you explain this to a colleague?

What personal *procedural rules* for understanding and integrating cultural considerations into your CBT practice have you developed?

- Try to identify a "when… then…" rule that you can implement to improve the cultural sensitivity of your CBT practice.
- What strategies are you going to put in place to facilitate the expansion of your socio-cultural awareness?

What specific actions could you take to increase your *reflection* on your cultural self-awareness and on the cultures of others, particularly related to the clients you see?

- What barriers prevent you from being able to step back and reflect on cultural difference? How could you surmount these barriers?
- What structures could you put in place?

SUGGESTED READING

Hays, P. A. (2013). *Connecting across cultures.* Los Angeles, CA: Sage.

Morgan, A. (2015). *Reading the world: confessions of a literary explorer.* London: Harvill Secker.

6

CLIENT FEEDBACK:

An Essential Input to Therapist Reflection

James Hawkins, Richard Thwaites and Beverly Haarhoff

LEARNING AIMS

- To detail research findings relating to client outcomes for psychological therapies over the past four decades
- To alert CBT therapists to the possibility that they may be inflating their perceived therapeutic competency
- To provide declarative knowledge about the importance of systematic collection of client feedback (e.g. routine outcome measurement) as an input to reflection within self-supervision or clinical supervision
- To provide procedural guidance to structure CBT therapists' reflection on feedback from clients who are not responding at expected rates early in therapy

INTRODUCTION

During earlier chapters of this book we have discussed the role of reflection in facilitating the ability of CBT therapists to deliver therapy with sensitivity, flexibility and artistry, while adhering to evidence-based models. We have also detailed the role of reflection in the development of therapist skills from initial training through to master therapists.

Both supervision (see Chapter 2) and self-supervision (see Chapter 3) have been discussed as potential forums for reflection, and procedural guidance on how to best use these has been provided. Within these chapters a whole range of inputs

to reflection have been discussed, including specific therapy events (e.g. client disengagement), therapist thoughts (e.g. *"This client will never get better with CBT"*,
"I don't want to upset my client with Exposure and Response Prevention"), therapist feelings
(e.g. anxiety) and therapist behaviours (e.g. therapist taking too much responsibility
in session, avoiding a hyperventilation experiment) that alert the CBT therapist to
the need for reflection. Within the current chapter we will examine in detail another
potential input to reflection, one that is much underused despite the evidence that it
could improve clinical outcomes dramatically: client feedback (for example, sessional
outcome data and routine ratings of the therapeutic alliance). This session-by-session
feedback is one answer to the common question of "What kind of reflection, on what
aspects of our practice, is likely to be particularly helpful in improving our effectiveness
as CBT therapists?"

As therapists do we know how many clients we help? Or which problems we are
more effective with? Are you highly effective in working with depression but less
effective with anxiety disorders? How do you know? How do you decide what training you need? Is it based on hard evidence or a gut feeling?

Within clinical services or research trials we can observe different levels of effectiveness, both overall and with specific disorders. In this chapter we argue that the use
of routine outcome measures provides valuable information on:

- Which of your clients are failing to improve?
- How many clients are you able to help effectively?
- Which presenting problems are you less effective with, and how might this be addressed
  in self-supervision, supervision or training?

This chapter also argues that there is a wealth of research data suggesting that
CBT therapists would benefit from reflection on those clients who are not making good or expected progress. This would help therapists to be in a position to
take action to prevent therapeutic drift (Waller, 2009), suboptimal therapy or
ultimately even client disengagement. It is also argued that to do this well we
need to improve our sessional monitoring of both symptom levels and of the
therapeutic alliance.

The first section of the chapter presents research that supports the generally beneficial effects of all established psychological therapies. It also highlights the embarrassing
lack of progress over the years in making psychological therapies, including CBT, still
more effective. The fact that many therapists can be lax when it comes to utilising
personal "practice-based evidence" regarding how clients are actually progressing, or
failing to progress, is explored. In addition, it has been found that there are significant
differences between individual therapists, with some therapists obtaining consistently
better client outcomes. This fact, in conjunction with the observation that therapists,
on the whole, show a marked tendency to overstate their competence, is explored in
relation to possible pathways to achieving better outcomes. Finally, structured self-
reflection on regular, systematically collected client feedback is proposed as a way of
correcting this situation, along with the likely benefits that this particularly productive
form of self-reflection can bring for CBT therapists and their clients. Clinical outcomes are identified as a key input to the other reflective processes discussed in this

book, such as self-supervision or supervision. Reflective practice is not a replacement for routine outcome measurement; routine outcome measurement is a key input into reflective practice.

It is important to note that while almost all the research reported in this chapter refers to psychological therapies in general, this of course includes CBT. CBT is widely accepted as an established evidence-based model. While this is not contested, it is possible that some CBT therapists may become complacent about their therapeutic competency simply because they identify as a CBT therapist and think "Well, I'm providing the most evidence-based treatment for their problem…", thus perhaps blocking a more reflective and curious stance regarding variation in their therapy outcomes.

WHAT DOES RESEARCH TELL US ABOUT THE EFFECTIVENESS OF PSYCHOLOGICAL THERAPY?

Outcomes for psychological therapy are pretty good, but largely stagnant

Psychological therapies have been shown to be effective. When treating people suffering from psychological disorders, psychological therapy achieves similar results to psychiatric drugs but typically with outcomes that are better maintained (Cuijpers et al., 2013; De Maat, Dekker, Schoevers & De Jonghe, 2006; Huhn et al., 2014). To put this into a broader context, psychiatric drugs themselves achieve results that are similar to outcomes produced by pharmacotherapy for general medical conditions – a major comparison of key meta-analyses found average effect sizes of 0.49 for psychiatric medications and 0.45 for general medical medications (Leucht, Hierl, Kissling, Dold & Davis, 2012). Effect size estimates are a very useful measurement method when meta-analyses need a common format to quantify the different outcomes of a number of individual research studies. When contrasting diverse diseases, one should treat simple effect size comparisons with considerable caution. The overall picture provided by these reviews is, however, still useful – the benefits achieved through psychological therapy are worthwhile and roughly comparable to treatment outcomes achieved across the whole field of medicine. In fact, hundreds of psychological therapy meta-analyses have shown effect sizes of approximately 0.6 (0.4 to 0.8) (Lambert, 2013). In the social sciences this is considered a "medium" to "strong" result (for Cohen's d). To clarify the statistics, an effect size of 0.6 means that 73% of those receiving psychological therapy have a better outcome than the average client who does not receive psychological therapy. Or to put it slightly differently, 64% of clients receiving psychological therapy achieve a "successful result" compared with only 36% of clients who are not receiving therapy. Increasingly, economic analyses are demonstrating how cost-effective these psychological therapy outcomes can be (Smith & Williams, 2013).

These are robust results, showing encouraging reductions of relapse and cost-effectiveness – so what's not to like about these benefits of psychological therapy? Well, since Smith, Glass and Miller's famous early estimate of an 0.85 effect size from a meta-analysis of 475 psychotherapy studies (Smith, Glass & Miller, 1980), research has failed to show any general improvement in psychotherapy outcomes over the subsequent 30 plus years (Lambert, 2013). When one considers the vast amount of effort that has been put into trying to make therapy more effective, this lack of improvement seems hard to understand (although interestingly one could make similar pessimistic claims for all the research money poured into trying to find more effective antidepressant medications). An example of this very disappointing lack of progress in CBT specifically is illustrated by a 2008 paper analysing the outcomes reported in 364 research studies of CBT treatment for anxiety disorders published over the last 40 years (Ost, 2008). Ost concluded that "the results showed that in most instances there were no significant changes in effect size across time" (2008, p. 5).

There are some scattered signs of progress but these signs are fairly few and far between. An awful lot of the "noise" around the many regular conferences and workshops seems to be more about therapy "fashions" than about genuinely important advances in the client outcomes that are achieved. In fact, when we look at the psychological therapy field in general, improved statistical methods suggest that we have been overestimating our effectiveness (Cuijpers et al., 2009; Lambert, 2013), and far from seeing progress, our results are actually worse than we were claiming three or four decades ago.

What of the therapist's contribution?

Depressingly, lack of progress in producing better outcomes over the decades is mirrored by similar findings for individual therapists, who, as a group, do not appear to show an improved rate of successful outcome relating to length of clinical training or experience. Research study after research study has shown that most therapists do not seem to get better results as they gain increasing professional experience. Outcomes achieved are typically unrelated to the therapist's qualifications, training, type of therapy, age and gender (Baldwin & Imel, 2013). Possibly experience with particular types of client difficulty may boost the helpfulness of therapists working in specific domains or with specific problems (Kraus, Castonguay, Boswell, Nordberg & Hayes, 2011), but even this common-sense finding waits for adequate replication. At least the position of psychological therapy may not be as dire as in medicine more generally, where a systematic review of 62 studies examining the link between physician experience and patient outcome found that in 52% of the studies increased years of experiences was associated with poorer performance on all outcomes and in 21% of the studies increased experiences was associated with worse outcomes on some measures and no difference on others (Choudhry, Fletcher & Soumerai, 2005). This review

identified an inverse relationship between years of experience and the quality of care provided, and in some studies, an inverse relationship with resultant
death rates as well. It is easy to reassure ourselves as psychological therapists that
at least with talking therapies we are not liable to produce such toxic damage
if we are not working optimally. This reassurance is hollow, though, and only
defensible if we are unaware of the increased disability and mortality associated
with persisting psychological distress. There is significant research demonstrating
this (Russ, Stamatakis, Hamer, Starr, Kivimaki & Batty, 2012; Saint Onge, Krueger
& Rogers, 2014; US Burden of Disease Collaborators, 2013; Whiteford et al., 2013)
and it is recognised that better management of psychological problems can change
subsequent risk. For example, a recent study showed that improved management
of depression in older adults was associated with a 24% decrease in death rates over
the eight years of follow-up (Gallo et al., 2013).

It is likely that many therapists are ignorant of the mortality increases associated
with poor treatment largely because, in contrast to poor surgical operations, clients
do not typically die in front of them. However, our clients, even those with common
mental health problems such as anxiety disorders and depression, who drop out of
treatment, may experience preventable poor psychological and physical wellbeing in
the future although we don't get to see the suffering once they disengage from our
services. It is our ethical duty to take advantage of research findings, both in the field
of specific CBT models but also in how we track and take action on clients' sessional
responses to the therapy we deliver.

Can individual therapists make a difference?

Despite this lack of overall improvement in the effectiveness of psychological
therapy over the last three or four decades, fascinatingly, and very importantly,
there is considerable variation in therapist effectiveness, although therapists themselves are poor at assessing their own success rates. While the vast majority of
psychological therapy research studies have not been designed to detect differences in the outcomes achieved by individual therapists, there are now several
research teams who have looked carefully at this area and found that there is very
significant variation between therapists (Anderson, Ogles, Patterson, Lambert &
Vermeersch, 2009; Baldwin & Imel, 2013; Lutz, Leon, Martinovich, Lyons & Stiles,
2007; Okiishi, Lambert, Eggett, Nielsen, Dayton & Vermeersch, 2006; Saxon &
Barkham, 2012; Wampold & Brown, 2005). To illustrate this point, a recent study
investigated the therapeutic effectiveness of 119 therapists treating 10,786 clients
across a range of UK adult primary care counselling and psychological therapy
services. Recovery rates were calculated using the standard Jacobson and Truax
(1991) criteria of reliable change to below the clinical cut-off post-treatment.
These researchers found that 19 "poor" therapists (16%) achieved only an average
43.3% recovery rate, 79 "good" therapists (66%) achieved a 58% recovery rate,
while 21 "excellent" therapists (18%) achieved 75.6% recovery rates (Saxon &
Barkham, 2012) (see Figure 6.1).

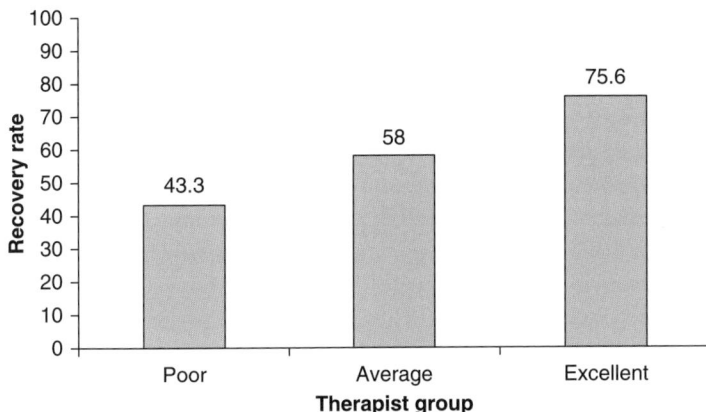

FIGURE 6.1   *Difference in recovery rates between therapists (Saxon & Barkham, 2012)*

In an even more recent paper looking at the outcomes of low intensity practitioners, Green et al. (2014) found that the 25% least helpful practitioners in their study produced effect sizes of about 0.2, while the most helpful 25% produced effect sizes of more than 0.9 (with the most effective practitioners getting considerably better results than even this impressive effect size). Looking at effect size for therapists allows us to understand the variance between therapists rather than the impossible aim of making all therapists at least average. Some therapists will always be less effective than others, but our aim is to reduce the variance of those who are below the best. The authors comment that these results should prompt further "therapist effects" research to sample both the characteristics and actual "in-session" behaviours of effective practitioners (Green et al., 2014). This will then identify what it is that effective practitioners are doing differently, and how this is actually clinically achieved.

What are the differences between the behaviours of the poor therapist and the average therapist? Basic skills around goal setting, focus, formulation and maintaining fidelity to the evidence base? What is the difference between average therapists and excellent therapists? Have the latter developed a storehouse of procedural guidance that they can reflect on and implement with their more challenging clients? Research suggests possibly so. There has been some research regarding the characteristics of therapists identified as "supershrinks" or "master therapists" (see Chapter 1 for more detail). These studies identify "unusually high levels of reflectivity" as an important quality that these therapists have in common (Rønnestad & Skovholt, 2001). It could be hypothesised, therefore, that this group of therapists would pay attention to, and reflect deeply upon, clients who are failing to achieve a positive outcome from therapy. It seems important to move towards investigating what these therapists actually do when they are faced with clients who fail to improve. For example, the in-session practice of the single "super-coach" in Green et al.'s paper (2014) would be a useful single-case study looking at their clinical decision-making and micro-skills when faced with clients who are not responding to initial evidence-based interventions. Imagine the huge improvement in service effectiveness, with the resulting major reductions in suffering, disability and death, if the minimally effective therapists could learn to be as helpful for their clients as a moderately effective therapist, never mind the excellent therapists!

An immediate problem with trying to implement such a potentially ground-breaking improvement strategy is that in most clinical practice nobody really knows which therapists are excellent, which are good, and which are poor. It certainly seems to be a waste of time to ask therapists themselves. Remember that Saxon and Barkham's study (2012) found that 18% of therapists were excellent, 66% were good, and 16% were poor. When mental health professionals were asked to rate their overall clinical skills and performance compared to others in their profession, 25% assessed themselves to be in the top 10%, the remaining 75% assessed themselves as above average, and none rated themselves as below average (Walfish, McAlister, O'Donnell & Lambert, 2012). As the poet Robert Burns (1785) wrote:

> O wad some Power the giftie gie us
>
> to see oursels as ithers see us!
>
> It wad frae mony a blunder free us,
>
> an' foolish notion

UTILISING CLIENT FEEDBACK AS AN INPUT TO REFLECTION

It has been suggested that a huge and still under-used resource is obtaining and acting on feedback about how our clients are, or are not, progressing. Although CBT therapists, in keeping with the empiricist principles of CBT, are trained and encouraged to use sessional symptom measures and regularly collect client feedback on therapy processes, it may be that the wrong questions are being asked, or that while some services are particularly good at outcome monitoring, many others may not be doing so well. For example, in England, sessional outcome data are a central part of the national Improving Access to Psychological Therapies programme (Department of Health, 2008). Each service and therapist aims to collect data on 90% of their clinical sessions in order to be able to provide accurate data on outcomes (whether the ending is planned or unplanned), but also so that the therapist can take action on clients failing to recover (whether that is stepping them up to a more intensive therapy, considering medication or just reflecting and changing the approach within sessions). Mandatory data collection by therapists, however, does not automatically necessarily ensure that it is effectively used. Once client feedback is collected it is possible that it is not well processed or reflected upon.

Further, it could be speculated that therapists practising in a private capacity may be less likely to use sessional or regular clinical outcomes. Some CBT therapists may hold unhelpful beliefs concerning the utility of regular monitoring. These can take the shape of beliefs regarding the client's reaction (e.g. "*Clients don't like filling in lots of forms*") or the value of symptom measurement (e.g. "*It's impossible to measure symptoms with questionnaires*", "*There isn't a perfect measure so why use an imperfect one*"). In addition, therapist avoidance and disorganisation (not having the appropriate clinical measures to hand) can further contribute to the failure to collect meaningful data.

One potentially helpful action and source of information for *all* therapists would be to routinely collect clear client feedback on what results are being achieved. It is difficult to improve without knowing whether one's efforts are moving one in the right direction or not. Imagine a darts player wanting to learn to get higher scores. How would he feel if he went to a trainer who said something like "No problem; you need more practice. Here, let me put this blindfold on you so that you have no accurate idea where your darts are landing on the dartboard. Now practise away!" How many hours of throwing darts at an invisible dartboard would be needed in order to become more effective? How many hours of training workshops and clinical practice do therapists' need to improve client outcomes that can be largely invisible to them as therapists? Even if therapists can say with some accuracy whether a client has improved or not while the client is attending therapy, would they actually have improved faster if they had not been coming to psychotherapy and was any improvement achieved despite the therapy intervention? We do not know. Very few therapists have any idea how effective they are. We are blindfolded darts players ignorantly hoping that continued practice will magically help us to achieve better results. It is no surprise that a meta-analysis of doctors found that increasing years of practice were typically associated with worse results (Choudhry et al., 2005), and for psychological therapists there seems little, if any, association between experience and client outcomes (Baldwin & Imel, 2013). We don't know where our darts are falling. In a study of 550 clients treated by 48 psychological therapists (22 licensed, 26 trainees), the therapists were told that previous research at the clinic involved had shown that about 8% of clients typically deteriorated during treatment. The therapists were asked to identify this group of clients. At the same time, the clients were monitored and their progress charted against a large database of previous client treatment progress charts. This actuarial system accurately identified 36 of the 40 clients who did worse – a 90% detection rate. The therapists predicted that only three of the 550 clients would deteriorate and only one of these three was in the 40 who did in fact worsen – a 2.5% detection rate where even the solitary accurate prediction was made by a trainee therapist and not one of the experienced practitioners (Hannan et al., 2005) (see Figure 6.2).

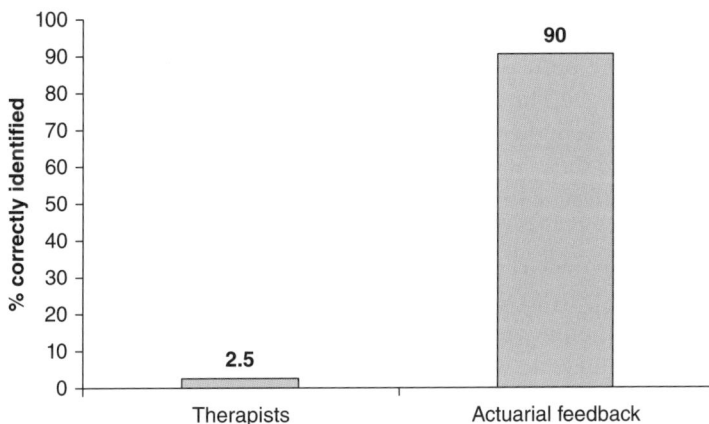

FIGURE 6.2 *Ability to identify clients at risk of treatment failure (Hannan et al., 2005)*

More recent research (Hatfield, McCullough, Frantz & Krieger, 2010) has come to similar conclusions, with the authors commenting that "therapists had considerable difficulty recognizing client deterioration, challenging the assumption that routine clinical judgment is sufficient" and noting "Outcome assessment strategies do exist to help clinicians detect client deterioration"(p. 25).

CLIENT-FOCUSED RESEARCH

About 20 years ago Howard and colleagues (1996) introduced a crucial new approach for improving our outcomes. They wrote:

> Treatment-focused research is concerned with the establishment of the comparative efficacy and effectiveness of clinical interventions, aggregated over groups of patients. The authors introduce and illustrate a new paradigm – patient-focused research – that is concerned with the monitoring of an individual's progress over the course of treatment and the feedback of this information to the practitioner, supervisor, or case manager. (Howard, Moras, Brill, Martinovich & Lutz, 1996, p. 1059)

This practice-based evidence complements the effectiveness of evidence-based practice. As Boswell and colleagues (2015) wrote about Howard et al.'s ground-breaking ideas:

> Their approach differed from traditional efficacy and effectiveness research, which focuses on the average response of participants in either experimental or naturalistic settings. As a complement to traditional nomothetic approaches, these researchers proposed directing attention to a more idiographic approach, asking 'Is this treatment, however constructed, delivered by this particular provider, helpful to this client at this point in time?' (Boswell, Kraus, Miller & Lambert, 2015, p. 7)

A recent paper commissioned by the US Department of Health and Human Services (Brown, Hudson Scholle & Azur, 2014) makes it clear that routine outcome monitoring is at the heart of an evidence-based strategy for improving delivery of effective psychotherapy. The authors review measures assessing the structure, process and outcomes of psychotherapy. They discuss the strengths and limitations of each type of measure and then emphasise that it is likely to be most helpful to focus on an assessment of the effectiveness and outcomes of care rather than other domains. The authors go on to underline that routine outcome monitoring can serve at least two purposes: (1) to help track client progress and identify individuals who fail to respond to treatment; and (2) to encourage client engagement in treatment. A recent paper on implementing routine outcome monitoring (Boswell et al., 2015) discussed the improved results achievable with this approach. They cite a meta-analysis of research studies which have explored the benefits of routine outcome monitoring (ROM) over treatment as usual (TAU) for clients who were predicted to have a negative outcome (Shimokawa, Lambert & Smart, 2010, cited in Boswell et al., 2015).

This showed the average at-risk client whose therapist received feedback did better than approximately 70% of at-risk clients where no feedback was given. By the end of therapy, 9% of those receiving feedback had deteriorated while 38% had achieved clinically significant improvement. Among at-risk clients, however, for those whose therapists did not receive feedback, 20% deteriorated while 22% clinically significantly improved. Overall results showed that, compared to standard TAU clients, those in the ROM feedback group were less than half as likely to experience deterioration and were about 2.6 times more likely to achieve reliable improvement.

The well-established "Outcome Questionnaire System" (Lambert, Burlingame et al., 1996) not only provides progress feedback but also asks clients judged to be at risk of deterioration to complete a 40-item measure of the therapeutic alliance, motivation, social supports and recent life events. Therapists are then given feedback on these areas, a problem-solving decision tree, and intervention suggestions to help them tackle issues that may be interfering with client progress. This intervention was referred to as a Clinical Support Tool that can function as a way of providing information and ideas for therapists to reflect and potentially act upon. When the outcomes of clients whose therapist received the Clinical Support Tool feedback were compared to the treatment-as-usual clients, the results showed that the average client in the Clinical Support Tool feedback group was better off than 76% of clients in the treatment-as-usual group. The rates of deterioration and clinically significant improvement among those receiving Clinical Support Tools were 6% and 53%, respectively. These results suggest that clients whose therapists used Clinical Support Tools with off-track cases have less than a quarter the odds of deterioration, while having approximately 3.9 times higher odds of achieving clinically significant improvement.

Much more research needs to be done, not least in assessing how well these very encouraging results hold up across more diverse populations (Davidson, Perry & Bell, 2014). There are a whole series of studies (Gilboa-Schechtman & Shahar, 2006; Gunlicks-Stoessel & Mufson, 2011; Lewis, Simons & Kim, 2012; Van, Schoevers, Kool, Hendriksen, Peen & Dekker, 2008) looking at treatment response trajectories (particularly with depression) and highlighting that, on average, encouraging outcomes in early psychotherapy sessions suggests that the client will do well over the full course of treatment. As Oscar Wilde underlined, however: "The truth is rarely pure, and never simple" (Wilde, 1965). There are question marks about how important it actually is to get particularly fast initial client progress to produce good post-treatment outcome. Recent careful work with a fairly large sample (N=362) of depressed clients treated with CBT (Vittengl, Clark, Thase & Jarrett, 2013) showed a variety of response trajectories (not just log-linear, but also linear and one-step) that produced similarly successful results. Other studies with depression (Percevic, Lambert & Kordy, 2006) and anxiety (Chu, Skriner & Zandberg, 2013) suggest that it is somewhat naïve to assume one requires rapid improvement to have any hope of satisfactory overall response. This seems even more probable when assessing more prolonged treatments, for example, a 50-session, two-year treatment of personality disorders where the first six sessions may primarily involve assessment (Bamelis, Evers, Spinhoven & Arntz, 2014). As Lambert has pointed out, "aspects of patient functioning show differential response to treatment, with more characterological (e.g. perfectionism) and interpersonal aspects of functioning responding more slowly than psychological symptoms" (Lambert, 2013 p. 189). He highlights that:

research suggests that a sizable portion of patients reliably improve after 7 sessions and that 75% of patients will meet more rigorous criteria for success after about 50 sessions of treatment. Limiting treatment sessions to less than 20 will mean that about 50% of patients will not achieve a substantial benefit from therapy (as measured by standard self-report scales). (Lambert, 2013, p. 188)

Lambert uses the memorable metaphor of how one decides when to remove the cast from someone's broken leg. He argues that standard, fixed, low doses of psychological therapy for all presenting clients are like an orthopaedic department insisting that all leg casts are removed after a set, minimal time instead of removing the cast only when sufficient healing has taken place. He points out that for psychological therapy a major unanswered question is "how long to continue with a treatment that the client has not yet responded to?"

Despite these caveats, the current overall research picture suggests that there is real value in careful routine outcome monitoring as an aid to meaningful reflection, especially for therapists who are committed to this process (de Jong, van Sluis, Nugter, Heiser & Spinhoven, 2012) and for clients who are not responding well. Remember dropout rates are high – for example, a meta-analysis of 34 effectiveness studies of CBT for depression found a mean dropout rate of 25% (Hans & Hiller, 2013). The research shows that we can, and need to, try harder to identify when we ourselves as therapists are being more or less effective, and then self-correct when necessary. We need to recognise that using routine outcome monitoring strategies to alert us to lack of client progress is very likely to outperform our surprisingly poor clinical judgement. It remains to be seen whether over time the regular reflective use of outcome measures actually develops improved accuracy of judgement in therapists.

HOW TO BECOME MORE EFFECTIVE THERAPISTS

The importance of client feedback

Developing literature on the characteristics of more effective therapists is throwing up some intriguing suggestions. One of these is that the difference between excellent therapists and their colleagues is particularly evident for more severe clients (Saxon & Barkham, 2012) and another is that "a portion of the variance in outcome between therapists is due to their ability to handle interpersonally challenging encounters with clients" (Anderson et al., 2009, p. 755). Interestingly, when depressed clients themselves were interviewed about difficulties in treatment, two of the themes emerging from the study were, first, that these clients diagnosed as suffering from Major Depressive Disorder (MDD) felt that there was a lack of clarity around their MDD diagnosis and insufficient explanations about the treatment, an absence of discussion around the causes of depression and no evaluation of the treatment provided. Clients in this study also felt that the treatment offered was not personalised and that there was an absence of clear goals. A second theme related to what was named "a precarious relationship with the clinician". Study participants described factors such as lack of trust, inappropriate professional guidance and attitudes reflecting this theme (van Grieken et al., 2014, p. 153). These are clients at risk of deteriorating or dropping out. Better monitoring and managing of these challenging cases is something virtually all therapists could benefit from. This is a strong argument for routine sessional outcome monitoring and alliance assessment as an input to therapist reflection. This seems especially beneficial for initially less effective therapists (Anker, Duncan & Sparks, 2009).

A recent helpful Canadian publication, which is freely downloadable from the internet, lists and describes ten routine outcome monitoring systems (Drapeau, 2012) and others continue to be added. As discussed earlier, the major Improving Access to Psychological Therapies (IAPT) initiative in England potentially provides a particularly useful new example for therapists (Brown et al., 2014), although currently the published sessional data are only being used to compare recovery rates between services and disorders and there is not yet widely available predicted session-to-session trajectories of improvement using the IAPT data. Hopefully this will emerge.

To summarise, research highlights the following important points about psychological therapy as it is currently practised:

- The field as a whole has been painfully slow at producing better client outcomes.
- The lack of clear correlation between qualifications and/or experience and improved therapist effectiveness strongly suggests that our training methods need to be improved.
- There are major differences between the effectiveness of different therapists, with some therapists achieving significantly higher rates of positive outcomes.
- Identifying and studying more effective therapists has the potential to be a useful research strategy. It is hoped that future research programmes will address this important area.
- In parallel with this, CBT therapists can try harder to identify when they are being more or less effective by attending to, and reflecting on, different aspects of client-generated feedback. This feedback should provide useful data for self-correction.
- Therapists often fail to accurately identify when their clients are doing poorly. This finding points to the importance of using routine outcome monitoring strategies in preference to relying on what appears to be the surprisingly poor clinical judgement of the majority of therapists.

THE WAY FORWARD

Tracking progress with clients as an input to reflection

The studies reviewed above convincingly show that improved reflection on regular sessional outcomes and alliance feedback from clients has the potential to make significant and much needed improvements to our helpfulness as therapists. The Clinical Outcomes in Routine Evaluation (CORE) (Evans, Connell, Barkham et al., 2002),

Outcomes Questionnaire (OQ) (Lambert, Finch & Maruish, 1999) and Partners for Change Outcome Management System (PCOMS) (Miller, Duncan, Sorrel & Brown, 2005) are all examples of monitoring methods and approaches that can be currently used (Drapeau, 2012), and in England there is the rapidly growing IAPT data (Department of Health, 2008) to compare ourselves to and learn from. It could be concluded that such monitoring, promising so many potential gains, would be an easy innovation to sell to CBT practitioners. It would, however, seem that this is not true (Boswell et al., 2015). There are many personal and organisational factors that resist this kind of change. For example, clinicians who believe they are overstretched and too busy may feel they are being asked to do more than they can cope with, there may be untested therapist beliefs regarding the willingness of clients to fill out clinical measures, the lack of a service structure to support the collection and storage of clinical data (e.g. software, database, etc.) and some clinicians may even feel a sense of relief when difficult-to-treat clients don't attend for a session or terminate therapy early.

Tracking progress with clients has the potential for increasing client engagement in therapy. The greatest gains, though, seem likely to accrue from identifying those clients who are not progressing at expected rates after roughly the initial 3–6 sessions of therapy. As discussed, a slower than predicted improvement rate is not necessarily indicative of a particular client being unable to benefit to a worthwhile extent from therapy, and it is not generally expected that a high percentage of clients will make sizeable improvements after 3–6 sessions, but a focus on slow improvers has been repeatedly shown to be an excellent use of reflection time and it is therefore likely to be very worthwhile to reflect on any clients that do not show adequate initial change. Ideally, this would be highlighted by some pre-agreed criterion, such as falling below the 25th percentile on a predicted trajectory of improvement with a well-validated assessment measure.

Often a good next step is to move from reflection to discussing the slow progress with the client (preferably recording the discussion for later reflective review and use in self-supervision or supervision). When outcome scores have not been progressing well, the following are useful points for therapist reflection and client/therapist discussion:

- What has been happening to the therapeutic alliance measures?
- Is there agreement on focus, specific goals and therapeutic methods?
- Does the client feel adequately understood and validated?
- Am I following an evidence-based model for the problem focus?
- Am I avoiding anything in the therapy?
- Have there been any external life events that have interfered with progress?
- What about the client's expectancies and motivation?
- Are there other ways of augmenting the therapy – for example, by bringing in their partner, friend or other family member, or by introducing a group intervention or training, or by upping the frequency of sessions, or by adding or altering medication or other biological interventions?

It makes sense to use or develop a checklist to work through with clients who are not on track. For example, the OQ feedback system achieved better outcomes through supplementing progress feedback by asking clients who were predicted to deteriorate to complete a 40-item measure of the therapeutic alliance, motivation, social supports, and recent life events.

CONCLUSION

To conclude, psychological therapy is a helpful and effective intervention for many mental health problems. On the downside, it has been very slow to increase the rates of effectiveness established three decades ago. This chapter is more broadly focused than preceding chapters in that it considers the current state of the effectiveness of all contemporary psychological therapies, including, but not specific to, CBT. To return to a question posed at the beginning of the chapter, "What kind of reflection, on what aspects of our practice, is likely to be particularly helpful in improving our effectiveness as therapists?" Routine outcome monitoring and organised reflection on cases that are not "on track" has been shown to have the potential to move the whole field forward in ways that both therapists and clients are likely to welcome.

CBT therapists, trained to value empirical evidence-based practice and the unique phenomenology each client brings to therapy, have a head start regarding improved outcome monitoring. CBT has produced, and continues to produce, an ever-expanding range of measures to quantify symptoms and processes, many having the potential to be used in a collaborative and client-focused manner. Collecting, and attending to, client feedback is one of the core competencies measured by both the Cognitive Therapy Scale (Young & Beck, 1988) and the Cognitive Therapy Scale-Revised (Blackburn et al., 2001). This is a competency that training courses and supervisors should be developing in novice CBT therapists.

The other chapters in this book which focus on the different structures for CBT therapist reflection will hopefully provide the reader with many different forums and guidelines to improve CBT therapists' reflection on all aspects of their therapy. This chapter, however, emphasises that early identification of whether or not CBT is proceeding in an optimal way is a paramount consideration. This means that CBT therapists, in line with the strong research indicators outlined in this chapter, need to recognise that regular outcome monitoring is a more effective way of doing this than clinical judgement alone. A truly reflective CBT therapist cannot ignore the valuable source of information that is client feedback.

TAKING IT FORWARD

What *declarative knowledge* have you learnt from reading this chapter?

- What do you feel are the most important points that emerge for you and your work from this chapter on the value of routine outcome monitoring?
- Was there anything that surprised or challenged you?
- Is there any additional information or knowledge that you now want to explore – what does it involve?

Developing *procedural skills*

- Would you like to try routine outcome monitoring in your own practice or, if you already use it, are there new adaptations that you would like to try?

- When will you review the outcomes of your clients? Before or after sessions? During self-supervision or supervision?
- Could you identify your own "when... then..." rule for when clients are failing to show progress or are deteriorating? How will you identify this and ensure that this is reflected and acted upon?

Using outcomes to inform your *reflections* on clients

- What would you need to do to ensure that outcome monitoring leads to effective reflection on your work?
- What might hijack or get in the way of genuine reflection?
- How will you move from reflection to action?

SUGGESTED READING

Boswell, J. F., Kraus, D. R., Miller, S. D., & Lambert, M. J. (2015). Implementing routine outcome monitoring in clinical practice: benefits, challenges, and solutions. *Psychotherapy Research, 25*(1), 6–19.

7

REFLECTION IN CBT TRAINING

Peter Armstrong

LEARNING AIMS

- To provide a declarative framework around CBT training and the role of reflection within such training
- To give readers using this framework procedural guidance to support the process of reflection as both trainers and trainees

INTRODUCTION

How should CBT trainers decide on what to teach and how? How should CBT therapists and would-be CBT therapists decide on the training they need? What reflections should inform development and selection of curricula? The answer appears to lie in more considered and structured reflection on training. Barnett and Coate (2005) observe: "Curriculum design in Higher Education is not yet a properly reflective practice. As a result … newly emerging curricula are often not what they should be" (p. 2).

They argue that **reflective curriculum** design results in better engagement between educators and students. A number of factors, however, currently inhibit reflective practice across the design, delivery and review of training. First is our lack of an overarching conceptual map. Bennett-Levy and colleagues (Bennett-Levy, Thwaites et al., 2009) follow Kolb (1984) in stressing the conceptual component of reflection, hence the conceptual material following here. Second is the assumption that we already know what to teach. CBT boasts a wealth of models of psychological disorders (e.g. Clark, 1986; Dugas & Robichaud, 2007) and processes (Nolen-Hoeksema, Wisco & Lyubormirsky, 2008). Shouldn't our training reflect this clinical evidence? Yes, as a general guide, but to fit specific training ventures to the needs of particular trainees in specific contexts, a more detailed reflective approach is called for. Finally, there are day-to-day obstacles to reflective training, for example corporate demands, market forces, calls on practitioners' time from other aspects of their employment, and demands on our attention from outwith the workplace, such as household and money matters, caring duties and friendships. Potential trainees may find financial support difficult to find; employers, under pressure to deliver increased volumes of treatment, may be reluctant to release staff; fatigue and work-stress affect practitioners' motivation to innovate and seek training.

We are not wilfully unreflective, but such circumstances militate against reflection and result in lower levels of trainer–trainee engagement, under- or over-ambitious training, training that is under-supported by organisations or at odds with organisational requirements, yielding reduced benefits to clients. I would argue that training devised and sought reflectively can bring these forces together to the maximum benefit to all concerned.

In order to improve reflection on CBT training, this chapter proposes a conceptual structure consisting of three levels (scope, goals and focus), which, used in sequence, will assist trainers and trainees in reflectively developing, selecting and reviewing training, and will also inform reflection on learning processes and systems during training.

A THREE-LEVEL CONCEPTUAL STRUCTURE TO FACILITATE REFLECTION ON TRAINING

Level one: scope of CBT training

In 2008, the Newcastle Cognitive & Behavioural Therapies Centre (NCBCT) (Armstrong, Freeston & Twaddle, 2008) proposed a framework in which the scope of a training venture is determined by three major influences: needs, drivers and capacity. Within this framework, optimal organisation and selection of training are construed as balancing these influences, from which it follows that mindful reflection upon them will benefit trainers and trainees alike. The more mindful of them we are, the better placed we are to make informed choices. Each is discussed in turn below.

Needs refers to the abilities and professional requirements of trainees directly related to the service clients receive, and to the difference between a current level of skill and/or knowledge and a higher level that would enhance the quality of their work, thereby better meeting their clients' needs. Trainers can easily begin their planning on the basis of a "product" they can market – a particular skill set or theoretical framework. While these are important factors (see capacity, below), training set up exclusively or too predominantly on this basis risks being ill-fitted in its content, level or methods to trainee needs. Further, trainers, trainees and their managers alike might easily experience a blurring between needs and the next concept, "drivers".

Drivers are the broader influences, organisational, professional and political, providing impetus for training and influencing its content and delivery. The most striking example in the UK is the Improving Access to Psychological Therapies (IAPT) project (Department of Health, 2008). Layard and colleagues had previously calculated the cost to the British economy of the national rates of depression and anxiety (Layard et al., 2006). Layard further calculated the cost of providing effective evidence-based psychological therapy against the economic benefits of improved rates of recovery, concluding that training and psychological treatment would pay for themselves through the increased economic contributions of those recovering from depression or anxiety disorders. When this was taken up by government, a centrally determined curriculum was promulgated across England (Liness & Muston, 2011), with new services initiated alongside new courses. Economic drivers therefore played an important role for these courses and the trainees entering them. Within the framework being described here, however, it does not constitute a need, as the overall economy of Britain is a contextual factor in the lives of clients and providers rather than a direct moment-to-moment experience, such as the cripplingly low mood of major depression, or practitioners' inability to deliver courses of Behavioural Activation (Martell, Dimidjian & Herman-Dunn, 2010). This is not to argue that needs-led training is "a good thing" and driver-driven training is "bad". Without IAPT drivers, many thousands of people would be denied the treatment they now receive (Department of Health, 2012).

It is important to recognise the difference between needs and drivers. Drivers set a broad context within which training may or may not be supported, favouring certain kinds of training over others. Needs, on the other hand, relate to particular practitioners' specific levels of knowledge and skill, and the quality of treatment they deliver. Drivers provide the broad brush-strokes of training; needs determine its fine-tuning. In the context of the IAPT project, an economic driver influenced what training was needed across the country; need determines what particular coaching and supervision particular trainees require.

Capacity refers to a range of factors affecting the abilities of trainer, trainees and environment to deliver, receive and use learning, both on a day-to-day "state" basis and according to more stable (though amenable to change) traits and abilities. These include: trainers' and trainees' levels of knowledge and skill in particular areas of practice or theory; trainers' ability to convey knowledge and trainees' readiness to acquire it; and rapidly changeable factors such as the energy, morale and motivation of trainers and trainees alike. The environment in which the training takes place is a significant capacity factor: the immediate physical environment of the teaching venue and the broader organisational/clinical environment into which trainees carry their learning. That immediate environment will impact on what can be addressed and what cannot (for example, skills practice, small group discussion); the broader environment will largely determine what will be sustained and what will not (for example, training in a set of therapy skills that can be well-directed in the teaching room but will not be supervised in the workplace is unlikely to have a lasting effect) (see Figure 7.1).

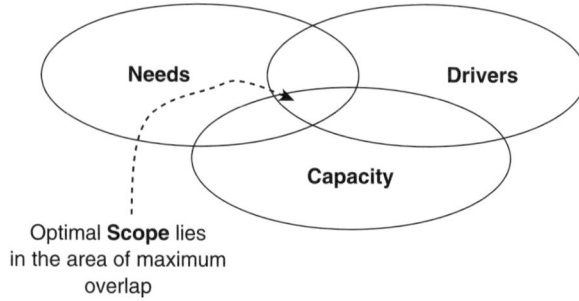

FIGURE 7.1   *The scope of training*

Since these three factors determine the scope of training (Armstrong et al., 2008), reflection on them can help trainers and trainees ensure that their training meets real need, is attuned to the organisational, political and social drivers that will sustain its delivery and application, and is well suited to the capacities of its deliverers and recipients.

Exercise: Reviewing a recent training experience

- Trainers, consider training in preparation or recently delivered.
- Trainees, reflect on future or recently completed training.

Questions are phrased prospectively (see Table 7.1), but can be adapted for retrospective use. If using retrospectively, weigh your findings regarding the issues raised here against how useful your learning was, and how well sustained it was.

TABLE 7.1   *Exercise: need, drivers and capacity*

	Trainer	Trainee
Need	What skill or knowledge will I help develop here? Affecting which aspect of trainees' work? How much do I know about their work and therefore their needs? If very little, what do I need to investigate? How? If training is offered too widely to allow me to get that specific knowledge, how clearly have I described its applicability to attendees' work?	How will this training affect what I offer clients? How will it alleviate their problems? How will it affect the kind of resource I am? How will it affect my development as a therapist? If I'm unclear on these issues, who do I need to consult? What questions to ask?
Drivers	Which policies (and whose) will affect the training's delivery, uptake and support? From which organisation(s) and professions are the trainees coming? How will their work context affect their receipt of training?	How does this training fit with the context and core business of my service? How does it relate to managerial agendas? Can I reasonably expect managerial support

	Trainer	Trainee
	Have the trainees chosen to, or been required to, attend? If unsure about wider organisational, professional or governmental agendas, what documents, websites, and policies should I consult? Who might help contextualise the training?	for the training? How can I show that in training me, the wider organisation or profession will benefit?
Capacity	To what extent do I have the knowledge and skill to deliver this training? Nowhere near? → It looks like I need to decline. It's a little beyond? → What's my learning plan? Well within? → How to guard against complacency? How am I placed right now to deliver (life-events, energy, morale, other demands on my time…)? What steps do I need to take if my answer here reveals obstacles? What are my main priorities right now? What support should I seek? From whom? What do I need to drop, delegate? How thoroughly will the outputs of training be supported? How should that level of post-training support affect its scope? What can I do to maximise support?	How ready am I for this training? When I look at my current levels of knowledge and skill, how do they relate to the training's challenge? Do I need to do other groundwork to be ready? Is it pitched at a level with insufficient challenge to helpfully stretch my efforts and imagination? If I can't answer these questions, who do I need to ask? How is the timing of this training? How much time, energy, and enthusiasm can I devote? If I need to prioritise it, what else do I need to change? If I have other priorities, do I need to reschedule the training? When I look at what the training will deliver, how much will I be able to use it in my work? How well matched to my role will it be? What supports will be available to me in order to use this learning?

Level two: the goals of training

The need for "SMART" goals (Specific, Measurable, Achievable, Relevant and Timely) is recognised. However, we should not neglect the need for goals to be meaningful to both trainees and trainers. It would be unrealistic to expect that every course or class could meet every participant's most meaningful goals. Realistic reflection on goals by trainers when devising and publicising training, and by potential trainees when selecting training, will therefore help them come together on both a realistic and a creative basis.

Types of goals relevant to training

There is a wide literature on the nature and effects of **approach** and **avoidance** goals in both the educational (Hullemen, Schrager, Bodmann & Harackiewicz, 2010) and mental health fields (Martell et al., 2010). Between these (apparent) opposites lie **maintenance** goals. These terms are largely self-explanatory:

- **Approach goals** are states (like satisfaction) and attributes (like competence in CBT) we wish to achieve or obtain
- **Avoidance goals** are states (like fear) and outcomes (like failure) we want to avert

These two kinds of goals relate to future conditions that we wish to achieve or avoid. The third kind of goal relates to already-existing conditions that we wish to keep:

- **Maintenance goals** are states (like good health) and attributes (like established skills and values) we wish to keep

In training, we commonly attend to approach goals. An example can be found in the high-intensity IAPT curriculum (Liness & Muston 2011), which gives two broad aims: "1: To develop practical skills in CBT for common psychiatric disorders such as depression and anxiety, 2: To develop critical knowledge of the theoretical and research literature relating to CBT", and specifies 11 objectives, for example: "At the end of the course, students will be able to... deal with complex issues arising in CBT practice". The key approach terms are "to develop" and "will be able to". Readers will have encountered similar goal-statements at the outset of training. Trainers may also elicit trainees' goals in attending a class, but a trawl through course prospectuses will rarely yield a list of avoidance or maintenance goals.

What is the relationship between these goal types, in particular between approach and avoidance? Much has been written on this in the mental health field, for example how depression (Dickson & MacLeod, 2004; Martell et al., 2010) is characterised by avoidance-dominated behaviour, absence of focus on approach goals, and reducing access to established and new rewards is associated with euthymia. There is an equivalent educational literature stressing the benefits of approach mentality (Elliot & Thrash, 2001).

Why attend to avoidance goals when there is evidence that following them leads to difficulties? The answer is that failure to reflect on them does not guarantee their absence. Trainees and trainers alike, guided by a series of explicit approach goals, may at the same time be guided by unstated, implicit, possibly unrecognised avoidance and maintenance goals. Is this problematic? Potentially, yes, since unrecognised goals are not subject to reflections that encourage engagement; nor are they amenable to discussion when disagreements and conflicts about goals and their achievement arise. But aren't these differences merely semantic – two sides of the same coin? For an academic review of that question see Hulleman, Schrager, Bodmann & Harackiewicz (2010). In order to experientially understand the difference between approach and avoidance goals imagine the following scenarios:

> **Playing a game – tennis or football**: imagine a player or team whose aim (approach) is to win. Put them on the court or field with another player or team aiming to avoid losing. Do they behave in the same way? Feel the same?

Picture a hill: one climber wants to get to the summit; another is primarily driven by not falling off the mountain.

In business: one person aims to make a profit, to grow their company; another guards against losses.

What differences do you note?

Now apply the principle to training.

- Trainees: How will your behaviour be affected if your primary aim is to improve your skills? In skills workshops? In supervision? In reviewing your clinical sessions? In contrast, how will it be if you are more concerned with not showing yourself up, in workshops, supervision, therapy sessions, or conversations?
- Trainers: Addressing a class can be anxiety-provoking. Apply the test to yourself. If your actions in the classroom or the supervision room or the examiners' meeting are driven by what you most want to achieve, how will they look? If, on the other hand, you feel uncomfortable and exposed in the trainer role, if you really don't want to make a fool of yourself, or if you are low on energy and you don't want to make extra work for yourself, how will that look?

"But" one might ask, "why would I put myself in this position (of being a trainee on a demanding course or running one) if I weren't driven by my approach goals?" Law, Elliot and Murayama (2012) studied the relationship between the approach and avoidance goals of undergraduates. They found the goal types strongly correlated – two sides of the same coin – when students' sense of competence was high, and weakly correlated when their sense of competence was low. In other words, when we are relatively confident in our skills, our approach and avoidance goals work in tandem, but when confidence is shaken, they come adrift from one another.

How should this affect our approach to training? Trainees and trainers alike at times find their sense of competence shaken. The experience of "deskilling", whereby trainees' perception of their competence declines markedly in the course of training, is well recognised in the therapy literature (Lombardo, Milne & Proctor, 2009). Likewise, trainers surprised by a difficult question from the classroom, or asked to teach a subject outside their established expertise, will know how self-doubt can arise. Feelings of anxiety or despondency can easily be triggered. How best can we ready ourselves for and respond to these?

- First, be prepared. When embarking on delivery or receipt of training, set time aside for honest reflection on goals: what do you really most want to achieve from the training? Record these approach goals. Check them for SMARTness but, more importantly, check that they really matter to you.
- Be honest with yourself about any feelings of anxiety or pessimism about the training: what you fear might happen, what you least want to happen. Record these avoidance goals.
- Put the two lists together. If Law et al.'s (2012) findings apply to you, and you are reasonably confident, you should find the lists are matching opposites (I want to

pass the course/don't want to fail; I want to be enthused/don't want to be bored). You might even find that you have constructed composite approach/avoidance goals where the match has already been made ("I want to feel challenged, but don't want to be out of my depth").

- Reflect on your past experiences of training or other challenges. Try to note down the "signs and symptoms" of being in approach-goal mode or in avoidance-goal mode.
- You might find it easier to voice approach goals rather than avoidance goals. These latter raise uncomfortable feelings, or might yield embarrassment when made explicit. But the discomfort might prove worthwhile because if they emerge covertly during the course of the training, you will be less able to address them. Look out for any avoidance goals that look as if they aren't the "flip side" of approach goals: these might suggest when we are at risk of becoming more avoidant than is helpful. If, as a teacher, I am afraid of appearing stupid, this might lead me to avoid tricky areas of theory or skill, to bluff my way out of tight corners, rather than admit "I don't know"; as a trainee, I might resist structuring CBT sessions if this seems to risk me losing my core counselling skills.
- Ask yourself: under what conditions you might lose touch with your approach goals and become more driven by your avoidance goals.
- Now spend time reflecting on your strengths – skills, competencies, difficult conditions you have mastered, successes. Note these down, because by focusing on what we already have and wish to keep, our maintenance goals (e.g. core interpersonal skills and values), we can increase the chances of our approach and avoidance goals remaining in healthy agreement. In this context, Montgomery, Croft and Hackmann (2010) note the value of emphasising existing skills when introducing practitioners to CBT.
- Who else might you share your reflections with (a supervisor, supportive peer) to help remind you of your approach goals, your strengths? Who might sensitively point out when you fall into unhelpful avoidance patterns, and then support you in getting back into approach mode?
- Think how best to record and refresh your reflections as you progress through the receipt of, or delivery of, training.

Level three: focus in CBT training (including moment-to-moment learning processes)

For the purposes of this chapter, a model linking the clinical supervision work of Inskipp and Proctor (1995) with the DPR model (Bennett-Levy, Thwaites et al., 2009) has been developed. The model applies the supervision categories of normative (relating to standards of practice and competence), formative (relating to the development of new abilities) and restorative (relating to the wellbeing of practitioners) to clinical training generally, proposing that these require, at different times, different levels of attention to the components of the DPR model. This can be construed as a "combination lock" whereby correct alignment accesses optimal learning activity (see Figure 7.2).

The model suggests that training partners first clarify which mode will best meet the goals of training: normative (recognition and observation of standards, steps necessary

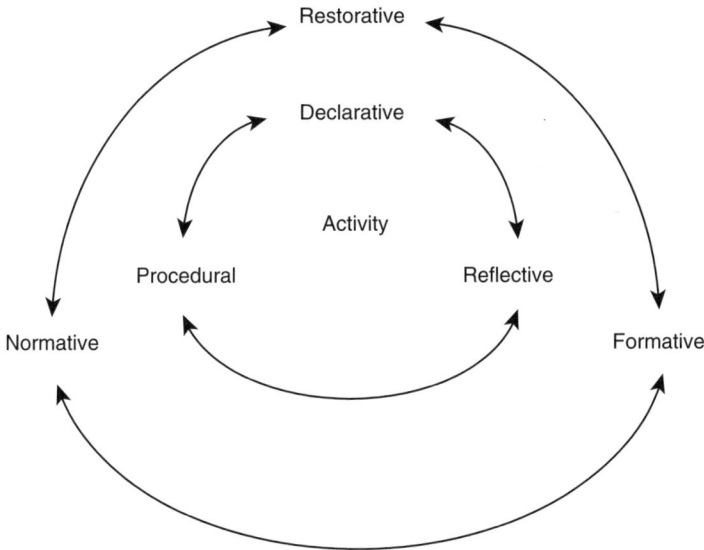

FIGURE 7.2 *Aligning mode and system*

to pass a course); formative, (progression towards and beyond norms or otherwise develop skills); or restorative (enhancement of wellbeing in the context of therapeutic work and its difficulties).

As with the Newcastle "cake stand" model of clinical supervision (Armstrong & Freeston, 2006), mode selection can be understood in two timeframes – longer-term selection guiding whole workshops or courses and moment-to-moment choices during training sessions – as participants respond to material encountered. That said, we should be cautious of radical short-timeframe mode-shifts if they lose focus on the legitimate overall goals already agreed.

Having established mode, consideration can be given to which of the DPR model's learning systems should be emphasised and when, for example, declarative (e.g. the theory and evidence underpinning treatment of depression), procedural (e.g. how to implement behavioural activation with artistry) or reflective. The reflective system can be used to integrate the declarative with the procedural, or at various points in training: for example, at the commencement of training, where partners are still building awareness of one another, at the conclusion of training, where they have gone through declarative and procedural change, or when puzzles arise, calling for pause rather than hurried avoidance of them.

In these moments, we are best placed to ask "What shall we *do*?" That is, how best to engage these learning systems, such that our mode-based goals are achieved? Trainers and trainees might usefully reflect on the times they have *begun* with this question, basing their choices on tradition, personal preference or on the unreflective, and therefore premature, application of Kolb's cycle (Kolb, 1984).

The following practical example illustrates the integration of learning mode with therapist skill acquisition system.

PRACTICAL EXAMPLE

The integration of learning mode with therapist skill acquisition system

Establishing the mode for the workshop "Understanding Clinical Supervision"

A trainer is commissioned to deliver a half-day workshop titled "Understanding Clinical Supervision", while, as part of the same programme, other trainers will provide guidance on the use of the Supervision Adherence Guidance Evaluation (SAGE) tool (Milne & Reiser, 2008), a measure for assessing supervisory competences. The trainer therefore puts normative considerations to one side as these are being dealt with in that other teaching. Next, he considers the emphasis on restorative and formative modes, concluding that both are relevant: supervision is a demanding role, and increasing awareness (formative) of conceptual models could help trainee supervisors manage difficulties in the supervision room such that supervision will be more interesting and enjoyable, and therefore less stressful (restorative).

Matching system to mode of learning in the workshop

The workshop title "Understanding Clinical Supervision" implies an emphasis on declarative knowledge, for example understanding the various models of CBT supervision. Taking into account the fact that this is a half-day workshop, and part of a longer programme, the trainer places less emphasis on skills (procedural) apart from the skill of formulating supervision processes using these models. He reflects on his clinical experience, in which knowledge of CBT models helped him to help others – making treatment more rewarding, enjoyable, less onerous. By extension, he predicts that by formatively developing trainees' declarative knowledge he should help the group restoratively. He has a hypothesis that the greater the transitional challenge for group members in becoming supervisors, the more this restorative mode will be called upon.

And so the declarative system will be emphasised, but lest he might simply stand up and talk for three hours, presenting numerous slides, it will be important to intersperse episodes of reflection between those of declarative exposition to help trainees internalise the models presented, compare them against their past and current experience, and inform the group's (and therefore his own) understanding and critique of the models. He is concerned now that there appears little or no emphasis on the procedural system, but reflects that there are occasions on which a declarative focus is appropriate, and reminds himself again of the workshop presenting the SAGE model of supervision (Milne & Reiser, 2008), with its correspondingly heavy emphasis on procedure. Further, he recalls, the procedural learning he wishes to promote is that of formulating supervision processes. He now has a clearer idea of what he and the trainees should do in the session.

Planning activity for the workshop

To reduce the chances of a declarative over-emphasis, trainees will first reflect on notable experiences of supervision – those they have loved and hated, as supervisors or supervisees. At this stage the trainer will not apply a conceptual framework, but will introduce a structure, because he has experience of asking people to reflect on strong feelings ("loved" or "hated"), when that strength of feeling reduced their ability to stand back far enough to reflect – instead they relived, ruminated or worried. So he will pair off trainees, giving each an opportunity to describe their experience, and tasking each with being *active* listeners, feeding back frequent summaries. He wants the trainees to return to these reflections throughout the workshop, so he asks them to write down the main themes in their discussions. In whole-group feedback, he will listen for themes that relate to the models he is about to expound and will introduce declarative vocabulary derived from the models. He will then describe the selected models, or parts of them, pausing after each mini-lecture for episodes of whole- or small-group reflection on how aspects of the model inform their understanding of their experiences and vice versa. He decides to support these reflections by providing diagrams of key concepts, for example "the seven eyes of supervision" (Hawkins & Shohet, 2006), inviting trainees to relate their original thoughts to the diagram and to try using the authors' terminology as they do so, thereby practising the procedure of formulating supervision.

This being a CBT supervision workshop, the temptation is to set homework "because that's what we do in CBT". But, in using this model, the trainer specifies an activity intended to consolidate the knowledge introduced in the workshop; that is further practising the procedure of formulating supervision issues as a regular part of writing up supervision notes, and thereby continuing the formative work done in the classroom. He will liaise with the presenter of the SAGE workshop to discuss how the largely declarative input of the current workshop will segue into the more procedural work to follow there.

Readers will note a general reflection of Kolb's (1984, 2000) and Honey and Mumford's (1992) learning cycles. These will now be explored further.

REFLECTION DURING TRAINING

Thus far we have reflected through stages of increasing specificity from scope, through goals, to selection of mode and system (focus). Now we look at reflection on learning processes as they emerge in the classroom, following the Kolb/Honey and Mumford model, with particular emphasis on Bennett-Levy and colleagues' central placement of reflection (Bennett-Levy, Thwaites et al., 2009; Thwaites et al., 2014). In keeping with the DPR model, and drawing on classroom experience that suggests learning seldom, if ever, progresses uniformly across the four phases of experiential learning, a harmonisation of the cycle and the DPR model is proposed whereby reflection is redrawn as the central hub of learning rather than as one point on its circumference (see Figure 7.3).

Concrete Experience

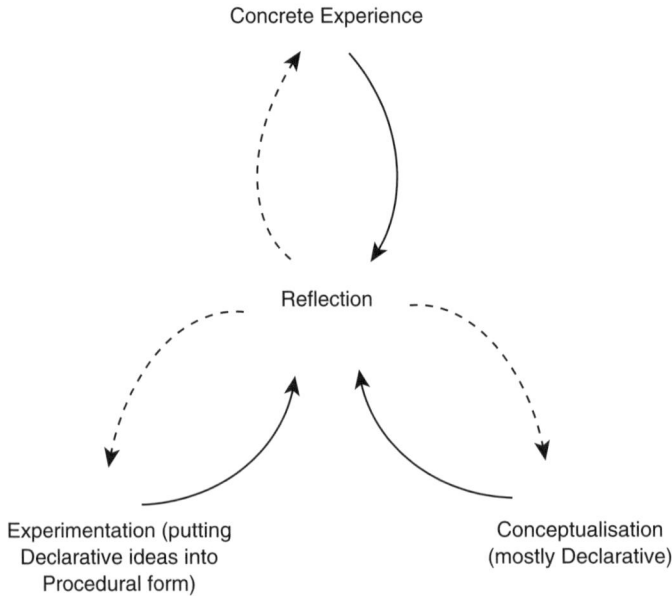

Reflection

Experimentation (putting
Declarative ideas into
Procedural form)

Conceptualisation
(mostly Declarative)

FIGURE 7.3 *Harmonisation of the experiential learning cycle and Bennett-Levy's DPR model*

This version suggests that reflection is the "engine" of learning in providing a place where new inputs from concrete experience (e.g. a therapy session), conceptual ideas (e.g. a theory lecture), and tentative experimentation (such as role-playing a new skill in supervision) can sit alongside each other, together with existing knowledge and skill and feelings about new inputs – comfort or discomfort, certainty and uncertainty. This placing together of new and established knowledge in the context of our immediate responses facilitates synthesis of ideas, feelings and actions, the outputs of which provide guidance for which of the content-rich learning phases we need to access next in order to carry learning forward: get more experience, knowledge, or to try a further experiment. In Figure 7.3, the solid lines indicate that successful learning necessarily feeds content through reflection, while the broken lines flowing from reflection indicate that the direction of that flow is always optional according to which phase needs to be accessed on the basis of the synthesis achieved during reflection.

PRACTICAL EXAMPLE

Undertaking a course of workshops on CBT for depression

Imagine you are undertaking a course of workshops on CBT for depression and at the same time you are treating some of your clients for that problem. Thus far your experience of CBT has been strongly influenced by foundational training where you learned about negative automatic thoughts, assumptions and beliefs (Beck, Rush, Shaw & Emery, 1979) and about "thinking errors" (black and white thinking, and so on). This week's workshop is on the subject of

Behavioural Activation (Martell et al., 2010). How might this proceed in terms of the model suggested in Figure 7.3?

First, you arrive at the workshop already in possession of the concrete experience of delivering therapy. Your trainer asks "Who is currently treating depression?" Hands go up and she asks "How's it going? What do you find is working? What difficulties do you run into? How does it feel to spend a lot of time working with a depressed person?" You're now being asked to reflect on the experience. Notice that you're not being asked to conclude anything, to give a lot of theory or evidence, to show that you *know*, or to change your mind about anything. You are simply being asked to stand back from and focus on your experience.

Now your trainer puts the cat among the pigeons. She summarises: "You seem to be spending a lot of time talking about your client's thoughts. How much time do you give to behaviour?" By doing this she is dipping a little into conceptualisation, but bringing you quite quickly back to reflection. It turns out that the group, like many CBT trainees, find thoughts, assumptions and beliefs much more interesting than reinforcement schedules, so she shares personal experience: how that used to be the case for her; that she now spends much more time addressing behaviour; that she used to think "Behaviourist" referred to a kind of soulless bogey-man who did unpleasant experiments with pigeons; now she wants to share something of her journey into working more behaviourally. Here she has referred back to her own concrete experience and is sharing some of her own reflections. She asks the group how they feel about "Behaviourist" and "Behaviourism", eliciting some similar reactions, some thoughts that behaviourism is simplistic, too basic for clients with complex needs. These are raw reactions on the group's part, best understood as a concrete experience in reaction to a conceptual subject. The trainer brings these reactions into reflection by the straightforward means of summarising and checking that she has understood the group's feelings.

She now gets very conceptual, asking a series of questions about positive and negative reinforcement, and about positive and negative punishment. As do many trainees (and more experienced therapists), the group gets very confused as they try to grasp these four apparently basic concepts. She feeds this back to them, facilitating reflection on the concrete experience of being confused, then asks how their confusion compares with their view that behaviourism is simplistic, inviting them to conceptualise their misconception of behaviourism. By now it's beginning to dawn on at least some of the group that perhaps their reasons for favouring thoughts over behaviour are questionable: perhaps they've been avoiding these confusing ideas and favouring those they find easier and more intriguing – thoughts – rather than basing their interventions on client need. That is, her guidance of the group has enabled synthesis of concrete experience with conceptual thought such that a new engagement with the subject matter is possible. Now she gives a brief lecture on the basic concepts of operant conditioning (Skinner & Ferster, 1957), asking the group to feed back their understanding, affirming when they are correct, gently correcting when they are not, thus helping them to reflect on their new learning rather than simply copy it down.

Now that the students' reflections have enabled a shift in attitude to the material, the group are better positioned to experiment, so the trainer invites

(Continued)

(Continued)

them to devise brief narratives illustrating their understanding of reinforcement and punishment. In this they will need to visit experimental territory ("Let's try out *this* story"), pausing reflectively to place their experimentally-generated material alongside their new concepts, yielding further synthesis.

And so the process continues.

The trainer's experience

The trainer has arrived equipped with at least three important aids: two key concrete experiences – of therapy and of undergoing a "conversion" to Behavioural Activation (so she both knows what it's like to be in the therapy room and has a fair chance of understanding how the group might react to her ideas); third, a good conceptual grasp of the ideas she wants to share. But she can't assume that the group will have the same negative feelings about behaviourism that she once held, so she engages in some joint reflection with them.

Reflecting on the group's reaction, she sees that they are largely where she once was, suggesting that they have learning needs in the conceptual zone, so she issues a conceptual challenge ("you're doing a lot on thought; not much on behaviour") before sharing some more reflections of her own transition. Now she elicits raw reactions to "behaviourist" – not yet reflections, but reactions that require shaping via her summaries. These help the group stand back from immediate responses in order to focus.

A further episode of reflection indicates a continued conceptual learning need, so she takes the learning task there. This is difficult for the group, and in her private reflections she notes their levels of discomfort. Simply getting confused and being shown you don't understand something isn't in itself a helpful learning experience, although it is necessary for the group to realise what they don't know.

So she realises the need for more reflection – again to help the group stand back from and focus on their confusion, to help normalise their getting confused about reinforcement and punishment; they also hear that the teacher has previously been in this same position, so the trainer–trainee alliance is nurtured while at the same time the group has a clearer sense of needing to learn.

Where does the learning need to take place? Here again, we see reflection giving direction: by reflecting on the group's level of understanding, the trainer sees that they don't yet have sufficient grasp of the material to take it into concrete experience in the therapy room, nor yet to support experimentation. Therefore she provides conceptual-declarative information in a lecture.

But she now needs to check what the group have grasped, so there follows further reflection via interactive feedback, which has at least two reflective functions: helping the group to look at their new understanding and helping her see where the learning need is now.

Finding that they are beginning to grasp the material, she recognises the need to put flesh on conceptual bones. But these are still new ideas, which just a few minutes ago the group thought too simplistic to use, so they are not ready to take them into the therapy room so she recognises the need to experiment. And so the cycle continues.

REVIEWING TRAINING

The model outlined in this chapter is intended to provide a structure for training partners' reflections on progress and process as they move through particular learning episodes as described in the above section, and as they move across the larger stages of training. The following are useful questions to ask, and are the learning cycles and systems:

- Working in sympathy?
- In keeping with the required mode of training?
- Working towards desired goals?
- In keeping with its optimal scope?

Table 7.2 lists a series of questions that trainers and trainees can ask themselves – perhaps most productively sharing questions and answers between one another. You will note that at this point the training partners are invited to review the training using the conceptual model in reverse order. That is, having worked outside inwards to construct the training, they now work inside outwards to review it. The left-hand column uses the workshop case example, described above; the right-hand column describes the questions' reflective focus. In this example, the exercise is assumed to be trainer-led, but similar questions can equally be asked by trainees and by managers facilitating training.

TABLE 7.2 *Reflective review of training*

Review...	Example	Reflect on...
General experience	"How have you found the workshop so far? Which bits have worked best? Or been tougher?"	concrete experience of being in the training room
Focus (Systems)	I've put some new information your way – what have you found out? Which ideas are clearest/least clear?	declarative uptake & challenges effectiveness of declarative teaching
	Here's a bit of a challenge: have a go at describing one of these ideas again (reinforcement, punishment…)	
	You've been practising using the model; how was that? How do you see that going in real therapy practice?	procedural uptake & applicability effectiveness in generating new skill; experimental options
	Let's think about one thing you'll do differently in your next therapy session.	
	I've a sense this was pretty challenging. How are you feeling about this? Have I got you curious? Do you feel up in arms about it?	ability to reflect on new material
Focus (Modes)	We wanted the workshop to help you move forward in treating depression. Where do you see yourselves improving – right now, or as you go away from the workshop? How will you keep progressing with this material?	formative movement & challenges

(Continued)

TABLE 7.2   *(Continued)*

Review...	Example	Reflect on...
	We don't always follow the evidence as rigorously as we could. When I look back on my own career, I can see courses of treatment that weren't up to standard. We're careful of "should" in CBT, but given your learning today, is there anything in your practice that really ought to change?	normative impact of training
	This can be challenging. It's hard to think "I might have acted differently with this or that client". Thinking about change can be difficult. I'm no different in that respect and I'm impressed with how the group has taken on the challenge. Well done. Two things I'd like you to do now: think how someone else in the group might be struggling right now and offer a thought that will help with that struggle. And to finish – if you're going to struggle to implement this work, how will you get support in supervision... from your peers...	personal & group restorative inputs
Goals	"Let's look at what we set out to achieve... and have achieved... haven't achieved... discoveries we made... new goals arising"	goal attainment, frustration, new generation
	"How does it feel to have arrived where we have... to still have further to go..."	
Scope	"How *much* have we got out of our work here? Is there more we might have done? Still have to do? Has the training stretched you? Far enough? Too far? Too little? Are there other supports that would have enhanced the training?"	capacity
	"How will our learning here be used with your clients... in supervision... in staff meetings... in service development"	need

drivers |

CONCLUSION

Thorough reflection takes time. We might baulk at this, but hurry seldom makes the most of opportunity. That aside, training partners can judge the balance between major reflective and briefer enquiring pauses in the course of training. In this they would mirror good therapy practice, as encapsulated in the following quote: "Feedback should be given/elicited throughout the therapy – with major summaries both at the beginning ... and end ... while topic reviews ... should occur throughout the session" (James, Blackburn & Reichelt, 2001, p. 6).

The case for this level of reflection on training parallels that in therapy. Evidence-based CBT calls for consistency, but not for a uniformity that would deny the unique needs of individuals. Evidence-based CBT is balanced, avoiding, on the one hand, ill-informed choice based solely on personal preference and, on the other hand, uniformity that denies the unique needs of individuals. Likewise, training should adhere to clinical evidence, but, via reflective engagement between participants, be characterised by the adaptability seen in the practice of all good CBT therapists, resembling that other discipline, Jazz, which the poet Richard Kell (2001, p. 98) has described as:

neither the grip

of perfect unity

nor the lax

unlovely scrimmage.

Trombone, clarinet, sax

like braiding water slip,

the image

of good community

TAKING IT FORWARD

What *declarative knowledge* have you gained from reading this chapter?

- How would you summarise the key points of this chapter to a colleague?
- Can you identify one new piece of declarative learning about the role of reflection pre-, during or post-training?

What *procedural rules* regarding the delivery of training can you develop?

- Try to identify a "when… then…" guidance that would help improve your planning for training? For example, "WHEN I sit down to plan training, THEN I first need to consider…"
- If you are currently more in the role of receiving training, what guidance can you take away for identifying your own goals for training?
- As we move from one area of our work to another, in this case from being a therapist to being a trainer or trainee, we access different parts of ourselves that need to use different rules. What rule adjustments do I need to make when I enter the role of trainer or trainee?

Can you think about how you best can bring *reflection* into your delivery or engagement in training?

- What would help you to reflect ahead of training?
- What strategies are you going to put in place to facilitate the engagement of your reflective system post-training?

- Training can raise strong feelings, such as annoyance at trainees who don't seem to want to learn, or resentment of trainers who seem to be undermining our established knowledge. How can I use the feelings that are likely to inhibit reflection as cues to encourage it?

SUGGESTED READING

This chapter is the first to consider the role of reflection in CBT training. The following recommended readings do not therefore directly address reflection in training but have been recommended to provide a broader context for the ideas presented.

Fennell, M. (2010). Training skills. In M. Mueller, H. Kennerley, F. McManus & D. Westbrook (Eds.), *The Oxford guide to surviving as a CBT therapist* (pp. 371–405). Oxford: Oxford University Press.

Rakovshik, S. G., & McManus, F. (2010). Establishing evidence-based training in cognitive behavioral therapy: a review of current empirical findings and theoretical guidance. *Clinical Psychology Review, 30,* 496–516.

8

EXPERIENCING CBT FOR YOURSELF:

Using Self-Practice and Self-Reflection (SP/SR) to Develop Therapeutic Competence and Metacompetence

*Richard Thwaites and
Beverly Haarhoff*

LEARNING AIMS

- To understand how practising CBT methods on yourself (self-practice: SP) and reflecting on this process (self-reflection: SR) can be used to develop and fine-tune CBT knowledge and skills, ultimately leading to greater flexibility and artistry
- To understand the evidence base for SP/SR as an experiential training and professional development strategy
- To identify the key principles in developing SP/SR programmes
- To learn how to apply these principles to developing your own informal examples of SP/SR

INTRODUCTION

Over the course of the history of CBT there has been a well-established recommendation that therapists should learn CBT by practising it upon themselves in an informal way. Back in 1995, Judith Beck advised CBT therapists "to gain experience with the basic techniques of cognitive therapy by practising them yourself before doing so with patients", pointing out that "trying the techniques yourself allows you to correct difficulties in application and putting yourself in the patient's role affords you the opportunity to identify obstacles (practical or psychological) that interfere with carrying out assignments" (Beck, 1995, p. 312). And Christine Padesky suggested that "To fully understand the process of the therapy, there is no substitute for using cognitive therapy methods on oneself" (Padesky, 1996, p. 288).

This made intuitive sense. Being in the "client's shoes" would give therapists a taste of how it might feel to experience a CBT intervention from the client's perspective, and they would then be more able to implement CBT in a sensitive and skilled manner, attuned to what the client may be experiencing. This became even more important when CBT further developed and therapists became increasingly likely to be working with clients with more complex and entrenched problems, such as personality disorders, which were more likely to present challenges in establishing and maintaining effective therapeutic relationships (Beck, Freeman & Associates, 1990). Over the years therefore, trainers and supervisors have, to varying degrees, encouraged therapists to practise aspects of CBT upon themselves.

In this chapter, a number of examples of the informal use of self-practice in CBT are examined. In these, the application is somewhat *ad hoc* and a formal reflective structure is not necessarily utilised. The remainder of the chapter details a targeted training method called Self-Practice/Self-Reflection (SP/SR) (Bennett-Levy et al., 2015). SP/SR is the first CBT training approach to involve the formalised practice of CBT on oneself (SP) followed by a structured process of reflection (SR) on the experience and implications of this for self (personal and professional). SR also involves the consolidation of declarative knowledge and the development of procedural rules for practice. In this chapter we will review the current evidence for SP/SR and then focus on SP/SR workbooks in facilitated groups as the most commonly used and researched method to deliver SP/SR, providing examples and guidance on how SP/SR programmes can be implemented. A typical programme will be outlined and an example of SP/SR in action provided. Key principles underlying the facilitation of effective SP/SR programmes will be delineated, emphasising the importance of participant engagement and fidelity to the model. In conclusion, some guidelines on how to develop your own informal or formal experience of SP/SR are provided.

EXAMPLES OF INFORMAL SELF-PRACTICE

Introducing self-practice within supervision to improve procedural skills

A supervisor notices that a supervisee is using thought diaries in a rote fashion without any understanding of the challenges or commitment involved and hypothesises that the supervisee would be able to use this intervention in a more sophisticated way if they had their own experience of using thought diaries to identify and challenge their own unhelpful thoughts. Here self-practice is introduced as a learning tool to improve procedural skills in utilising a specific therapeutic intervention (thought diary).

Introducing self-practice in supervision to address unhelpful therapist beliefs

A supervisor believes that a supervisee is avoiding using behavioural experiments with a particular client due to his own anxieties about the task. After a collaborative discussion, a conclusion is reached that there may be a possibility that the supervisee's avoidance is impeding therapy. The supervisor suggests that the supervisee completes a thought diary for homework to help him examine (and perhaps challenge) his beliefs about behavioural experiments and the client distress he predicts may result from the experiment.

Although these examples differ in their primary emphasis, in that the first example targets procedural skills and the second example is directed at belief change, self-practice is likely to impact on both the supervisee's beliefs and procedural skills. However, the extent to which the therapist is able to learn from their self-practice experience and transfer this into new learning (i.e. new procedural skills or new beliefs) largely depends upon their reflective processes and the scaffolding structures put in place by the supervisor to support reflection and learning.

Introducing self-practice in training to improve procedural skills

A trainer may ask participants in a half-day training session to engage in an experience of self-practice, such as a self-formulation task, in order to improve declarative and procedural skills around the task of developing formulations with clients. Or in a longer course, such as a whole module on anxiety disorders, a trainer might ask participants to engage in a series of related self-practice tasks over a number of teaching sessions (e.g. identifying a belief to be tested in a behavioural experiment, planning and carrying out the behavioural experiment and then reviewing the findings). In such an example the aim might be the development of procedural skills, with some potential increase in declarative knowledge (particularly if used with less experienced therapists). The degree to which such benefits are realised is again related to the ability of the trainer and learner to facilitate effective reflection upon the experience and ensure experience leads to new knowledge and skills.

Table 8.1 summarises how both informal and formal self-practice and self-reflection are utilised within CBT training and supervision. It illustrates the main aims, the extent of the reflective component and the overall intensity of the experience.

TABLE 8.1 *Examples of the usages of self-practice within CBT training, supervision and continuing professional development*

Type of self-practice experience	Main aim	Self-reflective component	Intensity (e.g. time, resources)
Specific practice of a one-off CBT task during training session e.g. participants formulating their own experience in an individually identified situation	Increase procedural skills relating to the task (and potential declarative knowledge for less experienced therapists)	No formal component but often includes group debriefing or discussion	**Low** Can take minutes during training session
Specific practice of a one-off CBT task agreed during supervision e.g. supervisee lacks confidence in the use of thought records so they agree a specific task with their supervisor involving the self-practice of using thought records between supervision sessions	Could be used to develop procedural skills or Could be targeted to change a therapy-interfering therapist belief	No formal component but often includes post-task discussion around the experience	**Low** Can take minutes between supervisions sessions
Practice of a series of connected CBT tasks during a training course e.g. implementing a behavioural experiment from start to finish	Increase procedural skills related to the task	No formal component but often includes group debriefing or discussion	**Moderate** Can take minutes or hours over a period of weeks
A formal SP/SR programme using a workbook e.g. the therapist completes a formal SP/SR programme (either alone, in pairs or in a group)	Develop procedural skills, increase self-awareness	Formal reflective component involves answering a series of targeted questions aimed at deepening experience and transferring learning into procedural skills. Usually involves the sharing of process reflections with a wider group to enhance learning	**High** Several hours per week over numerous weeks (e.g. 12 modules over 24 weeks)
Formal SP/SR programme via co-therapy e.g. participants are allocated a co-therapist and each have 10 sessions working with their therapist on a identified problem	Develop procedural skills, increase self-awareness	Formal reflective component involves answering a series of targeted questions aimed at deepening experience and transferring learning into actual procedural skills	**High** Several hours per week over numerous weeks

SELF-PRACTICE/SELF-REFLECTION (SP/SR)

SP/SR is a training strategy with a growing evidence base for improving therapist skills and knowledge (Gale & Schröder, 2014). It was initially developed by James Bennett-Levy during the late 1990s (Bennett-Levy et al., 2001) and has subsequently been implemented in a range of formats, countries and settings (educational establishments and clinical services) across a range of participant groups, including trainee CBT therapists (Chaddock et al., 2014), newly qualified CBT therapists (Haarhoff et al., 2011), experienced CBT therapists (Davis et al., 2015), trainee low intensity practitioners (Chellingsworth & Farrand, 2013), experienced low intensity practitioners (Thwaites et al., 2015), trainee clinical psychologists (Bennett-Levy et al., 2001) and clinical psychologists (Bennett-Levy, Lee, Travers, Pohlman & Hamernik, 2003). The first SP/SR workbook for CBT therapists has now been published (Bennett-Levy et al., 2015).

Reflection is a key aspect of SP/SR and the structured reflective processing is as important as the self-application of CBT techniques. The content of the structured reflection in SP/SR is often quite different from the usual reflection that takes place in CBT (e.g. in supervision) in that it also covers the therapist's own experience during the practice (both as a therapist and also in their wider personal life). The depth and quality of the self-reflection is influenced by the identified problem, pre-existing reflective skills, time commitment, interactions with other group members and the skill of the facilitator (Wood, 2014). The degree to which the self-practice leads to new learning is influenced by the quality of the self-reflection and also the commitment of the participant to alter therapy practice post-reflection. This might involve changing behaviour or cognitive processes in therapy sessions or in the therapist's wider personal life, ultimately enhancing procedural knowledge. As Bennett-Levy et al. (2015, p. 3) state, SP/SR is:

> an integrative training strategy that links the declarative understandings of CBT with procedural skills; integrates the conceptual with the interpersonal and the technical; and enhances the channels of communication between the "therapist self" and the "personal self". The self-experiential element of SP/SR facilitates the links; reflection provides the glue.

SP/SR can be delivered in a range of ways, each with different strengths and weaknesses (Thwaites et al., 2014). For example:

- A co-therapist method with participants alternating between the roles of therapist and client. Participants usually receive four to six sessions in each role (Bennett-Levy et al., 2003)
- Self-guided SP/SR from workbooks, for therapists wishing to "go it alone"
- Working through an SP/SR workbook with a supervisor
- Working through an SP/SR workbook with a colleague
- A group-based intervention in which participants work through a shared workbook covering therapeutic tasks typical of CBT over a period of six to 24 weeks (Bennett-Levy et al., 2001; Bennett-Levy et al., 2015; Chaddock et al., 2014; Davis et al., 2015; Farrand, Perry & Linsley, 2010).

The evidence base

In recent years the evidence base for SP/SR has steadily grown. The key finding from every SP/SR study published to date has been that therapists report that by experiencing CBT "from the inside out", their attitudes towards their clients change. For example, SP/SR gives therapists an understanding of the process of change and of the inherent difficulties of being in the client's shoes, thus increasing empathy and usually also improving their interpersonal skills (Bennett-Levy et al., 2015). A second key finding is that therapists report a strengthening in their reflective skills, something which is of great importance in acquiring further therapeutic skills and competency as this then allows them to learn more effectively from future experiences and go on to develop metacompetence (Thwaites et al., 2014). The reflective system is characterised as being "the engine" which drives lifelong learning as a therapist, particularly once basic therapy skills have been learned" (Bennett-Levy, Thwaites et al., 2009, p. 119). Table 8.2 summarises the current research findings on the outcomes of formal SP/SR programmes.

TABLE 8.2 *Summary of main SP/SR research findings (adapted and updated from Thwaites et al., 2014)*

Domain	Research findings
Declarative knowledge (knowledge that we might write about, talk about or read about)	• A clearer (Haarhoff et al., 2011) and deeper (Bennett-Levy et al., 2001) understanding of the CBT model (declarative knowledge)
Procedural skills (when and how we implement declarative knowledge in practice)	• Increased level of specific CBT skills (e.g. explaining model, process and tasks) (Bennett-Levy et al., 2001; Chaddock et al., 2014; Davis et al., 2015) • A specific primary impact on interpersonal aspects of therapist performance, such as empathic attunement and interpersonal communication skills (Bennett-Levy et al., 2003; Chaddock et al., 2014) • An increased understanding of the processes of change in therapy and potential difficulties in making changes (declarative knowledge) (Bennett-Levy et al., 2001; Bennett-Levy et al., 2003) • Increased self-awareness and knowledge of self (Bennett-Levy et al., 2001) • Increased therapist flexibility and creativity (Bennett-Levy et al., 2003) • Better understanding of CBT processes, specific therapeutic methods and the development of a therapeutic style (Laireiter & Willutski, 2003)
Reflective skills (using our experiences to learn which skill to apply to which client under which set of circumstances at which point in time in therapy)	• Increased self-reflection skills (both during and after sessions) (Bennett-Levy et al., 2003)

Domain	Research findings
Therapist beliefs	• Changes in beliefs relating to both therapist self and personal self (Chaddock, 2007; Davis, 2008; Fraser & Wilson, 2010) • Change in unhelpful therapist beliefs about themselves (both the therapist self and the personal self) (Davis, 2008).

The first meta–synthesis of SP/SR research (Gale & Schröder, 2014) identified three key areas, namely the individual's experience, outcomes of SP/SR and the training implications of SP/SR. A number of themes are listed within each area as shown below. All of these are consistent with our experiences of facilitating SP/SR programmes.

First, in terms of the individual's experience of SP/SR, there were five main observations:

1. Being in the client's shoes helped the therapist to develop a greater understanding of the potential experience of the client and with this a "deeper sense of knowing".
2. Increased self-awareness of their thoughts, feelings, behaviours and an associated greater understanding of themselves.
3. A realisation, through personal changes, that therapy can be life-changing.
4. An increased understanding of the potential difficulties with CBT techniques based on their experience.
5. A greater appreciation of the potential for negative experiences through therapy (e.g. accessing painful memories or being exposed to difficult feelings).

Second, with respect to the outcomes of SP/SR, the study found changes in the following areas:

1. An increased experience of empathy for clients, particularly around the difficult process of change.
2. The transfer of a new way of "knowing" CBT to therapy, for example more skilled use of interventions, anticipation of potential pitfalls and greater ability to address difficulties.
3. A greater understanding of the CBT model and an increased ability to communicate the model to clients.
4. An increased understanding of the role of the therapist as a guide and of the importance of the therapeutic relationship.
5. An increased sense of confidence and competence in the use of therapeutic techniques and an ability to reflect on actions leading to greater flexibility and experimentation.

Third, in terms of training implications, the key themes were:

1. A recognition of the value of SP/SR as a learning method.
2. The importance of others in gaining benefit from SP/SR (e.g. being part of a group of peers, working with another individual such as a co-therapist or a tutor).
3. A recognition of the crucial role of written reflections.
4. A recognition that the benefits of SP/SR can be lifelong.

As these studies attest, in the last 13 years the evidence base for SP/SR has grown and we would suggest that it now supports the usage of formal workbooks, both in training and also as part of continuing professional development. However, the published research to date is based on self-report and the next stage will involve investigating the objective impact of SP/SR on therapist behaviours and observed competence and then, finally, clinical outcomes (Thwaites, Bennett-Levy & Haarhoff, 2015).

Using SP/SR workbooks with groups

SP/SR workbooks have typically involved 6–12 SP/SR modules completed over a period of between 12 and 24 weeks. The SP exercises are generic CBT interventions rather than disorder- or protocol-specific interventions, and are used to identify, conceptualise and intervene to address the identified problem. Examples would be using the five areas model to understand how the different elements of a problem interact to maintain the problem, employing an activity diary to increase engagement in valued and necessary activities and using thought records to challenge unhelpful thinking patterns (Bennett-Levy et al., 2015).

The starting point in the workbook is the identification (by the therapist) of a professional or personal issue of mild to moderate severity (not one causing major emotional distress). The problem needs to have an emotional charge but participants are cautioned against choosing a problem which is acute or related to a significant current life issue such as bereavement or other significant loss.

At the end of each SP exercise a number of SR questions guide the participant through the SR process and the participant reflects on the experience of trying out the CBT interventions for themselves. The questions guide the participant to first reflect on the implications for self and then to broaden this enquiry and ask what relevance this experience has for their professional experience with clients.

What does a typical SP/SR workbook programme look like?

Feedback from therapists and trainees contemplating "signing up" to an SP/SR programme suggests that it can often be hard to imagine what this might involve. An overview of the steps involved in setting up an SP/SR programme is provided below to illustrate the process.

- Potential participants receive information about the benefits of SP/SR, ideally have a chance to discuss this with someone who has previously taken part in a similar programme, and have the chance to ask questions.
- The group discusses and agrees an acceptable framework regarding safety and confidentiality (e.g. use of names or pseudonyms, timescales for modules).

- All participants develop their own Personal Safeguard Strategy (PSS). SP/SR does not always feel comfortable and for very small numbers it can go beyond discomfort and the individual may require additional support. The PSS details a series of steps participants can take if they become distressed by the programme. For example, an initial step might be to discuss the problem with an identified colleague. If the upset or emotion persists, the second step would be for a participant to consult with their supervisor. Participants can spend time discussing how they might monitor their emotions to distinguish between normal strong emotional responses and an emotional response that becomes something to worry about. Clearly, identifying a support person is recommended.
- Participants are now ready to commence the programme. The starting point is to identify a challenging problem area – either in a work-related context or in their personal lives. As described above, this would be of moderate severity, meaningful enough for them to want to change but not so severe that it is likely to become too distressing during the programme. An example might be reducing perfectionism with clients or working on unhelpful beliefs about oneself as a therapist.
- Participants then continue to work on their identified problem, first constructing a working formulation of the identified problem and developing individualised goals, and then spending a week applying one or more specific CBT interventions (whether assessment or change-focused) to themselves (SP), recording the content of their SP in the workbook. Note the SP content is not shared with the wider group.
- Following completion of each SP module, participants work through a series of structured reflective questions designed to promote and fine-tune reflection on the SP experience and enhance learning about: the intervention, CBT in the wider sense, the personal self and also the therapist self.
- As a final step, participants post their initial reflections on the *process* of the SP/SR (note, not the *content*) on a web-based discussion board or other shared medium, such as verbal or written feedback in a group situation. Participants then comment on each other's experiences, ask questions and share learning. Such iterative commenting allows both a deepening of the reflective process and also a sharing of learning from fellow participants. Useful aspects of sharing reflections on process include gaining an understanding of the commonalities, and differential reactions, to CBT interventions. Without this, novice therapists can make the assumption that their response is the same response that will occur in others or conversely that their response is very different and cause for concern.

SP/SR in action

In order to provide a flavour of a typical week's SP/SR activity we will describe an SP module designed to help the therapist identify their unhelpful thinking and behaviour. This example has been adapted from the only currently published SP/SR workbook manual (Bennett-Levy et al., 2015). To contextualise this example, during the earlier modules participants will have identified either a work-based or personal problem and completed baseline measures. They will also have spent considerable time developing a formulation of their own specific problem. The SP exercise is followed by an example of structured SR questions.

PRACTICE EXAMPLE

Identifying unhelpful thinking and behaviour

Self-Practice (SP)

1. Participants are asked to complete thought diaries in order to become more aware of their own negative automatic thoughts (NATS). They are then encouraged to "unpack" these NATS using the "downward arrow" technique to guide questioning (Greenberger & Padesky, 1995).
2. During the second section of the SP, participants are encouraged to consider a range of maintenance processes (for example, cognitive biases, selective attention, escape, avoidance, safety behaviours) that may be playing a role in their individual problem situation.
3. The final SP task requires that the participant starts to map out personal maintenance cycles using the identified processes.

Self-Reflection (SR)

After completing the SP exercises, participants are asked to complete the following reflections:

- What did you notice about your experience of identifying negative automatic thoughts? How easy or difficult was it? How much did you believe the thoughts? Was there any difference in your level of belief at a "gut level" and at a "head level?"
- Having identified your own NATs, does this influence how you might work with clients to help them identify their NATs? How might you adjust or change your customary rationale? What do you think might be important for them to know in advance?
- Were you able to map out a personal maintenance cycle(s)? Did you learn anything from this experience? Were there any surprises?
- Think about your current caseload and bring to mind one of your most difficult clients. How might the maintenance cycles that you have identified in yourself have an effect on your attitude and/or your behaviour with this particular client?
- What might be the best way to introduce the idea of maintenance cycles to your clients? What might be the best ways to develop them over the course of treatment?
- What are the key things you have learned during this module that you would like to remember?"

(Adapted with permission from Bennett-Levy et al., 2015, pp. 98–119.)

As can be imagined, completion of such a module can be a demanding and time-intensive process and to achieve maximum benefit from this type of SP/SR programme it is recommended that the completion of each module is spread over at least two weeks, requiring between 1–3 hours' worth of time per week. For many individuals, such a time commitment may not be possible at a particular point in their lives or career, due to competing personal, emotional or occupational time constraints. Other options for such individuals wishing to learn experientially would be to spread the module content over a greater number of weeks, utilise a less intensive SP/SR programme or develop your own less formal experience of self-practice and self-reflection.

INTRODUCING AN SP/SR PROGRAMME AS PART OF CBT TRAINING OR CONTINUING PROFESSIONAL DEVELOPMENTS: KEY PRINCIPLES

Freeston, Thwaites and Bennett-Levy (in preparation) have identified a number of principles which should be considered in the planning stage of an SP/SR programme. These key principles are based on theory and the practical experience of implementing a number of SP/SR programmes. While some of these principles are specific to formal SP/SR programmes, many of them can be adapted and applied to the introduction of less formal experiences of SP/SR, whether in a supervision or training context. These include:

1. **Take into account the Zone of Proximal Development** (Vygotsky, 1978). What learning stage is the individual at, and what scaffolding do they need to learn effectively outside their current capacity? As a supervisor, if you are planning a self-practice exercise about the use of thought diaries, consider the novice supervisee's current knowledge of accessing beliefs and identifying hot cognitions. What structures do they need to put in place to scaffold this activity, and what knowledge and skills do they already have that can function as a platform for development?
2. **Ensure a match between the content learning needs of the practitioner(s) and the content of the self-practice**. It can be counterproductive to implement an SP/SR programme or even an informal self-practice exercise on a CBT technique that is not appropriate for the participant to be using. For example, providing an SP/SR programme on identifying and working with schema-level beliefs is likely to be confusing and detrimental to novice therapists doing an introductory course on CBT, where all their experience is in working at the level of negative automatic thoughts, emotions and behaviours relates to the here-and-now. Exceptions may be made if the exercise has a clear rationale and is explicitly badged as an activity not to be utilised in day-to-day clinical work.
3. **Understand the likely change processes for individuals as SP/SR introduces new experiences of CBT**. For example, a number of studies have demonstrated a period of destabilisation or deskilling for some participants during early stages of SP/SR (e.g. Thwaites et al., 2015). Participants can report becoming aware of "what they don't know" (Bennett-Levy & Beedie, 2007). Signposting and normalising such reactions in advance can be both validating and anxiety-reducing.

4. **Do not make assumptions about initial reflective ability**. Earlier SP/SR tasks might be focused on developing reflective capacity and using prompts to help participants move towards reflection-in-action.

DESIGNING YOUR OWN SP/SR: KEY PRINCIPLES

For CBT therapists wanting to develop a personal mini–experience of SP/SR the following guidelines are suggested:

> **Be clear on your main goals.** Do you want to increase your knowledge and skill of a particular intervention? Do you want to fine-tune your artistry in how you use specific interventions by having a greater understanding and clearer "when...then..." procedural rules? Do you want to change therapy-interfering beliefs of your own? Do you want to use self-practice of CBT to make changes in your wider life?

> **Be clear on how much time you can commit.** Are you thinking of a one-off exercise or a longer-term series of practices? The length of time and degree of commitment will obviously be influenced by the desired outcomes. Be realistic. As we all know, good intentions do not always lead to the time commitments we would like!

> **Be honest with yourself about your initial reflective ability.** Do you naturally recall thoughts, feelings and behaviours following events? What makes it easier or harder to reflect in the moment? What thoughts or feelings are you more likely to avoid?

> Bennett-Levy et al. (2015) provide information on how to establish a structure that supports effective reflection based on feedback from previous SP/SR participants. These suggestions range from practical tips on finding a location and time where you are unlikely to be disturbed, to guidance on enhancing recall through the use of multisensory inputs and how to gain maximum benefit by linking personal and professional reflections.

> **How will you support the SP/SR?** Will you do this alone, with a colleague or will you use clinical supervision or a mentor to provide support? Think about and record a plan of what actions you would take if the SP/SR brings up unanticipated difficulties (see Personal Safeguard Strategy (PSS)).

> **Will you be sharing your process reflections with anyone?** Be clear on the difference between reflections on content (for your eyes only) and reflections on process. It can often be very useful to share the latter, especially if the other person is undertaking a similar experience of self-practice.

> **Monitor your outcomes.** Once you've worked out what you want to achieve, measure your progress with belief ratings, behaviour counts, mood ratings, ratings of perceived competence – whatever captures the desired changes. For more experienced therapists, the main skill improvements from SP/SR are noticed during the sessions with the most challenging clients (rather than on average for all clients) so consider this in developing your outcome monitoring (Chapter 6 will give you some ideas about how to do this.)

Be gentle and compassionate with yourself. Experiencing CBT from the inside can often lead to awareness of what could be done differently or perhaps more skilfully or with more sensitivity – this is one of the aims! Be prepared for a temporary perception of deskilling. Try to avoid judging yourself for any difficulties in engaging or making changes and use such thoughts as further inputs into the self-practice – these are just more thoughts or behaviours to be accepted and then addressed.

CONCLUSION

SP/SR is a focused training strategy with a growing evidence base supporting its efficacy in the development and fine-tuning of CBT skills, particularly those concerning the interpersonal or process aspects of therapy. Currently, the strongest evidence is for workbook-based programmes that follow the key delineated principles of SP/SR. It is important to distinguish this from SP/SR programmes that do not follow best practice, and more informal "mini-experiences" of SP/SR. This is not to suggest that the latter might not be useful, but, as we have discussed, there are important principles based on research into formal SP/SP programmes which we recommend as likely to maximise benefit. In addition, as previously mentioned, for a small minority of participants, SP/SR has proved challenging, resulting in some emotional distress and confusion. For this reason we emphasise the importance of proper preparation and participants developing their PSS, as described above.

This chapter has provided guidance on how you can introduce self-practice as a learning strategy in supervision or training. It has also provided initial guidance on how to implement your own "mini-experience" of practising CBT on yourself and reflecting on the experience to develop new learning. As a final inspiration to develop your own experience of SP/SR, consider the quote below (which is typical of many SP/SR participants) and reflect on whether experiencing CBT from the inside might bring something new to your practice.

> I have to say that I have gained such a lot of insight into what it might feel like from the client perspective when they pitch up for help and that this experiential process has helped me to change lots of small things about the way I interact with clients, how I explain things, and the compassion I feel for those clients who take a long time to get us (often those with multiple failure to engage…, DNA [do not attend], don't complete homework or disengage). (SP/SR participant)

TAKING IT FORWARD

What *declarative knowledge* have you learnt from reading this chapter?

- What has stood out for you in reading this chapter? Has anything surprised you?
- Have you learned anything new about the ways that SP/SR can be used to develop CBT skills?
- What is the most important take-home message for you in terms of new knowledge?

How might you use an informal experience of self-practice or a formal SP/SR programme to develop or fine-tune a *procedural skill*?

- What would your goal be in planning your own experience of SP/SR? What procedural skill would you want to develop or improve?
- How could you best turn your own personal experience of applying CBT to yourself into a new way of doing things in therapy?
- How might you move from personal experience via reflection to the development of a new procedural rule?
- What might act as a barrier to doing things differently?
- What could you put in place to remind you to apply your new way of doing things?
- How could you review and evaluate this?

Try to identify a structure that would work best for you to engage your *reflective system* following an experience of self-practice?

- What are the conditions under which you would be best able to review your experience and bring to mind your bodily sensations, feelings, thoughts and behaviours?
- What questions might you ask yourself to turn a self-practice experience into new learning about CBT?
- How might you note this new learning to avoid it being forgotten?

SUGGESTED READING

Bennett-Levy, J., Thwaites, R., Haarhoff, B., & Perry, H. (2015). *Experiencing CBT from the inside out: a self-practice/self-reflection CBT workbook for therapists.* New York: Guilford Press.

9

REFLECTION IN LOW INTENSITY CBT:

Challenges and Practice-Based Innovations

Paul Farrand, Kat Rayson and Laura Lovis

LEARNING AIMS

- To understand the development of the Psychological Wellbeing Practitioner role and training within the context of the Improving Access to Psychological Therapies (IAPT) programme
- To articulate the challenges faced in developing reflective skills in the wider practitioner-level mental health workforce
- To show how evidence-based teaching and training strategies can support the development of reflective skills during and post-training in these groups

INTRODUCTION TO PSYCHOLOGICAL WELLBEING PRACTITIONERS

The Improving Access to Psychological Therapies (IAPT) programme and low intensity CBT

In 2008 the IAPT programme was established in England to implement the National Institute for Health and Clinical Excellence guidelines for the treatment of depression

(NICE, 2004a) and anxiety disorders (NICE, 2004b). The implementation of a new model of delivering psychological therapies, in particular CBT, called Stepped Care was developed (NICE, 2004a, 2004b, 2011a). It was recognised that existing psychological therapy services could not meet the excess demand being placed on them without a very large increase in mental health funding. A new approach to delivering these evidence-based treatments was therefore needed, leading to a revolution rather than evolution in service delivery (Bennett-Levy et al., 2010). Part of this revolution included the introduction of a new competency-based workforce called Psychological Wellbeing Practitioners (PWPs) into primary care.

Stepped Care and low intensity CBT

The PWP workforce was developed to work at Step 2 of a Stepped Care model of service delivery to support low intensity CBT interventions for mild to moderate high-prevalence mental health problems (Bennett-Levy et al., 2010). These low intensity CBT interventions are commonly in the form of written or computer/internet-based CBT self-help materials capable of being supported face-to-face, via the telephone, email, or instant messaging.

The implementation of low intensity CBT provides services with the capacity to assess and treat a larger number of clients than more traditional forms of psychological therapy. This is as a consequence of PWPs typically providing clients with a 30–40 minute assessment (Farrand & Williams, 2010), followed by intervention support sessions lasting up to 30 minutes (British Psychological Society, 2012b). The average number of support sessions varies, but around five sessions is typical (IAPT, 2010). Shorter and fewer support sessions enable PWPs to have caseloads of between 60 and 100 clients, and therefore they are described as working with a high-volume caseload. Clients are regularly reviewed (at least every four weeks) within case management supervision (see Chapter 2 for the distinctions between different models of supervision) and can be stepped up to receive high intensity treatment or to secondary care if necessary (NICE, 2011b).

While placing low intensity demands on service resources, the demands placed on the clients are likely to be equally as high as those experienced with high intensity CBT. Potentially, the demands may be even higher given the greater expectation that the client works through the self-help materials between support sessions.

Psychological Wellbeing Practitioner: a new type of practitioner mental health workforce

Previously, implemented workforces in England, which share similar roles to PWPs, such as that of the Graduate Mental Health Worker, have been categorised as paraprofessional (Farrand, Confue, Byng & Shaw, 2009), with NICE also recognising PWPs as "Paraprofessional: a staff member who is trained to deliver a range of specific healthcare interventions, but does not have NHS professional training, such as a psychological wellbeing practitioner" (NICE, 2011b, p. 52). However, such categorisation contradicts other definitions of a paraprofessional, which identify such a practitioner as "…a person to whom a particular aspect of a professional task is delegated, but who is not licensed to practise as a fully qualified professional" (Oxford English Dictionary [Online], 2015). While the latter definition has potentially been appropriate in describing previous roles, such as that of the Gradate Mental Health Worker (GMHW) (Farrand, Duncan & Byng, 2007), sharing some similarities with PWPs with respect to supporting CBT self-help, it fails to capture the additional responsibilities undertaken by PWPs. Furthermore, the PWP role differs from that associated with a paraprofessional given that, within a Stepped Care model of mental health delivery, they undertake a role that is distinct from other "professionals", and therefore their tasks are not delegated. However, while not reflecting a paraprofessional role, the role of the PWP does also differ from that associated with high intensity therapy roles. These roles often require the therapeutic use of self as agent for change, but this is not identified as being necessary for the successful support of low intensity CBT (Richards, Lovell & McEvoy, 2003). Instead, PWPs develop a range of competencies specifically required to support the delivery of low intensity CBT (Roth & Pilling, 2007a).

With the potential of the PWP role being demonstrated within the IAPT programme (Clark et al., 2009), other countries, such as Hong Kong and Australia, are currently developing a similar workforce to support the delivery of low intensity CBT interventions. The implementation of low intensity CBT interventions into mental health service delivery is also gaining momentum in European countries, in particular Holland, Belgium and Sweden. Across these countries, however, there may be slight variations in the composition of the low intensity CBT self-help interventions, especially away from the focus on "single strand" interventions (IAPT, 2010). While it seems likely that differences in the PWP workforce may emerge between countries, including with respect to the workforce name, it seems likely that the focus on supporting low intensity CBT self-help materials will remain. With consideration of such a focus, discussions are currently under way within the British Psychological Society (BPS) to recognise PWPs as representing a practitioner workforce. Within the discipline of psychology such developments have the potential to run alongside related developments in practitioner roles in other areas, such as education, healthcare, business and law.

The English experience: Psychological Wellbeing Practitioners (PWPs)

Prior to training, PWPs and those entering "practitioner" roles in other areas come to the role with a variety of experiences. PWPs are not required to have a "professional" background upon entry to training, although the reality is that the role attracts some applicants who already hold a core profession, such as occupational therapy or mental health nursing in particular. More often, however, and being an expectation of entry to training, trainee PWPs will have some limited experience of mental health working. This may be in the voluntary sector or in organisations where there is a high likelihood of exposure to people with mental health problems, such as housing charities. This does not assume that trainee PWPs come with experience of delivering psychological interventions, but at least they have some understanding about the demands and challenges that may be placed on them when working in mental health settings. The lack of previous experience, however, does often mean that trainee PWPs are inexperienced reflectors and particularly lack experience in reflective writing.

Since the implementation of the IAPT programme, PWP workforce attrition rates have been high. It has been suggested that a large number of applicants to PWP training posts are treating the role as a stepping-stone towards other careers, which was not the original intention of the IAPT programme. In particular, an increase in applications to high intensity CBT or clinical psychology training programmes has been identified (BABCP/IAPT, 2011). The intention to move into different roles could potentially influence the way PWP trainees instrumentally prioritise the assessed components of the programmes over those that may enhance or extend their clinical competency.

PWP curriculum overview

Prior to the IAPT programme, roles such as Graduate Mental Health Workers existed in some English regions and supported low intensity CBT (Farrand, Duncan & Byng, 2007). Given the wide variation in the training, functions and impact of this role, the training of a similar PWP workforce was standardised in the IAPT programme to support implementation. IAPT worked in partnership with education providers and leading professionals to develop a clear competency framework for PWPs (Roth & Pilling, 2007a) alongside a standardised and prescriptive national training curriculum (Richards, Farrand & Chellingsworth, 2011; Richards & Whyte, 2011).

PWP training is principally delivered as a Post Graduate Certificate. Fulfilling the desire to widen access to training for people with a wide educational background, such as qualifications at undergraduate diploma or equivalent, a route for non-graduate study at undergraduate degree level was also required. This means that trainees on the non-graduate route may lack experience of not just reflective writing but academic writing more generally.

The PWP training course is delivered across four modules:

1. Engagement and Assessment of Patients with Common Mental Health Problems
2. Evidence Based Low Intensity Treatment for Common Mental Health Disorders

3. Values, Policy, Culture and Diversity
4. Working within an Employment, Social and Healthcare Context. (Richards & Whyte, 2009, p. 8)

Trainees attend 25 days' teaching at the university and 20 university-directed study days to be undertaken in the workplace, requiring trainees to take responsibility for their own learning. This places greater demands on the trainee PWP to both coordinate their own learning experiences alongside facilitating learning opportunities within the clinical setting.

Having to negotiate their own learning within clinical settings has been identified by many trainees as a challenge. In particular, such challenges have been identified with respect to the different demands being placed on the trainee and the clinical service. Within the IAPT programme, recommendations were made that trainees should not start assessing or treating clients until they have completed and passed the competency assessments in Modules 1 and 2. However, in some cases, trainees were required to take on a caseload of clients before this time as a result of pressures placed on IAPT services to meet waiting time targets. While trainees therefore had directed study days set aside within the curriculum to reflect on the development of their competency in the clinical method, service-level pressures upon them may have left them with little time to reflect on their practice.

The focus on reflection in the assessment of PWPs during training

Trainees are assessed through:

1. A competency assessment for each of the modules addressing assessment, treatment, engagement with case management supervision and adaptations to practice to accommodate diversity. Competency assessments are undertaken within the university and based upon a simulated role-play scenario with an actor briefed in advance to undertake the role of a client.
2. A written reflective commentary based upon a video recording of each of the competency assessments.
3. Written exams addressing topics covered across each module.

While the reflective commentaries and exams carry equal academic weighting, competency assessments are marked as PASS/FAIL only. As such, marks contributing to the overall programme award solely consist of those awarded for the written assessments.

ROLE OF REFLECTION IN PWP TRAINING

The Declarative Procedural Reflective (DPR) model of therapist skill acquisition (Bennett-Levy, 2006) provides a useful framework to describe how PWP training programmes seek to develop and assess a range of skills associated with competent clinical practice (Bennett-Levy et al., 2010) (see Chapter 1). Trainees are able to demonstrate their declarative knowledge in the exam, procedural skills within the competency assessments and their reflective ability through the reflective commentaries. The focus on developing reflective capacity is considered essential to skill development, enabling practitioners to build on conceptual (declarative) knowledge and procedural skills, and is identified as the process that enables novice practitioners to move towards expert (Bennett-Levy, 2006).

The importance placed on reflection within PWP training is outlined in the national training educator support materials:

> Reflection: all teaching and learning activities should promote PWP trainees' ability to reflect on their own performance and personal development. Learning activities and assessments should incorporate reflection by PWP trainees on what they have done well and how they could improve their performance, linked to an understanding of the rationales for particular skills and an ability to accurately identify their use. (Richards & Whyte, 2009, p. 10)

The process of reflection provides a means through which intentional learning can be achieved. While reflection can take place at an unconscious level, using it as a tool for learning is reliant on it being conscious (Marton & Booth, 1997). Through reflection, trainees can explore their actions, thoughts and feelings to develop action plans for improving their future practice, with time set aside to achieve these objectives through the directed learning days.

Problems with reflection in the training of PWPs

When PWP trainees are learning to reflect, their reflection tends to be very descriptive. Clinical educators on the IAPT PWP training programmes have highlighted how the written reflections undertaken by the trainees are largely centred on a purely descriptive account of what happened, and what may be done differently, in their practice (Chellingsworth & Farrand, 2013). Such reflections are rarely informed by reference to the appropriate literature to help the trainees critically evaluate their practice and become truly critically reflective practitioners.

Levels of reflection

Observations that initial reflections of PWP trainees tend to be descriptive are consistent with research exploring levels of reflection among student teachers undertaking training programmes (Hatton & Smith, 1995). The Hatton and Smith (1995) model of reflection identifies four distinctive categories of written reflection.

TABLE 9.1 *Categories of written reflection (Hatton & Smith, 1995) with examples*

Descriptive writing: Practitioner places emphasis on gaining required skills and behaviours.	"I did not summarise information effectively throughout the assessment. I therefore missed important opportunities for the patient to feel they had been listened to and heard, and to check that I had understood and noted down information from the patient's dialogue correctly. I need to mention this in my next supervision session."
Descriptive reflection: Practitioner attempts to provide reasons for their actions through the application of the literature.	"During the assessment with my patient there were several occasions when she clearly became distressed, my patient disclosed having difficult thoughts such as 'I'm useless'. It would have been appropriate at this point to show verbal empathy by giving an empathy statement such as 'its sounds like you've been having some very distressing thoughts'. Not using verbal empathy appropriately may have impacted on the therapeutic relationship and patient engagement as Cahill et al. (2008) report the use of common factors as important to patient outcome."
Dialogic reflection: Represents a third, more demanding level of reflection emerging when competing claims for good practice are considered. The practitioner may therefore engage in an inner dialogue alongside discussions with other professionals to generate new understanding and insights.	"I feel I followed the very structured LI model for assessments (Richards & Whyte, 2009) well. This method of assessment within IAPT is important to LI working as it helps enable services to improve access to interventions (Farrand & Williams, 2010). But at times, my patient appeared to become frustrated with this very structured approach, perhaps thinking I was not responding sufficiently to their emotional distress before moving on in the assessment. This I feel in turn impacted on my therapeutic relationship. A good therapeutic relationship can be achieved when a patient-centred approach and common factor skills are used effectively (Mead & Bower, 2002). I intend to take this potential conflict to supervision to discuss with my supervisor how I can successfully incorporate and develop my skills in these areas within the LI assessment model."
Critical reflection: Characterised by a consideration of the broader historical, social and political contexts in which events take place.	"The quality of the therapist–patient relationship is the most consistently reported predictor of treatment outcome (Norcross, 2002). Cahill et al. (2008) proposes that 30% of outcome is due to 'common factors' which primarily involve the therapeutic relationship. This highlights the importance of me always displaying good common factor skills when working with patients. I believe, however, that my focus on getting the specific factors correct was to the detriment of my common factor skills. There is, however, contradictory evidence to suggest that specific factors are more important to the the therapeutic relationship (Blow et al., 2007). The importance of both common and specific factors to the therapeutic relationship has therefore been highlighted in the literature. This would indicate that if I display both common and specific factors sufficiently, I will improve patient engagement and outcomes, which would contribute to better overall service recovery rates."

These are presented in Table 9.1, alongside an example of each, informed by the IAPT PWP Post Graduate Certificate training programme.

According to this model, these distinctive forms of reflection represent a developmental hierarchy, which students progress through as their skills in reflection improve. This would offer an explanation as to why the reflections of an experienced practitioner may be quite different in quality from those generated by a PWP trainee who may be at the earlier stages of the model. The DPR model (Bennett-Levy, 2006) provides further support for the development of reflective skill with experience. The model suggests that during the initial stages of training PWP trainees lack the procedural knowledge to inform how and when to use acquired skills and have not yet progressed through to the later stages of the model. It may therefore need to be recognised that paraprofessional practitioners often lack the experience to reflect in a more critical way during the initial stages of training.

Lack of previous clinical experience

Differences in the quality of reflective writing on the PWP training course may also represent the often minimal levels of experience the trainees have on entering the PWP training programme. This lack of experience is amplified given the diverse nature of the backgrounds and clinical practice experience of trainee PWPs in comparison to those already having a professional background. When entering psychological therapy training programmes directed at professionals, previous clinical experience often represents essential entry criteria. It has, however, been suggested that this explanation linking lack of experience to poor reflective capacity is incomplete. Experience alone does not constitute learning but is dependent upon the meaning and value the learner attaches to the experience (Kolb, 1984). Additionally, therefore, PWP trainees may still need to develop values to attach to their experiences and hence undertake reflection.

The focus on self in reflective writing

Writing in the first person represents a key expectation associated with written reflections (Tummons, 2011). Depending on the trainee's previous experience, this may be uncomfortable given that previous written assignments may have been penalised for the use of first person pronouns or for drawing on personal experience. PWP trainees may therefore not be familiar with writing in this way, thus impacting on what they write reflectively. This therefore discourages genuine self-examination in the written reflections of trainee PWPs that can lead to reflections that are superficial or strategic in nature (Hobbs, 2007).

Conflicting demands placed on trainee PWPs

Course providers in a variety of disciplines include written reflection assessed assignments as part of their programme assessment. There is, however, some debate about whether written reflection will remain authentic and effective when included as an assessed component on a programme (Tummons, 2011). The biggest area of concern arises with respect to trainees viewing reflective assignments as a university requirement linked to assessment, rather than a process towards skills and self-development (Tummons, 2011). Focus on assessment prevents trainees from engaging in the "deeper" form of learning required to undertake good quality reflective assignments (Ramsden, 2003). While this is likely to be experienced to some extent across all programmes employing written reflections as part of assessment, there are several reasons as to why there may be a greater impact on PWP or practitioner training programmes more generally:

- There are a large number of PWP trainees entering the role to gain higher qualifications and further experience to progress onto other careers in psychological therapies. This may lead them to prioritise achieving higher grades at the expense of using reflective writing as a tool to enhance their clinical skills and competencies.
- Within the PWP training programme, the large emphasis placed on the assessment of reflective assignments and the weighting these have towards the overall programme award encourage an instrumental rather than deeper level of learning.
- Practitioners undertaking training are generally doing so while holding down their first role and working within their employing service when not attending university training days. The demands placed on trainees may prevent them from approaching their written reflective assignments at a deeper level with reflections remaining largely descriptive (Richardson & Maltby, 1995).
- Practitioners may also be new to their roles, and indeed, in some cases, new to full-time employment. They may therefore be reluctant to write an honest account of a particular moment or event due to the perception of a need to protect their identity and to avoid exposing themselves to too much scrutiny (Tummons, 2011). This may also raise concerns regarding the authenticity of trainee reflective writing (Wenger, 1998).

SUPPORTING REFLECTION IN THE TRAINING OF PSYCHOLOGICAL WELLBEING PRACTITIONERS

Given difficulties surrounding the written reflections of trainee PWPs moving beyond descriptive writing (Hatton & Smith, 1995), it is clear that ways to support trainees to move beyond this level reflection are required. This is especially important given that an emphasis on simply practising reflection is not sufficient (Kolb, 1984).

Promote self-assessment

"Self-assessment schedules" have been shown to provide a structured way to promote a deeper level of reflection in students alongside an increased understanding concerning the requirements of reflection (Bain, Mills, Ballantyne & Packer, 2002). These have been identified to promote a deeper level of reflection by:

- requiring students to revisit their own reflections leading to developments in thought and understanding
- increasing student awareness of deficits and variations in their current level of reflection and what it is expected of them
- encouraging students to monitor and become more aware of their reflective processes.

Make the requirements associated with reflection more explicit

Examination of the written guidance concerning the expectations and components of a written reflection suggest that university programmes may need to be more explicit (Rai, 2006). Rather than exploring the value and meaning of experiences, students may think the expectation is to outline what they know about the experience (MacLellan, 1999). This is consistent with PWP trainees who tend to provide a narrative account of what they did or didn't do in the session as opposed to using their knowledge to reflect upon and evaluate their practice.

Feedback

Providing trainees with more targeted feedback has been shown to highlight areas of development in reflective capacity and provide a further way to enable better appreciation of the expectations placed on them (Samuels & Betts, 2007). As with many training programmes, the time to provide individual feedback to trainees is often restricted. Universities should therefore provide written materials and worksheets to support PWP trainees and other practitioners in using models of reflection and encouraging deeper levels of reflection.

Modelling practice

Modelling has been shown to be an effective way to support the development of reflective writing (Moon, 2004), further supported through providing examples of reflective writing. Educators could model reflective writing by providing examples of anonymised trainees marked reflective assignments alongside the mark provided. Additionally, formative and summative feedback on trainee's reflective writing may help to develop this skill further.

Provide a structured learning context to support reflection

Previous research has highlighted how trainees on professional training programmes may find it difficult to find the time to focus upon the development of their reflective capacity (Boud & Walker, 1998). Although this was a consideration within the PWP national curriculum with inclusion of the 20 university directed learning days in the workplace, it was still apparent that many trainees were not using the time to develop their skills in reflection. To overcome this limitation it may be helpful to provide trainees with a more structured learning context to support practice in reflection within the workplace (Boud & Walker, 1998). Several PWP training programmes have therefore directed trainees to use a number of university-directed workplace learning days to engage in a self-practice, self-reflection (SP/SR) structured approach to CBT training (Bennett-Levy, 2006). As proposed by the DPR model of therapist skill development (Bennett-Levy, 2006), SP/SR can be used in conjunction with other training techniques, such as role-play during course hours and within the university-directed time.

Within the structured approach to SP/SR several training programmes have required trainees to practise the low intensity (LI) CBT clinical interventions on themselves, or with a colleague during role-play, during service-based learning days and then post their reflections on an online reflective blog by a given deadline (Farrand, Perry & Linsley, 2010). The blogs are non-assessed and capable of being viewed by all members of that specific training cohort to facilitate peer and tutor feedback. They are, however, read and themed by the course tutors and used to inform the agenda for up to 10 hours of clinical skills supervision provided as part of the training programme. Using online blogs in this way can result in several benefits with respect to the development of reflective capacity (Farrand, Perry & Linsley, 2010):

- Blog posting deadlines make it more likely trainees will actively engage in the SP/SR process
- Trainees are able to use the blogs of other trainees to challenge and develop their own practice
- Peer-supported reviews provide alternative perspectives shown to be of value to trainees (Richert, 1990)
- Blogs support the provision of formative assessment feedback by tutors capable of being viewed by other trainees in the cohort, making them less apprehensive in being open and honest in their reflections (Tummons, 2011).

The use of the internet, such as through online blogs (Farrand, Perry & Linsley, 2010) or online message boards (Thwaites et al., 2015; Chapter 8, this volume), therefore present the potential to support structured approaches such as SP/SR in the development of reflective capacity in the PWP's workplace during training, or the development of competencies and metacompetencies post-training (Thwaites et al., 2015).

SUPPORTING REFLECTION IN QUALIFIED PSYCHOLOGICAL WELLBEING PRACTITIONERS

As discussed, reflective capacity is central in enabling psychological therapists and practitioners to learn from clinical experience and refine their skills (Bennett-Levy, 2006). Due to the condensed nature of the PWP training course, however, a structure to facilitate the continued development of reflective skills post-training is potentially of benefit.

Supporting continued reflection through supervision

PWPs receive weekly clinical case management supervision, alongside monthly clinical skills supervision (Turpin & Wheeler, 2011). Case management supervision can enable PWPs to reflect on their practice. However, given the priority on case discussion, limits may be encountered regarding the depth to which reflection can be undertaken (see Chapter 2). Potentially, therefore, the greater time available within clinical skills supervision provides a more appropriate option for in-depth reflective practice.

IAPT supervision guidance does not specify exactly how clinical skills supervision should be delivered and what techniques may be appropriate (Turpin & Wheeler, 2011). One possible use could therefore be to provide a supportive space for PWPs to reflect on their clinical practice and experience while receiving support from the supervisor to help frame difficulties and, through reflection, enhance clinical reasoning and stimulate ongoing development. The focus of clinical skills supervision would therefore not be restricted to enabling the PWP to simply learn new skills, but to enhance their reflection to enable them to apply existing knowledge and skills from other contexts to the new situation.

There are a number of ways in which the formative function of clinical skills can be met, making PWP reflection a regular feature on the clinical skills supervision agenda. What supervision activity might be appropriate for the PWP will depend upon the level of skills and expertise they currently have in the topic area. Helpful strategies proposed for inclusion within supervision to enhance the reflective system include (Bennett-Levy, 2006):

- Reflective attitude
- Self-Practice/Self-Reflection
- Reflective/Socratic supervision

- Self-supervision
- Reflective writing
- Reflective reading.

Working with high caseloads can often mean PWPs do not prioritise reflective practice and it is therefore essential that this is supported through the supervision process. While supervisors can facilitate this through supervision discussion, the ability to reflect on practice should not purely be dependent on the supervisor asking the right questions. Instead, the use of an established model of reflection would be helpful to support the development of these skills both inside and outside the supervision process.

Structure for reflection

While PWPs develop skills in reflective writing as part of their training, due to the variable levels of experience in mental health upon entry to training these skills can be highly variable. There are many different reflective models that can be applied, but applying a model that can be used by both novice and experienced reflectors may be particularly helpful.

The Rolfe, Freshwater and Jasper (2001) reflective model involves the PWP identifying an area of practice to be considered with reflection which is then stimulated by them asking three questions regarding this area: **"What?"**, **"So what?"** and **"Now what?"** Types of helpful questions for PWPs to consider at different stages of their reflective process, alongside an indication of the best times to ask these during the supervision process, can be seen in Table 9.2.

TABLE 9.2 *Helpful questions to ask within reflection (Rolfe, Freshwater & Jasper, 2001) and where most appropriate within the supervision process*

What...	So what...	Now what...
...is the problem/difficulty?	...does this tell me/teach me?	...do I need to do differently to do things better (literature)?
...was I trying to achieve?	...did I base my actions on?	(supervision)?
...actions did I take?	...other knowledge can I bring to the situation (literature)?	
...were the consequences?		
Before supervision	*Before and during supervision*	*During and after supervision*

While the delivery of clinical skills supervision is variable, a common feature often involves supervisory discussion of a client presenting with a specific difficulty. To support reflection during such supervisory discussions, the use of a "Reflection Record" (Figure 9.1) based upon the Rolfe et al. (2001) reflective model, with instructions to inform use, may encourage the PWP to reflect on the client presentation before, during and after supervision.

Reflection Record		
Name of PWP:	**Name of supervisor:**	**Date of next clinical skills supervision:**

To be completed before clinical skills supervision

Section 1: Description and context of event

Section 2: What…is the problem/difficulty? …was I trying to achieve? …actions did I take? …were the consequences?

Section 3: So what…does this tell me/teach me? …did I base my actions on? …other knowledge can I bring to the situation (literature)?

Supervision question:

To be completed at clinical skills supervision

Section 4: Now what…do I need to do differently to do things better?

Section 5: Action plan… What practical steps can I take to achieve the above?

FIGURE 9.1 *Example of a Reflection Record*

Instructions for the use of a Reflection Record

1. The PWP identifies a recent incident from their practice and completes Sections 1 and 2, the "**What...?**" of the Reflection Record.
2. The PWP then completes Section 3, the "**So what...?**" of the record, considering if relevant literature can be applied in this section (but it is not essential).
3. The PWP considers Section 4, the "**Now what...?**" of the record, noting down any ideas. This section will also be discussed further and completed during supervision.
4. The PWP formulates a suitable supervision question based on reflection so far.
5. The Reflection Record, completed to Section 3, the "**So what...?**" part of the record, is taken to supervision to present the reflective process completed to this point and to stimulate discussion with supervisor and/or peers.
6. Section 4, the "**Now what...?**" part of the record, is completed by the PWP during the supervision session.
7. Section 5, also completed during the supervision session, is used to establish an "**Action plan**" to inform practice or further development.
8. The PWP and supervisor now have a written record of the "**Action plan**", the implementation of which can be reviewed at the next supervision session.

Using SP/SR to support continued reflection in Psychological Wellbeing Practitioners

Using SP/SR as an approach to help promote and structure effective and continued professional development to enhance clinical competency beyond initial training has been highlighted (Bennett-Levy et al., 2001; Davis et al., 2015). There is now also emerging evidence highlighting the benefits of SP/SR for PWPs in the development of competencies and metacompetencies when dealing with clients that challenge standard LI CBT protocols, thereby informing adaptation and flexibility in the LI method (Thwaites et al., 2015; see Chapter 8). The continued use of SP/SR post-training therefore gives qualified or experienced PWPs a strategy for behaviour change, skills change and self-rated belief change. Such findings have implications for post-training development, as a means for PWPs to enhance their skills.

Supporting continued reflection in PWPs through Continuing Professional Development

While Continuing Professional Development (CPD) takes many forms, with respect to PWPs it is often delivered in the format of training workshops or "master-classes" provided by educational providers or services themselves. Although useful, events such as these can be ineffective unless learning is supported through supervision afterwards (Beidas, Edmunds, Marcus & Kendall, 2012; Lyon, Stirman, Kerns & Bruns, 2011). Indeed, both adult learning theory (Kolb, 1984; Schön, 1983) and the supervision literature (Bennett-Levy, 2006) highlight the seminal role of reflection, supported through the supervision process, as the key element that enhances skill development. Such skill development may also be further enhanced through the use of "Reflection Worksheets", which are provided during and 1–4 weeks following these training events, especially when email prompts are used to support completion (Bennett-Levy & Padesky, 2014).

Ultimately, the training of PWPs is undertaken to improve outcomes for the clients. The use of Reflection Records after training cannot ensure that therapists acquire the skills that are necessary for effective treatment, but supervisors are able to continually access and check the process of skill development (Milne, 2009) and provide further ways of supporting the PWP skill development through reflection.

CONCLUSION

With a focus on the practitioner PWP workforce, which has been developed across England as part of the IAPT programme, this chapter has identified several challenges that those undertaking practitioner roles in mental health settings may face when developing their reflective practice:

* Limited mental health working experience
* Training and workplace demands of the role
* Previous educational experience
* Limited time available within the training to fully develop competency in reflection
* Desire to move beyond PWP role quickly.

Although these are significant and important barriers, training providers and services can encourage and enhance reflection by:

* making reflection requirements more explicit
* promoting self-awareness
* providing constructive feedback on reflection
* modeling reflective writing
* ensuring that the assessment weighting placed on reflective assignments that contribute towards the overall programme award is not too large
* introducing non-assessed opportunities to practise reflection through SP/SR
* considering ways to support the development of reflection beyond the initial training, either within the workplace or by supporting reflection in training events, providing opportunities for continuing professional development.

A review of the national PWP training curriculum is currently under consideration and presents the potential to address some of the challenges experienced with respect to reflection in a psychological practitioner workforce. Hopefully this chapter will be useful in informing this development, alongside the training of roles similar to that of PWPs at an international level. Furthermore, developments in other training programmes directed at psychological practitioner roles in areas outside mental health may find the overview of challenges and solutions helpful.

TAKING IT FORWARD

What *declarative knowledge* have you gained from reading this chapter?

- What has stood out for you in reading this chapter? Has anything surprised you?
- What do you think are the main challenges for low intensity CBT practitioners in developing reflective practice?

What *procedural rules* are you starting to change or develop, having reflected on this chapter?

As an LI CBT practitioner

- How can you overcome some of the barriers unique to your role that might get in the way of effective reflection?
- When you do reflect, at what level do you think this is taking place? What do you need to do to improve your level of reflection?

As an LI CBT supervisor (if relevant)

- What level of reflection do your LI CBT supervisees display?
- What can you do in your role to increase your supervisees' levels of reflection?
- Identify one clear "when... then..." rule that can guide your future supervisory behaviours.

As an LI CBT trainer (if relevant)

- What level of reflection do your students display?
- What can you do as an educator to increase your students' levels of reflection during and after training?

What strategies are you going to put in place to facilitate the engagement of your *reflective system*?

As an LI CBT practitioner

- When engaging in continuing professional development, how can you use reflection to enhance your learning?
- What techniques can you use independently and in supervision to support your reflective practice?
- How do you feel about using the "Reflection Record" within your practice? What could get in the way of your using this technique? How can you overcome this?

As an LI CBT supervisor (if relevant)

- How can you support your supervisees to use structured written reflections such as the "Reflection Record"?
- Use SP/SR to practise using a "Reflection Record" to enhance the support you can provide to the practitioners you supervisee.
- Consider the ways you could provide feedback on your supervisees' use of reflection.

As an LI CBT trainer (if relevant)

- How can you structure training programmes or CPD workshops to ensure reflection is an essential element?
- What tools could your students use to enhance their reflection?
- What needs to be in place to support these tools?

SUGGESTED READING

Bennett-Levy, J. (2006). Therapist skills: a cognitive model of their acquisition and refinement. *Behavioural and Cognitive Psychotherapy*, *34*(1), 57–78.

Hatton, N., & Smith, D. (1995). Reflection in teacher education: towards definition and implementation. *Teaching and Teacher Education*, *11*(1), 33–49.

Richardson, G., & Maltby, M. (1995). Reflection-on-practice: enhancing student learning. *Journal of Advanced Nursing*, *22*(2), 235–242.

Rolfe, G., Freshwater, D., & Jasper, M. (2001). *Critical reflection for nursing and the helping professions: a user's guide*. Basingstoke: Palgrave.

Tummons, J. (2011). 'It sort of feels uncomfortable': problematising the assessment of reflective practice. *Studies in Higher Education*, *36*(4), 471–483.

10

USING SELF-REFLECTION TO PROMOTE CBT THERAPIST SELF-CARE

Beverly Haarhoff and Richard Thwaites

LEARNING AIMS

- To heighten CBT therapists' awareness of unique therapy-related challenges to therapist self-care
- To encourage CBT therapists to conduct a self-reflective assessment of their current work-related stressors
- To help CBT therapists use reflection to promote self-care in the service of preventing burnout and maximising wellbeing

INTRODUCTION: WHAT IS SELF-CARE?

Self-care, involves making an active choice to take care of yourself in terms of basic physical needs (eating, sleeping and exercise) and also in the emotional, interpersonal, occupational and spiritual arenas (Ziguras, 2004). Therapist self-care is made up of several different components, namely: knowing what self-care is, recognising the challenges to self-care and knowing how to enhance therapist self-care. In this chapter we make three broad assumptions. First, that self-care is an idiosyncratic construct. One size does not fit all, and although there are a number of frequently recommended strategies we will not be prescriptive regarding how each individual therapist institutes self-care. Second, CBT therapists have a good knowledge of the many CBT self-care strategies routinely recommended to clients, for example: behavioural activation, increasing pleasurable activities, relaxation, practising Mindfulness–Based Cognitive Therapy (MBCT), maintaining a healthy work–life balance, managing sleep, challenging unhelpful thoughts, becoming more self-compassionate, and learning how to solve problems and make decisions. Third, although most CBT therapists accept that applying these strategies would be similarly useful in their own lives, the problem lies in recognising the need for therapist self-care, and then in taking the necessary steps to put tried-and-tested self-care strategies in place. We will therefore concentrate on how to utilise self-reflection to identify the need for self-care in the therapeutic context, and to recognise the obstacles to implementing self-care strategies.

In this chapter we focus on how self-reflection can facilitate *active choice* regarding our self-care as CBT therapists. Any discussion of therapist self-care needs to be set against that which threatens or undermines self-care in CBT therapists. The chapter therefore outlines a number of unique occupational challenges facing therapists. The experience of therapist stress and distress is usefully viewed as occurring on a continuum (Baker, 2003), with what would be considered normal or transient levels of stress, emotional arousal or depletion at one end and conditions such as vicarious and secondary traumatisation, compassion fatigue and burnout situated at the more extreme end of the continuum. A clarification of these terms will be provided in order to assist CBT therapists recognise the level of stress they may be experiencing. Improving self-care, reducing unhelpful levels of stress and reducing the likelihood of burnout requires self-awareness and knowledge, two key elements developed through reflection. To this end we look at the importance of continuous and *constructive* self-assessment to identify sources of stress in the professional and personal context. We then emphasise the importance of using reflection to formulate the factors that predispose, precipitate and maintain the individual CBT therapist's vulnerability to stress, and suggest ways of constructing individualised action plans to counteract stress and improve self-care.

Returning to a theme emphasised in previous chapters, we recommend that identifying personal, spiritual and cultural strengths can increase therapist resilience to occupationally-generated stress. We also advocate an honest appraisal of our weaknesses and vulnerabilities as therapists. Mindfulness-Based CBT, self-compassion and Self-Practice/Self-Reflection are flagged as particularly relevant self-care strategies for CBT therapists and the chapter concludes with the importance of recognising and dealing with common barriers to therapist self-care. We hope the chapter will be useful to CBT practitioners at all levels of experience and that the ideas contained in the chapter can also be usefully adapted by CBT supervisors and trainers. Much of what has been included in this chapter could equally apply to anyone identifying as a therapist, although the way in which we conceptualise a framework for reflecting on therapist self-care will reference many of the principles of CBT discussed in previous chapters.

CHALLENGES TO CBT THERAPIST SELF-CARE

Being a therapist is consistently reported as an extremely rewarding occupation. Many therapists experience a great deal of satisfaction in this role and feel privileged to play a part in facilitating psychological healing (Norcross & Guy, 2007).

However, individuals employed in what is characterised as the caring professions (doctors, nurses, psychological practitioners, etc.), report suffering from disproportionately high levels of stress when compared to the general population. In addition, the role of psychological therapist presents a number of unique challenges (Tyler & Cushway, 1998), the most notable of which is that the vast proportion of the working day involves concentrated interpersonal engagement in the context of other people's emotional distress and cognitive and behavioural difficulties. In some instances, such as working with clients who experience severe addictions, trauma, sexual abuse or who have problems in the forensic arena, the exposure to high levels of clients' distress, or client accounts of dangerous antisocial behaviour, is relentless and extremely intense (Kottler, 2012). Even in these situations the therapist is generally expected to stay present and engaged, form empathic, helpful and supportive connections with clients, and at the same time, understand complex predisposing, precipitating and maintaining factors, manage risk, make decisions and/or recommendations in what are often uncertain and ambiguous situations. Many psychological practitioners will also at some point in their career experience the impact of client suicide, either directly as the client's therapist or indirectly as a member of a team or service (Hendin, Pollinger Haas, Maltsberger, Szanto & Rabinowicz, 2004). In addition, the working environment generally demands accountability and there is the possibility of client complaints that can, in some instances, result in legal repercussions. Therapists are also bound by many ethical considerations, confidentiality being one such expectation. This means therapists cannot easily "unload" events from their working day when with friends or family, or even talk about or point to successes.

Furthermore, as we have discussed in Chapter 4, therapists are also expected to develop a high degree of self-awareness, regulate their emotional responses to upsetting material, and in many instances use their personal emotional responses as an important sources of information relevant to conceptualising clients' difficulties (Leahy, 2007; Safran & Segal, 1996; Young et al., 2003). To complicate matters even further, many client difficulties are of an interpersonal nature and habitual, unhelpful interpersonal transactions often continue to play out in the therapeutic relationship (Beck, 2011). Therapists are fallible human beings and some will have had past experiences which may make them vulnerable to particular transactional styles (for example, they may have been bullied, abused or taken advantage of in their family of origin), and the life experience of many clients often mirrors the therapist's experience. We all experience loss, work stresses, difficult relationships, problems with our friends and relatives and, from time to time, difficulties with dysfunctional behaviours. Given all of these factors, it is therefore not surprising to find that therapists are vulnerable to experiencing a variety of occupationally-related stress conditions, including depression, anxiety, relationship problems, vicarious and secondary traumatisation, compassion fatigue, substance abuse and burnout (Kottler, 2012; Orlinsky, Rønnestad & Helge, 2005; Sayyedi & O'Bryne, 2003).

Therapists in training are identified as a group who are particularly vulnerable to high levels of stress (Cushway, 2005; Rønnestad & Skovholt, 2003). Stringent academic requirements, lack of relevant declarative and procedural knowledge, fear of negative evaluation, performance anxiety and a growing awareness of gaps in knowledge are just some of the factors that especially affect this group (Bennett-Levy & Beedie, 2007).

THE STRESS CONTINUUM

Definition of terms

Everyone experiences stress, which, for the purposes of this chapter, we broadly define as a response to a situation which activates and intensifies cognitive, emotional, physiological reactions and behavioural consequences which, in many instances, can result in actions that can be positive and helpful to the individual, spurring us on to do better and achieve more (McEwan, 2008). In the context of this chapter, however, we focus on the negative consequences of stress, which include the whole gambit of negative emotions (anxiety, anger, sadness or guilt), unpleasant physiological arousal, cognitions which may reflect a sense of not being able to cope, being overwhelmed, helpless or hopeless, resulting in unhelpful or self-defeating behaviours. Stress can also have physiological consequences and worsen conditions such as obesity, diabetes, cardiovascular and gastrointestinal problems and negative behavioural consequences such as work avoidance, poor eating habits and alcoholism. For example, nurses have been found to have higher mortality from stress-related causes and doctors have been observed to have relatively high rates of alcoholism (Tyler & Cushway, 1998).

In this chapter, we emphasise the role of cognitive processes in self-induced stress. The transactional model of stress offers an explanation for the role of cognition, positing the idea that stress arises from the interaction between the individual's primary appraisal of the context or environment in which they find themselves, as threatening or dangerous, and a perceived sense of not being able to cope, feeling overwhelmed or powerless to manage the perceived or actual challenge (Lazarus, 1966; Lazarus & Folkman, 1984). This model is commonly expressed as the tendency to overestimate danger and available resources and underestimate coping.

The following stress-related psychological conditions are identified as unique to the helping professions: compassion fatigue (Bride, Radey & Figley, 2007), vicarious traumatisation (Harrison & Westwood, 2009), secondary traumatic stress (Pearlman & Saakvitne, 1995) and burnout. Although there is some degree of overlap between these conditions, the literature distinguishes each as follows.

Compassion fatigue describes a situation where the therapist experiences a sense that they have given out so much empathy and compassion that there is no more left to give (Bride, Radey & Figley, 2007). Empathy has become blunted and the "emotional empathic response jug" is empty.

Vicarious traumatisation is when the therapist experiences the client's trauma as if it were their own trauma, visualising the occurrence (Harrison & Westwood, 2009).

In *secondary traumatic stress* the therapist experiences the same symptoms as the traumatised client (Pearlman & Saakvitne, 1995).

Burnout is defined as "a psychological syndrome of emotional exhaustion, depersonalisation, and reduced personal accomplishment that can occur among individuals who work with others in some capacity" (Maslach, 1993, p. 20). Burnout can include aspects of all the conditions described above. Signs and symptoms of burnout include: difficulties in staying present with the client, poor attention, impatience with clients and colleagues, feeling suspicious and judgemental of clients, feeling resistant about going to work, being bored, having a sense that no one is supportive, feeling isolated and alienated, feeling that work is predictable and boring, and constantly fantasising about doing something else (Kottler, 2012). From a CBT perspective, burnout encompasses changed thoughts, emotions, physiological responses and behaviour. Signs and symptoms should present for some weeks to signify these conditions (we all experience "off" days from time to time). It may be useful at this point to reflect on the conditions described above and place yourself on a continuum of stress, which ranges from normal levels of stress through to burnout.

SELF-ASSESSMENT

Identifying sources of therapist stress

The first step in implementing or improving self-care is to conduct a thorough self-assessment. This means identifying and reflecting on different sources of therapist stress and reflecting on the current personal relevance of each. The following stress-related domains are identified: client-related stress (which includes the impact of client suicide), work-related stress, event-related stress and self-induced stress (Kottler, 2012). In addition to these we will look at the particular stressors involved in CBT training.

Client-induced stress

Most clients who have engaged on a course of CBT want help, understand the reasons why they have entered therapy, and are pleased and/or relieved to have the opportunity to receive help. Clients generally grasp the principles of CBT, understand the idea of active involvement in CBT and recognise the importance of personal responsibility for addressing their difficulties and effecting positive change regarding their identified problems. In such cases, establishing a positive, collaborative working relationship does not present any difficulty and the process of therapy is a rewarding experience for therapist and client. However, in some instances, some clients may have developed problematic ways of managing their interpersonal transactions. This can mean unregulated emotional outbursts, behaving in ways that can be interpreted as unreliable or deceitful, seeming to exploit the mental health services in a variety of ways, becoming overly dependent on the therapist, or having unrealistic expectations regarding what therapy can achieve and becoming angry, and even litigious, if these expectations are not met (Beck, 2011).

Other forms of client-induced stress can result from the complexity and/or severity of the problems experienced by the client. This can mean that the therapist may witness the client deteriorating, becoming increasingly suicidal or inclined to self-harm or to harm others. Some therapists might blame themselves for this deterioration and experience anxiety, guilt, hopelessness and sadness. Other therapists may start to experience anger, resentment, fear and even extreme feelings such as hatred and despair. Therapists who work with clients who have experienced or inflicted trauma are witness to the presentation of what can be terrible accounts of deprivation, torture, sexual abuse and violence, all of which can vicariously traumatise the therapist.

Client suicide

The impact of client suicide is always very profound. There is an identified lack of research in this area. Most studies have been conducted with psychiatrists, who experience extremely high rates of patient suicide, with up to 50% of psychiatrists experiencing a patient suicide at some point in their career (Hendin et al., 2004). However, about 25% of other mental health practitioners will have experienced a client suicide at some point in their professional life. Serious personal and professional effects have been noted. Personal reactions can be stress, guilt, social withdrawal and loneliness, increased self-doubt, lack of confidence, feelings of isolation, anger, and symptoms of anxiety and depression. The professional implications often include lengthy administrative investigation of the event, which can be frightening for the practitioner, who may fear litigation or retribution. Other observable professional consequences can be that the practitioner becomes more defensive, is more inclined to use mental health legislation, may be subject to self-doubt, finds decision-making more difficult and, in some instances, it can lead to early retirement (Foley & Kelly, 2007).

Work-related stress

Obvious work pressures include time pressure related to unmanageable caseloads or shortages of suitable staff, difficult colleagues, insufficient or incompetent supervision, lack of professional development support, continual changes and restructuring of services, competency requirements, and so on. In addition, broad social changes, such as "globalisation", "informationalism", the emergence of the "network society" and the "manageralism, risk and the audit society" (Frost, 2010), have led to significant changes in the workplace. All of these social changes have positive and negative effects. Globalisation has meant a closer connection with, and need to consider, factors operating far beyond what would be considered familiar territory.

For example, increasingly culturally diverse populations present new clinical challenges (see Chapter 5).

Informationalism describes a situation where most professionals are literally swamped with a continual stream of information which is ever more readily available through the internet. CBT therapists who generally pride themselves on delivering evidence-based practice can, under these conditions, experience a sense of being left behind, never knowing enough, and not being able to see a way to catch up. The network society means increasingly close connections with many individuals and groups. This of course can be enormously rewarding but also brings stress. Needing to respond immediately to emails and to be continually up to date with new technologies of communication can be very challenging to some CBT therapists. Finally, the emphasis on managed care, cost-effective treatment, competency demands and frequent auditing can leave CBT therapists frustrated and alienated in the workplace.

Event-related stress

Event-related stress includes various real-life crises, for example divorce, bereavement, moving home, loss of employment, health, money and family problems and developmental transitions. It can also include stress-related events which might occur in the therapist's personal life but which impact on their work situation. All of these events can take their toll in different ways and present different challenges for therapists.

Self-induced stress

Self-induced stress often relates to therapists' underlying beliefs about self, clients and the course of therapy (Beck, 2011; Leahy, 2007). Underlying vicious cycles of beliefs, emotions and behaviours point to common therapist patterns, such as perfectionism, fear of failure, self-doubt, fear of being judged and evaluated by others and need for approval. Chapter 4, in discussing the therapeutic relationship, considers therapist beliefs in relation to therapy. However, therapist beliefs, as identified by the Therapist Schema Questionnaire (Leahy, 2001) or self-schema (see Young et al., 2003), described in Chapter 4, also have relevance to therapist cycles that can undermine self-care. The schema "subjugation", "self-sacrifice" and "unrelenting standards" are characterised as the "schema triad trap" (Young et al., 2003). This constellation of schema is common in CBT therapists (Haarhoff, 2006; Young et al., 2003) and can clearly lead to a deleterious experience of stress. Stress can also result from feelings of incompetency and, indeed, real incompetency and lack of skill and knowledge. What has come to be known as the "imposter syndrome" (Clance & Imes, 1978), which is excessive self-doubt in high achievers coupled with a belief that at any moment one's perceived lack of knowledge and skill will be discovered, is common in therapists at all levels of experience and can lead to ongoing anxiety and stress. There is also a suggestion that the constant need to be aware of one's own emotional and interpersonal issues can be stressful (Sayyedi & O'Bryne, 2003). This last stressor is of course very dependent upon the extent to which the therapist is able to deal with their personal issues.

- Take a moment to reflect on each of these domains and consider the relevance of each one to your own experience.

Stress and the trainee CBT therapist

Although there has been a paucity of research in this area, trainee psychotherapists, psychologists and nurses generally report high levels of stress relating to the experience of training in the mental health field (Cushway, 1992). We have both been involved with the training of CBT therapists for many years and have observed that trainee CBT therapists (who are often from diverse professional backgrounds) can sometimes report high levels of stress. CBT training can present particular challenges to therapists trained in other modalities. As part of training some trainees in postgraduate programmes can be required to work with clients in a manner that strictly complies with the theoretical principles and practical application of the CBT model. This involves what can be perceived as considerably more "scrutiny" than the practitioner may be accustomed to. For example, there is an emphasis on recording all therapy sessions, either in audio or visual form. The tapes are then reviewed by the supervisor and are regularly evaluated using structured rating scales such as the Cognitive Therapy Scale (Young & Beck, 1988), Cognitive Therapy Scale-Revised (Blackburn et al., 2001) or Assessment of Core CBT Skills (ACCS) (Muse, McManus, Rakovshik & Kennerley, 2014) to assess the trainee for the application of CBT competencies, which are increasingly delineated (Roth & Pilling, 2007a).

Supervision nearly always takes place in pairs and requires that the trainee shares their therapy tapes with both supervisor and fellow supervisee. Very often CBT trainees experience high levels of performance anxiety, and have a tendency to be self-critical and avoidant. CBT training is often at a postgraduate level and it is not unusual for therapists originally trained in other psychotherapeutic modalities to retrain as CBT therapists. These therapists can be particularly vulnerable to an experience of deskilling and diminished confidence as they learn to use an unfamiliar structure (for example, collaborative agenda setting, guided discovery, taking a more active role, eliciting feedback).

Trainee therapists can also experience considerable amounts of stress as they begin to confront the gap between what they know and what they recognise they need to know in terms of achieving competency as a CBT therapist. This can lead to a perception that they are not as competent as they thought they were initially which can result in a sudden drop in confidence (Bennett-Levy & Beedie, 2007). It has been observed that as a problem-focused, evidence-based, short-term therapy, CBT can result in a supervision style that focuses on identifying and correcting errors and missteps rather than being supportive, nurturing and encouraging. Leahy (2001) also suggests that CBT, with its emphasis on structure and evidence, may attract individuals who are less tolerant of the ambiguity and uncertainty that inevitably turn up in the therapeutic context.

Self-formulation of CBT therapist stress

Self-reflection of course plays a pivotal role in self-assessment. You have already considered the various domains of therapist-related stress in the context of your particular experience. Recognising formulation as a core CBT principle (Beck, 1995; Kuyken et al., 2009), it is useful to formulate and understand the way in which stress may figure in your life. There are a variety of ways to do this. However, we recommend that an extended five-part model (Padesky & Mooney, 1990) is a useful template. Figure 10.1 shows an example of a formulation template.

Environmental or situational factors: In this instance, reflecting on the domains of clinically-related stress discussed above, namely client, work-related, event-related, self-induced and training-related stress, is relevant. It is also useful to consider your close relationships. Is anyone complaining that you are not available or not having any fun, or that you are angry all the time, or boring?

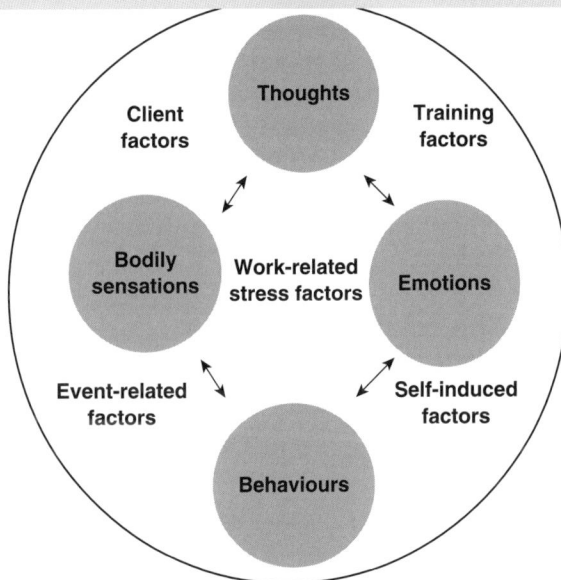

FIGURE 10.1 *"Stress" self-formulation five-part model (adapted from Padesky, C.A., & Mooney, K.A. (1990). Presenting the cognitive model to clients.* International Cognitive Therapy Newsletter, *6, 13–14. (Available from http://padesky.com/clinical-corner/publications) © 1986 Christine A. Padesky, www.padesky.com. Reprinted with permission.)*

Emotions: Are you overly anxious, angry, guilty, bored, frustrated, irritable or sad? You may like to rate the intensity of any emotions you identify on a personal visual analogue scale. If your emotions are particularly intense, utilising some of the symptom identification rating scales you use in your workplace could perhaps give you a clearer picture. Some scales you could employ are the Patient Health Questionnaire-9 (PHQ-9) (Kroenke & Spitzer, 2001) and the Generalised Anxiety Disorder seven-item scale (GAD-7) (Spitzer, Kroenke, Williams & Löwe, 2006).

Thoughts about work: For example, "Work is a pain, too hard, boring, upsetting, confusing or frightening". "My client(s) are difficult, not improving, unexpectedly dropping out of treatment etc."

Behaviour: Are you constantly complaining, staying late at work, leaving early repeatedly, avoiding work, pretending to be sick, drinking or eating too much, forgetting appointments, or neglecting work commitments?

Bodily Sensations: Are you often tired, sleep-deprived, ill or tense?

Reflecting on your self-formulation, consider the following:

- Are there significant work-related issues in my current situation? Are these inside or outside my control?
- Are there significant client-related stressors in my current situation? Trauma-related work? Particular clients identified as difficult?
- Are events in my life or outside work impacting on me as a CBT therapist?
- Have I detected any self-defeating therapy-related patterns or cycles? For example, am I working too hard, seeking perfectionism, experiencing self-doubt, avoidance, perceived lack of competence, actual lack of competence, performance anxiety, need for approval or self-sacrifice?
- If your self-formulation indicates a significant amount of work-related stress you can use the template shown in Figure 10.2, which details a specific work-related example, to unpack and understand your particular stress-inducing factors with greater clarity. Formulating some of the therapy behaviours that feed into professional stresses can help move towards a plan to make changes. For example, most therapists report that one factor that makes their working lives more difficult is seeing clients for repeated sessions when they are failing to engage or are unable to benefit from the therapy, yet most therapists will experience occasions when they hold onto such clients that they should discharge (Delgadillo, Gellatly & Stephenson-Bellwood, 2015). This creates longer term stress but allows the therapist to avoid a difficult conversation or decision in the short term. Understanding the beliefs and pressures that lead therapists to act in this way can help them to change their behaviour. It can be very useful to use this template to discuss your situation with someone else, a supervisor or trusted colleague. Chapter 4 also provides a useful resource regarding the identification of possible unhelpful therapist schema, beliefs and assumptions.

After completing your overall functional analysis of therapy–related stress you may like to review where you positioned yourself on the stress continuum you previously constructed.

If you have placed yourself at the more extreme end of the continuum it is recommended that you look for support beyond that which can be offered by this book and we suggest you consult with your close family, trusted colleagues, supervisor, manager or general practitioner. It may be time to consider taking a break, as in extended leave, or seeking personal therapy.

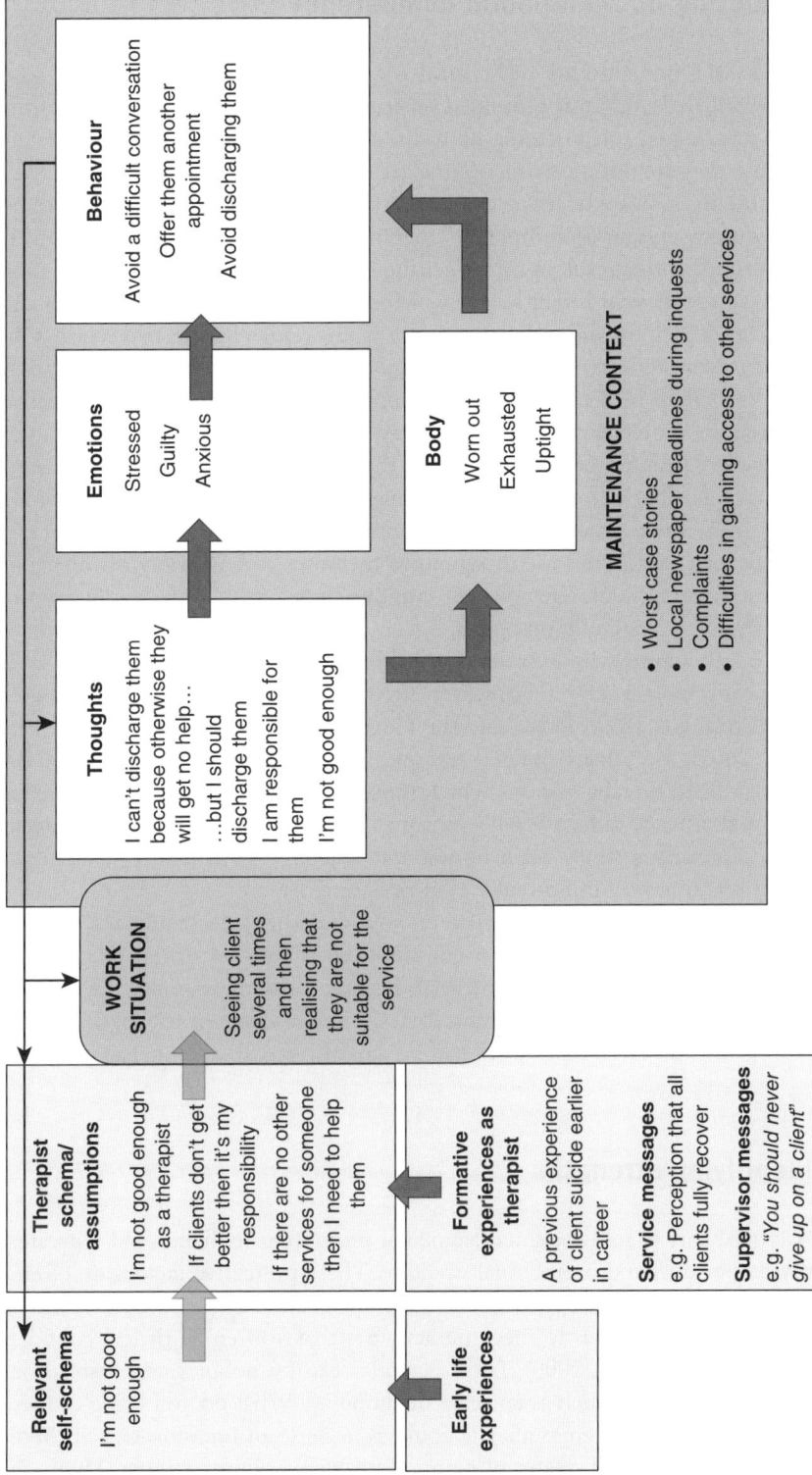

PROBLEM

I find myself holding on to clients who aren't appropriate for our service (e.g. high risk, failing to benefit) because it makes me think that I am letting them down. This leads to me feeling stuck and worn out by having to see clients who don't get better; I start to feel like a bad therapist and want to leave my job.

Behaviour

Avoid a difficult conversation

Offer them another appointment

Avoid discharging them

Emotions

Stressed

Guilty

Anxious

Body

Worn out

Exhausted

Uptight

Thoughts

I can't discharge them because otherwise they will get no help...
...but I should discharge them

I am responsible for them

I'm not good enough

MAINTENANCE CONTEXT

- Worst case stories
- Local newspaper headlines during inquests
- Complaints
- Difficulties in gaining access to other services

WORK SITUATION

Seeing client several times and then realising that they are not suitable for the service

Therapist schema/assumptions

I'm not good enough as a therapist

If clients don't get better then it's my responsibility

If there are no other services for someone then I need to help them

Relevant self-schema

I'm not good enough

Formative experiences as therapist

A previous experience of client suicide earlier in career

Service messages
e.g. Perception that all clients fully recover

Supervisor messages
e.g. "You should never give up on a client"

Early life experiences

FIGURE 10.2 *Example of a longitudinal formulation of therapist behaviours that can lead to burnout*

Reflecting on therapeutic competency

Many CBT therapists are self-critical and at times this is unfounded. In some cases, however, self-criticism is grounded on truthful acknowledgement of gaps in knowledge or competence, or facing up to the fact that some clients may be deteriorating because they are not receiving optimal treatment. Unfortunately a relatively common response to this state of affairs can be therapist avoidance, shying away from challenge or trying to present a "competent" therapist front. These actions maintain the status quo or, sadly, often result in things getting worse. A more self-nurturing approach is to try to discover what might be going wrong. Reflecting honestly on gaps and weakness can be helpful and support self-care if this results in effective action. Chapters 2 and 3 present reflective models to use in supervision and self-supervision which can be very helpful in determining what might be the challenge and negotiating a way to progress more helpfully. Another way forward is to collect and act upon client feedback. Chapter 6 highlights research that shows that many therapists fail to collect adequate feedback from clients regarding therapy progress or lack of progress and often overestimate their ability as therapists. Reflecting on client feedback gathered directly or through the use of symptom measures and a variety of other self-report measures, can facilitate therapist self-empowerment by showing us what we are doing well and what we could do better.

CBT therapists who are concerned about competency can also use reliable assessment tools such as self- and observer-rated scales, for example the Cognitive Therapy scale (Young & Beck, 1988), and the Cognitive Therapy Scale-Revised (Blackburn, et al., 2001), to evaluate difficult sessions. Using such scales requires the CBT therapist to record therapy sessions which move self-assessment forward in the sense that it allows for more objective self-evaluation of technical, conceptual, interpersonal and micro counselling skills. Such honest and objective assessment can highlight weaknesses but also, very importantly, confirm strengths.

Kottler (2012) suggests that every now and then we conduct a personal "hazard" assessment, asking ourselves questions regarding our formulation skill, ability to develop constructive therapeutic relationships, set therapy limits, stay present in the therapeutic hour and manage boundaries. A self-assessment tool to assess competencies against the CBT framework can be downloaded at www.ucl.ac.uk/CORE/.

Identifying strengths

A crucial part of self-assessment, aimed at promoting resilience and self-care, is identifying personal and professional strengths. These protective factors are often omitted in both our work with clients and in our own self-assessment. One of the best ways to discover strengths is to focus on activities that you enjoy or feel confident about (Mooney & Padesky, 2000). These activities can be hobbies, recreational or routine activities you enjoy, such as cooking or shopping! What do you bring to these activities that make them enjoyable? It could be a sense of humour, tenacity, intelligence, physical strength and dexterity or good problem-solving abilities. Think about this as a personal talent quest. Also think about your cultural and spiritual strengths (see Chapter 5). We have observed that our clients and the therapists who have participated in Self-Practice/Self-Reflection programmes (see Chapter 8) very often shy away from acknowledging their strengths, having underlying beliefs regarding the importance of being modest and never "blowing your own trumpet". If you are one of these individuals, asking people close to you what they think your strengths are can be very revealing and surprising. Other useful CBT strategies are using a personal positive data log to collect evidence of your strengths in a variety of areas beyond work.

If you need to improve self-care and develop resilience against burnout, recognising your strengths can be very helpful when you come to devise an action plan.

- Reflecting on your self-formulation in the context of all the factors discussed above can you discern precipitating, predisposing, maintaining stress-related factors in your current situation?
- How can you utilise your strengths to develop a plan to improve self-care in the workplace? For example, if you have a great sense of humour could you use this more at work? If you are a good organiser with good social skills, how could you use these skills to have more fun at work?

USING REFLECTION TO PROMOTE SELF-CARE AS A CBT THERAPIST

Reflect on how you would like things to be

A useful self-reflection exercise can be to consider how you would like things to be regarding your work situation and to construct an alternative formulation to mirror a new more adaptive way of being, incorporating the strengths you identified in your self-assessment. For example, what alternative strength-based thoughts and behaviours could you substitute? What alternative underlying belief or schema would you like to work towards supporting self-care? The five-part model can also be used to do this. Other CBT models such as the Old System/New System alternative conceptualisation (Padesky, 2005) and Old and New Ways of Being (Bennett-Levy et al., 2015) are also useful frameworks.

Self-care, mindfulness and self-compassion

Developing mindfulness, which usually relies upon some form of regular meditation practice, is increasingly found to be positively correlated with a number of important mental health benefits which include improved emotional regulation, attention, self-awareness, emotional attention, feeling happier and generally experiencing a sense of wellbeing, and intellectual alertness, as well as increased empathy and compassion for self and others (Ryan, Safran, Doran & Muran, 2012). Initially entering the mental health field as a treatment for individuals diagnosed with Borderline Personality disorder (Linehan, 1993) and chronic recurring depression (Segal, Williams & Teasdale, 2012), mindfulness is a therapeutic intervention now utilised across a variety of diagnostic presentations (Germer, Siegal & Fulton, 2005). Compassion Focused Therapy (CFT), developed by Gilbert (2009), is also proving to be a versatile therapeutic strategy that can help clients build a more self-nurturing and compassionate view of themselves. CFT emphasises the importance of mindfulness practice as a pathway to building increased self-compassion. Recently, some researchers have begun to consider that developing therapist mindfulness and self-compassion may improve therapist competency in a number of important ways that may be particularly beneficial in building a positive therapeutic alliance, which is widely recognised as a significant common factor promoting positive therapy outcome. It is beyond the scope of this chapter to discuss mindfulness and self-compassion as self-care strategies, but we would like to encourage CBT therapists to reflect on ways in which these strategies (perhaps less familiar than the more obvious CBT strategies, such as balanced activities and managing negative thoughts) can be integrated into professional life, during training and ongoing professional development. There are many web-based resources which can be used to support mindfulness practice, for example, see www.mindfulselfcompassion.org/meditations.

Self-Practice/Self-Reflection

Chapter 8 describes SP/SR as an experiential training and professional development strategy and documents the supporting research outlining many therapist benefits. Working through an SP/SR workbook, such as the one recommended in Chapter 8, can be a useful tool to support therapist self-care, containing as it does structured SP/SR exercises guiding the CBT therapist through the steps towards constructing a new and more sustaining way of being.

BARRIERS TO THERAPIST SELF-CARE

Finally, it is important to reflect on how self-care has actually figured in your professional life (and beyond). It can be useful to look at your immediate cognitive-emotional responses to this question. Is there a "*Yes, of course this is something I regard as important, practise and know a lot about*" or does the question evoke a sense of unease with thoughts such as "*This is indulgent, selfish and will lead to laziness and sloth*" or even the ironic "*What on earth is self-care?*"

There are many obstacles to self-care generally. Quite often it just seems too hard, too time-consuming, too difficult and even too boring. Many behaviours and habits running counter to self-care, such as alcohol consumption, binge eating or avoidance, offer a quick fix. Basic self-care principles, such as developing a healthy lifestyle, require discipline, and of course the ubiquitous enemy "time" has to be harnessed. Other barriers lie in our self-defeating cycles of cognition and behaviour, such as perfectionism, need for approval and performance anxiety. These cycles keep us trapped if they are not identified and challenged. There can also be a belief that individuals who practise self-care are narcissistic, self-indulgent and prone to self-pampering.

There is no easy solution to overcoming these barriers. However, using reflection to clearly identify and formulate the factors which may be compromising your ability to take care of yourself, and developing a structured view of how you would like things to be, should enable you to implement a constructive action plan to enhance your self-care as a CBT therapist.

CONCLUSION

We have left the self-care chapter to last, not because we think it unimportant, but because we think it the most important chapter. Metaphors such as "*Why should parents in aeroplanes put the oxygen mask on before their children when the plane is experiencing problems?*" or "*Why is it important for aid workers to eat well even though all around people are starving?*", which are so often used with clients to explain why they should prioritise their therapy commitment, hold for therapists even more strongly. You cannot care for others effectively unless you take care of yourself.

TAKING IT FORWARD

What *declarative knowledge* have you gained from reading this chapter?

- How might you go about increasing your knowledge regarding therapist self-care?
- Do you need to find out more about vicarious and secondary traumatisation and burnout? How can you do this?
- How could you find out more about the benefits of mindfulness and self-compassion?

What *procedural rules* regarding your self-care as a therapist can you develop?

- Have you identified clear work-related triggers for stress? Can you make a list of triggers, for example "When *trigger*... then..."?
- What steps can you take to address any client-based, work-based or event-based difficulties you may have identified?
- If you have identified self-induced defeating patterns, can you think of ways to address these?
- How will you know if you need support? What support can you rely on? How can you go about asking for support?

- How can you use your CBT declarative knowledge in a helpful procedural manner? For example, "*When* I behave, think or feel…, *then* I could…".
- What barriers stand in your way when it comes to recognising stress? Can you develop some rules for overcoming barriers? For example, "When *obstacle…*, then…".
- What barriers stand in your way when you consider improving self-care?

What strategies are you going to put in place to facilitate the engagement of your *reflective system* regarding self-care?

- How are you going to remember to "check in with yourself" or reflect on your wellbeing or self-care regime?
- Would it be useful to set a reminder or have a regular time in which to review your wellbeing and self-care regime?

SUGGESTED READING

Bennett-Levy, J., Thwaites, R., Haarhoff, B., & Perry, H. (2015). *Experiencing CBT from the inside out: a self-practice/self-reflection workbook for therapists*. New York: Guilford Press.

Germer, C. (2009). *The mindful path to self-compassion*. New York: Guilford Press.

Kottler, J. (2012). *The therapist's workbook*. Hoboken, NJ: John Wiley & Sons.

Teasdale, J. D., Williams, M., & Segal, Z. (2014). *The mindful way workbook: an 8-week program to free yourself from depression and emotional distress*. New York: Guilford Press.

REFERENCES

American Psychological Association. (2005). APA 2020: a perfect vision for psychology. *American Psychologist, 60*, 512–522.

Anderson, T., Ogles, B. M., Patterson, C. L., Lambert, M. J., & Vermeersch, D. A. (2009). Therapist effects: facilitative interpersonal skills as a predictor of therapist success. *Journal of Clinical Psychology, 65*, 755–768.

Anker, M. G., Duncan, B. L., & Sparks, J. A. (2009). Using client feedback to improve couple therapy outcomes: a randomized clinical trial in a naturalistic setting. *Journal of Consulting Clinical Psychology, 77*, 693–704.

Armstrong, P. V., Barton, S., Twaddle, V., Thwaites, R., & Platz, S. (2007, July). Developing interpersonal competencies in cognitive behavioural therapy: the challenges for trainers. Paper presented at the 5th World Congress of Cognitive and Behavioural Therapies, Barcelona.

Armstrong, P. V., & Freeston, M. H. (2006). Conceptualising and formulating cognitive therapy supervision. In N. Tarrier (Ed.), *Case formulation in cognitive behaviour therapy: the treatment of challenging and complex clinical cases* (pp. 349–371). London: Routledge.

Armstrong, P. V., Freeston, M. H., & Twaddle, V. (2008). CBT trainers: principles and practicalities. Unpublished manuscript, Newcastle Cognitive and Behavioural Therapies Centre, Newcastle-Upon-Tyne, United Kingdom.

Arntz, A., & Van Genderen, H. (2009). *Schema therapy for borderline personality disorder.* Chichester: Wiley-Blackwell.

BABCP/IAPT (British Association for Behavioural and Cognitive Psychotherapies/Improving Access to Psychological Therapies). (2011). Recruiting inexperienced Psychological Wellbeing Practitioners (PWP) to high intensity trainee posts: a threat to IAPT services. Joint Statement and Recommendations: Improving Access to Psychological Therapies. NHS, UK. Retrieved from www.iapt.nhs.uk/silo/files/iaptbabcp-pwp-statement-august-2011-final.pdf (accessed 30 May 2015).

Bain, J. D., Mills, C., Ballantyne, R., & Packer, J. (2002). Developing reflection on practice through journal writing: impacts of variations in the focus and level of reflection. *Teachers and Teaching: Theory and Practice, 8*, 171–196.

Baker, E. K. (2003). *Caring for ourselves: a therapist's guide to personal and professional well-being.* Washington, DC: American Psychological Association.

Baldwin, S. A., & Imel, Z. E. (2013). Therapist effects: findings and methods. In M. J. Lambert (Ed.), *Bergin and Garfield's handbook of psychotherapy and behavior change* (6th ed., pp. 258–297). Hoboken, NJ: John Wiley & Sons.

Bamelis, L. L., Evers, S. M., Spinhoven, P., & Arntz, A. (2014). Results of a multi-center randomized controlled trial of the clinical effectiveness of schema therapy for personality disorders. *American Journal of Psychiatry, 171*, 305–322.

Barnett, R., & Coate, K. (2005). *Engaging the curriculum in higher education*. Maidenhead, UK: McGraw-Hill.

Beck, A. T. (1976). *Cognitive therapy and the emotional disorders*. New York: International Universities Press.

Beck, A. T., Emery, G., & Greenberg, R. L. (1985). *Anxiety disorders and phobias: a cognitive perspective*. New York: Basic Books.

Beck, A. T., & Freeman, A., & Associates. (1990). *Cognitive therapy of personality disorders*. New York: Guilford Press.

Beck, A. T., Freeman, A., Davis, D. D., & Associates. (2004). *Cognitive therapy of personality disorders* (2nd ed.). New York: Guilford Press.

Beck, A. T., Rush, A. J., Shaw, B. F., & Emery, G. (1979). *Cognitive therapy of depression*. New York: Guilford Press.

Beck, J. (1995). *Cognitive therapy: basics and beyond*. New York: Guilford Press.

Beck, J. (2011). *Cognitive therapy for challenging problems: what to do when the basics don't work* (2nd ed.). New York: Guilford Press.

Beidas, R. S., Edmunds, J. M., Marcus, S. C., & Kendall, P. C. (2012). Training and consultation to promote implementation of an empirically supported treatment: a randomized trial. *Psychiatric Services*, *63*, 660–665.

Bennett, S., Flett, R., & Babbage, D. (2007, November). The adaptation of cognitive behavioural therapy for adult Maori clients with depression: a pilot study. In M. Levy, L. W. Nikora, B. Masters-Awatere, M. Rua, & W. Wiatoki (Eds.), *Proceedings of the national Maori and Pacific psychologies symposium* (pp. 83–91). Hamilton, NZ: Maori and Psychology Research Unit University of Waikato.

Bennett-Levy, J. (2006). Therapist skills: a cognitive model of their acquisition and refinement. *Behavioural and Cognitive Psychotherapy*, *34*, 57–78.

Bennett-Levy, J., & Beedie, A. (2007). The ups and downs of cognitive therapy training: what happens to trainees' perception of their competence during a cognitive therapy training course? *Behavioural and Cognitive Psychotherapy*, *35*, 61–75.

Bennett-Levy, J., & Lee, N. K. (2014). Self-practice and self-reflection in cognitive behaviour therapy training: what factors influence trainees' engagement and experience of benefit? *Behavioural and Cognitive Psychotherapy*, *42*, 48–64.

Bennett-Levy, J., Lee, N., Travers, K., Pohlman, S., & Hamernik, E. (2003). Cognitive therapy from the inside: enhancing therapist skills through practicing what we preach. *Behavioural and Cognitive Psychotherapy*, *31*, 143–158.

Bennett-Levy, J., McManus, F., Westling, B. E., & Fennell, M. (2009). Acquiring and refining CBT skills and competencies: which training methods are perceived to be most effective? *Behavioural and Cognitive Psychotherapy*, *37*, 571–583.

Bennett-Levy, J., & Padesky, C. A. (2014). Use it or lose it: post-workshop reflection enhances learning and utilization of CBT skills. *Cognitive and Behavioral Practice*, *21*, 12–19.

Bennett-Levy, J., Richards, D., & Farrand, P. (2010). Low intensity CBT interventions: a revolution in mental health care. In J. Bennett-Levy, et al. (Eds.), *The Oxford guide to low intensity CBT interventions* (pp. 3–18). Oxford: Oxford University Press.

Bennett-Levy, J., & Thwaites, R. (2007). Self and self-reflection in the therapeutic relationship: a conceptual map and practical strategies for the training, supervision and self-supervision of interpersonal skills. In P. Gilbert & R. Leahy (Eds.),

The therapeutic relationship in the cognitive-behavioural psychotherapies (pp. 255–281). London: Routledge.

Bennett-Levy, J., Thwaites, R., Chaddock, A., & Davis, M. (2009). Reflective practice in cognitive behavioural therapy: the engine of lifelong learning. In J. Stedmon & R. Dallos (Eds.), *Reflective practice in psychotherapy and counselling* (pp. 115–135). Milton Keynes, UK: Open University Press.

Bennett-Levy, J., Thwaites, R., Haarhoff, B., & Perry, H. (2015). *Experiencing CBT from the inside out: a self-practice/self-reflection workbook for therapists*. New York: Guilford Press.

Bennett-Levy, J., Turner, F., Beaty, T., Smith, M., Paterson, B., & Farmer, S. (2001). The value of self-practice of cognitive therapy techniques and self-reflection in the training of cognitive therapists. *Behavioural and Cognitive Psychotherapy, 29*, 203–220.

Blackburn, I. M., James, I. A., Milne, D. L., Baker, C., Standart, S., Garland, A., & Reichelt, F. K. (2001). The revised cognitive therapy scale: psychometric properties. *Behavioural and Cognitive Psychotherapy, 29*, 431–446.

Blenkiron, P. (2010). *Stories and analogies in cognitive behaviour therapy*. Chichester: Wiley-Blackwell.

Blow, A., Sprenkle, D., & Davis, S. (2007). Is who delivers the treatment more important than the treatment itself? The role of the therapist in common factors. *Journal of Marital and Family Therapy, 33*, 298–317.

Boswell, J. F., Kraus, D. R., Miller, S. D., & Lambert, M. J. (2015). Implementing routine outcome monitoring in clinical practice: benefits, challenges, and solutions. *Psychotherapy Research, 25*, 6–19.

Boud, D., & Walker, D. (1998). Promoting reflection in professional courses: the challenge of context. *Studies in Higher Education, 23*, 191–206.

Bride, B. E., Radey, M., & Figley, C. R. (2007). Measuring compassion fatigue. *Clinical Social Work Journal, 35*, 155–163.

Brinson, J., & Cervantes, J. (2003). Recognising ethnic/racial biases and discriminatory practices through self-supervision. In J. Kottler & W. P. Jones (Eds.), *Doing better: improving clinical skills and professional competence* (pp. 106–127). New York: Brunner-Routledge.

British Association for Counselling and Psychotherapy (BACP). (2007). *Ethical framework for good practice in counselling and psychotherapy*. Lutterworth: BACP.

British Psychological Society (2012a). Guidelines and literature review for psychologists working therapeutically with sexual and gender minority clients. Retrieved from www.bps.org.uk/sites/default/files/images/rep_92.pdf (accessed 30 May 2015).

British Psychological Society. (2012b). *Psychological wellbeing practitioner training: accreditation handbook* (3rd ed.). Leicester: British Psychological Society. Retrieved from www.bps.org.uk/system/files/Public%20files/2013_pwp_handbook_3rd_ed_final.pdf (accessed 30 May 2015).

Brown, J., Hudson Scholle, S., & Azur, M. (2014). *Strategies for measuring the quality of psychotherapy: a white paper to inform measure development and implementation*. Washington, DC: Mathematica Policy Research for US Department of Health and Human Services.

Burns, R. (1785). *To a louse*. Robert Burns Plus. Retrieved from www.robertburns. plus.com/louse.htm (accessed 30 May 2015).

Butler, A. C., Chapman, J. E., Forman, E. M., & Beck, A. T. (2006). The empirical status of cognitive behavioural therapy: a review of meta-analyses. *Clinical Psychology Review*, *26*, 17–31.

Cahill, J., Barkham, M., Hardy, G., Gilbody, S., Richards, D., Bower, P., Audin, K., & Connell, J. (2008). A review and critical appraisal of measures of therapist patient interactions in mental health settings. *Health Technology Assessment*, *12*, 5–18.

Cannadine, D. (2000). *The rise and fall of class in Britain*. New York: Columbia University Press.

Carlson, E. (2008). *The lucky few: between the great generation and the baby boomers*. New York: Springer.

Carroll, M. (1996). *Counselling supervision: theory, skills and practice*. London: Cassell.

Carroll, M. (2009). Supervision: critical reflection for transformational learning (part 1). *The Clinical Supervisor*, *28*, 210–220.

Carroll, M. (2010). Supervision: critical reflection for transformational learning (part 2), *The Clinical Supervisor*, *29*, 1–19.

Carroll, M., & Gilbert, M. (2011). *On being a supervisee: creating learning partnerships* (2nd ed.). London: Vukani Publishing.

Chaddock, A. (2007). Can the use of a self-practice/self-reflection approach enhance the therapeutic skills and attitudes of trainee cognitive-behavioural therapists? Unpublished DClinPsy thesis. University of Newcastle-upon Tyne, Newcastle-upon-Tyne, UK.

Chaddock, A. (2013). The therapeutic relationship: big deal or no deal? In *Low intensity cognitive behaviour therapy: a practitioner's guide* (pp. 69–84). London: Sage.

Chaddock, A., Thwaites, R., Bennett-Levy, J., & Freeston, M. H. (2014). Understanding individual differences in response to self-practice and self-reflection (SP/SR) during CBT training. *The Cognitive Behaviour Therapist*, *7*, e14.

Chellingsworth, M., & Farrand, P. (2013, July). Is reflective ability a predictor of clinical competency? Paper presented at the 41st Annual Conference of the British Association of Cognitive and Behavioural Psychotherapies, London.

Chen, D. C., & Englar-Carlson, M. (2003). From self-regulation to self-supervision: lessons from sport psychology to the practice of therapy. In J. A. Kottler & W. P. Jones (Eds.), *Doing better: improving clinical skills and professional competence* (pp. 177–199). New York: Brunner-Routledge.

Chigwedere, C., Fitzmaurice, B., & Donohoe, G. (2014, July). Can SP/SR be a credible equivalent for personal therapy? Paper presented at the 42nd British Association of Behaviour and Cognitive Psychotherapy, Birmingham.

Choudhry, N. K., Fletcher, R. H., & Soumerai, S. B. (2005). Systematic review: the relationship between clinical experience and quality of health care. *Annals of Internal Medicine*, *142*, 260–273.

Chu, B. C., Skriner, L. C., & Zandberg, L. J. (2013). Shape of change in cognitive behavioral therapy for youth anxiety: symptom trajectory and predictors of change. *Journal of Consulting and Clinical Psychology*, *81*, 573–587.

Clance, P. R., & Imes, S. (1978). The imposter phenomenon in high achieving women: dynamics and therapeutic intervention. *Psychotherapy Theory, Research and Practice*, *15*, 241–247.

Clark, D. (1986). A cognitive approach to panic. *Behaviour Research and Therapy, 24,* 461–470.

Clark, D. (2011). Implementing NICE guidelines for the psychological treatment of depression and anxiety disorders: the IAPT experience. *International Review of Psychiatry, 23,* 375–384.

Clark, D. M., Layard, R., Smithies, R., Richards, D. A., Suckling, R., & Wright, B. (2009). Improving access to psychological therapy: initial evaluation of two UK demonstration sites. *Behaviour Research and Therapy, 47,* 910–920.

Cox, C. I. (1982). Outcome research in cross-cultural counseling. Unpublished manuscript.

Cuijpers, P., Sijbrandij, M., Koole, S. L., Andersson, G., Beekman, A. T., & Reynolds, C. F. (2013). The efficacy of psychotherapy and pharmacotherapy in treating depressive and anxiety disorders: a meta-analysis of direct comparisons. *World Psychiatry, 12,* 137–148.

Cuijpers, P., van Straten, A., Bohlmeijer, E., Hollon, S. D., & Andersson, G. (2009). The effects of psychotherapy for adult depression are overestimated: a meta-analysis of study quality and effect size. *Psychological Medicine, 40,* 1–13.

Cushway, D. (1992). Stress in clinical psychology trainees. *British Journal of Clinical Psychology, 31,* 169–179.

Cushway, D. (2005). Stress in trainee psychotherapists. In V. Varma (Ed.), *Stress in psychotherapists* (pp. 18–34). London: Routledge.

Davidson, K., Perry, A., & Bell, L. (2014). Would continuous feedback of patient's clinical outcomes to practitioners improve NHS psychological therapy services? Critical analysis and assessment of quality of existing studies. *Psychology and Psychotherapy: Theory, Research and Practice, 88,* 21–37.

Davis, M. L. (2008). The impact of a self-practice/self-reflection programme on the therapeutic skills and beliefs of experienced cognitive-behavioural therapists. Unpublished DClinPsy thesis. University of Newcastle-upon Tyne, Newcastle-upon-Tyne, UK.

Davis, M. L., Thwaites, R., Freeston, M. H., & Bennett-Levy, J. (2015). A measurable impact of a self-practice/self-reflection programme on the therapeutic skills of experienced cognitive behavioural therapists. *Clinical Psychology and Psychotherapy, 22,* 176–184.

de Jong, K., van Sluis, P., Nugter, M. A., Heiser, W. J., & Spinhoven, P. (2012). Understanding the differential impact of outcome monitoring: therapist variables that moderate feedback effects in a randomized clinical trial. *Psychotherapy Research, 22,* 464–474.

Delgadillo, J., Gellatly, J., & Stephenson-Bellwood, S. (2015). Decision making in stepped care: how do therapists decide whether to prolong treatment or not? *Behaviour and Cognitive Psychotherapy, 43,* 328–341.

De Maat, S., Dekker, J., Schoevers, R., & De Jonghe, F. (2006). Relative efficacy of psychotherapy and pharmacotherapy in the treatment of depression: a meta-analysis. *Psychotherapy Research, 16,* 566–578.

Dennin, M. K., & Ellis, M. V. (2003). Effects of a method of self-supervision for counselor trainees. *Journal of Counseling Psychology, 51,* 69–83.

Department of Health. (2008). *Improving access to psychological therapies implementation plan: national guidelines for regional delivery.* London: Department of Health.

Department of Health. (2012). *IAPT three-year report: the first million patients*. London: Department of Health.

Dickson, J. M., & MacLeod, K. (2004). Approach and avoidance goals and plans: their relationship to anxiety and depression. *Cognitive Therapy and Research, 28*, 415–432.

Drapeau, M. (2012). Ten tools for progress monitoring in psychotherapy. *Integrating Science and Practice, 2*, 1–45.

Dugas, M. J., & Robichaud, M. (2007). *Cognitive-behavioral treatment for generalized anxiety disorder: from science to practice*. New York: Routledge.

Dunning, D. (2011). The Dunning-Kruger effect: on being ignorant of one's own ignorance. In J. Olson & M. P. Zanna (Eds.), *Advances in experimental social psychology* (Vol. 44, pp. 247–296). New York: Elsevier.

El-Leithy, S. (2014). Working with diversity in CBT. In A. Whittington & N. Grey (Eds.), *How to become a more effective CBT therapist: mastering metacompetence in clinical practice* (pp. 44–61). Chichester: Wiley Blackwell.

Elliot, A. J., & Thrash, T. M. (2001). Achievement goals and the hierarchical model of achievement motivation. *Educational Psychology Review, 12*, 139–156.

Erickson, R., & Goldthorpe, J. (2010). Has social mobility in Britain decreased? Reconciling divergent findings on income and class mobility. *The British Journal of Sociology, 61*, 211–230.

Eubanks, C. F., Muran, J. C., & Safran, J. D. (2015). Rupture resolution rating system (3RS): manual. Unpublished manuscript. Mount Sinai-Beth Israel Medical Center, New York.

Evans, C., Connell, J., Barkham, M., Margison, F., McGrath, G., Mellor-Clark, J., & Audin, K. (2002). Towards a standardised brief outcome measure, psychometric properties and utility of the CORE-OM. *British Journal of Psychiatry, 180*, 51–60.

Fanon, F. (1969). *The wretched of the earth*. London: Penguin.

Farrand, P., Confue, P., Byng, R., & Shaw, S. (2009). Guided self-help supported by paraprofessional mental health workers: an uncontrolled before-after cohort study. *Health and Social Care in the Community, 17*, 9–17.

Farrand, P., Duncan, F., & Byng, R. (2007). Impact of graduate mental health workers upon primary care mental health: a qualitative study. *Health and Social Care in the Community, 15*, 486–493.

Farrand, P., Perry, J., & Linsley, S. (2010). Enhancing self-practice/self-reflection (SP/SR) approach to cognitive behaviour training through the use of reflective blogs. *Behavioural and Cognitive Psychotherapy, 38*, 473–477.

Farrand, P., & Williams, C. (2010). Assessment in low intensity psychological therapy. In J. Bennett-Levy, et al. (Eds.), *The Oxford guide to low intensity CBT interventions* (pp. 89–103). Oxford: Oxford University Press.

Fennell, M. (2010). Training skills. In M. Mueller, H. Kennerley, F. McManus, & D. Westbrook (Eds.), *The Oxford guide to surviving as a CBT therapist* (pp. 371–405). Oxford: Oxford University Press.

Fernando, S. (2003). *Cultural diversity, mental health and psychiatry: the struggle against racism*. London: Brunner, Routledge.

Foley, S. R., & Kelly, B. D. (2007). When a patient dies by suicide: incidence, implications and coping strategies. *Advances in Psychiatric Treatment, 3*, 134–138.

Fraser, N., & Wilson, J. (2010). Self-case study as a catalyst for personal development in cognitive therapy training. *The Cognitive Behaviour Therapist, 3*, 107–116.

Freeston, M., Thwaites, R., & Bennett-Levy, J. (in preparation). Horses for courses: designing, adapting, and implementing self-practice/self-reflection programmes. Manuscript in preparation.

Frost, N. (2010). Professionalism and social change: the implications of social change for the 'reflective' practitioner. In H. Bradburt, N. Frost, & M. Zukas (Eds.), *Beyond reflective practice: new approaches to lifelong learning* (pp. 15–24). London: Routledge.

Gale, C., & Schröder, T. (2014). Experiences of self-practice/self-reflection in cognitive behavioural therapy: a meta-synthesis of qualitative studies. *Psychology and Psychotherapy: Theory, Research & Practice, 87*, 373–392.

Gallo, J. J., Morales, K. H., Bogner, H. R., Raue, P. J., Zee, J., Bruce, M. L., & Reynolds, C. F. (2013). Long-term effect of depression care management on mortality in older adults: follow-up of cluster randomized clinical trial in primary care. *British Medical Journal, 346*, f2570.

Germer, C. (2009). *The mindful path to self-compassion.* New York: Guilford Press.

Germer, C. K., Seigal, R. D., & Fulton, P. R. (Eds.). (2005). *Mindfulness in psychotherapy.* New York: Guilford Press.

Gilbert, P. (2009). *The compassionate mind.* London: Constable.

Gilbert, P., & Leahy, R. (Eds.). (2007). *The therapeutic relationship in the cognitive behavioral psychotherapies.* London: Routledge.

Gilboa-Schechtman, E., & Shahar, G. (2006). The sooner, the better: temporal patterns in brief treatment of depression and their role in long-term outcome. *Psychotherapy Research, 16*, 374–384.

Gordon, P. K. (2012). Ten steps to cognitive behavioural supervision. *The Cognitive Behaviour Therapist, 5*, 71–82.

Green, H., Barkham, M., Kellett, S., & Saxon, D. (2014). Therapist effects and IAPT psychological wellbeing practitioners (PWPs): a multilevel modelling and mixed methods analysis, *Behaviour Research and Therapy, 63*, 43–54.

Greenberger, D., & Padesky, C. (1995). *Mind over mood: change how you feel by changing the way you think.* New York: Guilford Press.

Grey, N., Deale, A., Byrne, S., & Liness, S. (2014). Making CBT supervision more effective. In A. Whittington & N. Grey (Eds.), *How to become a more effective CBT therapist: mastering metacompetence in clinical practice* (pp. 269–283). Chichester, UK: Wiley.

Gunlicks-Stoessel, M., & Mufson, L. (2011). Early patterns of symptom change signal remission with interpersonal psychotherapy for depressed adolescents. *Depression and Anxiety, 28*, 525–531.

Guterres, A. (2013). Remarks by Antonio Guterres, United Nations Commissioner for refugees, at the launch of humanitarian country strategies and requirements for 2014 including Syria regional response plan. Retrieved from www.unher.org (22 April 2015).

Haarhoff, B. (2006). The importance of identifying and understanding therapist schema in cognitive therapy training and supervision. *New Zealand Journal of Psychology, 35*, 126–131.

Haarhoff, B., & Farrand, P. (2012). Reflective and self-evaluative practice in CBT. In W. Dryden & R. Branch (Eds.), *The CBT handbook* (pp. 475–492). London: Sage.

Haarhoff, B., Gibson, K., & Flett, R. (2011). Improving the quality of cognitive behaviour therapy case conceptualization: the role of self-practice/self-reflection. *Behavioural and Cognitive Psychotherapy, 39*, 323–339.

Haarhoff, B., & Kazantzis, N. (2007). How to supervise the use of homework in cognitive behaviour therapy: the role of trainee therapist beliefs. *Cognitive and Behavioural Practice, 14*, 325–332.

Haarhoff, B., Thwaites, R., & Bennett-Levy, J. (2015). Engagement with self-practice/ self-reflection as a professional development activity: the role of therapist beliefs. *Australian Psychologist, 50*, 322–328.

Hannan, C., Lambert, M. J., Harmon, C., Nielsen, S. L., Smart, D. W., Shimokawa, K., & Sutton, S. W. (2005). A lab test and algorithms for identifying clients at risk for treatment failure. *Journal of Clinical Psychology: In Session, 61*, 155–163.

Hans, E., & Hiller, W. (2013). Effectiveness of and dropout from outpatient cognitive behavioral therapy for adult unipolar depression: a meta-analysis of nonrandomized effectiveness studies. *Journal of Consulting and Clinical Psychology, 81*, 75–88.

Harrison, A. (2013). Social mobility: Britain remains deeply divided. *BBC News Education and Family*. Retrieved from www.bbc.com/news/education-24566926 (accessed 30 May 2015).

Harrison, R. L., & Westwood, M. J. (2009). Preventing vicarious traumatisation of mental health therapists: identifying protective practices. *Psychotherapy, Research, Theory, Practice, Training, 46*, 203–219.

Hatfield, D., McCullough, L., Frantz, S. H. B., & Krieger, K. (2010). Do we know when our clients get worse? An investigation of therapists' ability to detect negative client change. *Clinical Psychology and Psychotherapy, 17*, 25–32.

Hatton, N., & Smith, D. (1995). Reflection in teacher education: towards definition and implementation. *Teaching and Teacher Education, 11*, 33–49.

Hawkins, P., & Shohet, R. (2006). *Supervision in the helping professions.* Maidenhead, UK: Open University Press.

Hays, P. A. (2006). Introduction: developing culturally responsive cognitive behavioral therapies In P. A. Hays & G. Y. Iwamasa (Eds.), *Culturally responsive cognitive-behavioral therapy: assessment, practice and supervision* (pp. 3–19). Washington, DC: American Psychological Association.

Hays, P. A. (2009). Integrating evidenced-based practice, cognitive-behaviour therapy and multicultural therapy: ten steps for culturally competent practice. *Professional Psychology, Research and Practice, 40*, 354–360.

Hays, P. A. (2013). *Connecting across cultures: the helper's toolkit.* Los Angeles, CA: Sage.

Hendin, H., Pollinger Haas, A., Maltsberger, J., Szanto, K., & Rabinowicz, H. (2004). Factors contributing to therapists' distress after the suicide of a patient. *American Journal of Psychiatry, 161*, 1442–1446.

Henrich, J., Heine, S., & Norenzayan, A. (2010). The weirdest people in the world? *Behavioural and Brain Sciences, 33*, 61–135.

Hobbs, V. (2007). Faking it or hating it: can reflective practice be forced? *Reflective Practice: International and Multidisciplinary Perspectives, 8*, 405–417.

Honey, P., & Mumford, A. (1992). *The manual of learning styles.* Maidenhead, UK: Peter Honey Publications.

Howard, K. I., Moras, K., Brill, P. L., Martinovich, Z., & Lutz, W. (1996). Evaluation of psychotherapy: efficacy, effectiveness, and patient progress. *American Psychology, 51*, 1059–1064.

Huhn, M., Tardy, M., Spineli, L. M., Kissling, W., Forstl, H., Pitschel-Walz, G., Leucht, C., Samara, M., Dold, M., Davis, J. M., & Leucht, S. (2014). Efficacy of pharmacotherapy and psychotherapy for adult psychiatric disorders: a systematic overview of meta-analyses. *JAMA Psychiatry, 71,* 706–715.

Hullemen, C. S., Schrager, S. M., Bodmann, S. M., & Harackiewicz, J. M. (2010). A meta-analytic review of achievement goal measures: different labels for the same constructs or different constructs with similar labels? *Psychological Bulletin, 136,* 422–449.

IAPT (Improving Access to Psychological Therapies). (2010). Good practice guidance on the use of self-help materials within IAPT services. NHS: Improving Access to Psychological Therapies. Retrieved from www.iapt.nhs.uk/silo/files/good-practice-guidance-on-the-use-of-selfhelp-materials-within-iapt-services.pdf (accessed 12 January 2012).

Inskipp, F., & Proctor, B. (1995). *The art, craft and tasks of counselling supervision: part II, becoming a supervisor.* Twickenham, Middlesex: Cascade.

Jacobson, N. S., & Truax, P. (1991). Clinical significance: a statistical approach to defining meaningful change in psychotherapy research. *Journal of Consulting and Clinical Psychology, 59,* 12–19.

James, I. A., Blackburn, I. M., Milne, D., & Freeston, M. (2004). Supervision Training and Assessment Rating Scale for Cognitive Therapy (STARS-CT). Unpublished manuscript. Doctorate in Clinical Psychology, University of Newcastle-Upon-Tyne, UK.

James, I. A., Blackburn, I. M., & Reichelt, F. K. (2001). *Manual of the Cognitive Therapy Scale – Revised (CTS-R).* Northumberland, Tyne & Wear NHS Trust. Retrieved from www.ed.ac.uk/polopoly_fs/1.155959!/fileManager/CTSRmanual.pdf (accessed 1 April 2014).

James, I. A., Milne, D., & Morse, R. (2008). Microskills of clinical supervision: scaffolding skills. *Journal of Cognitive Psychotherapy, 22,* 29–36.

Jennings, L., Goh, M., Skovholt, T. M., Hanson, M., & Banerjee-Stevens, D. (2003). Multiple factors in the development of the expert counselor and therapist. *Journal of Career Development, 30,* 59–72.

Jones, W. P., & Harbach, R. L. (2003). A syllabus for self-supervision. In J. A. Kottler & W. P. Jones (Eds.), *Doing better: improving clinical skills and professional competence* (pp. 51–66). New York: Brunner-Routledge.

Katzow, A. W., & Safran, J. D. (2007). Recognizing and resolving ruptures in the therapeutic alliance. In P. Gilbert & R. Leahy (Eds.), *The therapeutic relationship in the cognitive behavioural therapies* (pp. 90–103). London: Routledge.

Keegan, D. (2013). Supervision. In *Low intensity cognitive behaviour therapy: a practitioner's guide* (pp. 293–317). London: Sage.

Kell, R. (2001). *Collected Poems 1962–1993.* Belfast: Lagan Press.

Kilminster, S. M., & Jolly, B. C. (2000). Effective supervision in clinical practice settings: a literature review. *Medical Education, 34,* 827–840.

King, M. (2003). *The Penguin history of New Zealand.* Auckland, NZ: Penguin.

Knapman, J., & Morrison, T. (1998). *Making the most of supervision in health and social care.* Brighton, Sussex: Pavilion Publishing.

Kolb, D. A. (1984). *Experiential learning: experience as the source of learning and development.* Englewood Cliffs, NJ: Prentice-Hall.

Kottler, J. A. (2003). When therapists supervise themselves. In J. A. Kottler & W. P. Jones (Eds.), *Doing better: improving clinical skills and professional competence.* (pp. 1–9). New York: Brunner-Routledge.

Kottler, J. A. (2012). *The therapist's workbook.* Hoboken, NJ: John Wiley & Sons.

Kraus, D. R., Castonguay, L., Boswell, J. F., Nordberg, S. S., & Hayes, J. A. (2011). Therapist effectiveness: implications for accountability and patient care. *Psychotherapy Research, 21,* 267–276.

Kroenke, K., & Spitzer, R. L. (2001). PHQ-9: a new depression diagnostic and severity measure. *Journal of General Medicine, 16,* 606–613.

Kuyken, W., Padesky, C., & Dudley, R. (2009). *Collaborative case conceptualization: working effectively with clients in cognitive-behavioral therapy.* New York: Guilford Press.

Laireiter, A.-R., & Willutzki, U. (2003). Self-reflection and self-practice in training of cognitive behaviour therapy: an overview. *Clinical Psychology and Psychotherapy, 10,* 19–30.

Laireiter, A.-R., & Willutzski, U. (2005). Personal therapy in cognitive behavioural therapy: tradition and current practice. In J. Geller, J. Norcross & D. Orlinski (Eds.), *The psychotherapists' own psychotherapy: patient and clinician perspectives* (pp. 41–51). Oxford: Oxford University Press.

Lambert, M., Finch, A. E., & Maruish, M. E. (Eds.). (1999). *The use of psychological testing for treatment planning and outcomes assessment* (2nd ed., pp. 831–869). Mahwah, NJ: Lawrence Erlbaum Associates.

Lambert, M. J. (2013). The efficacy and effectiveness of psychotherapy. In M. J. Lambert (Ed.), *Handbook of psychotherapy and behavior change* (6th ed., pp. 169–218). Hoboken, NJ: John Wiley & Sons.

Lambert, M. J., Burlingame, G. M., Umphress, V., Hansen, N. B., Vermeersch, D. A., Clouse, G. C., & Yanchar, S. C. (1996). The reliability and validity of the outcome questionnaire. *Clinical Psychology and Psychotherapy, 3,* 249–258.

Langs, R. (1979). *The supervisory experience.* New York: Aronson.

Law, W., Elliot, A. J., & Murayama, K. (2012). Perceived competence moderates the relation between performance-approach and performance-avoidance goals. *Journal of Educational Psychology, 104,* 806–819.

Layard, R., Clark, D., Bell, S., Knapp, M., Meacher, B., Priebe, S., Turnberg, L., Thornicroft, G., & Wright, B. (2006). *The depression report: a new deal for depression and anxiety disorders.* The Centre for Economic Performance's Mental Health Policy Group. London: London School of Economics.

Layden, M. A., Newman, C. F., Freeman, A., & Morse, S. B. (1993). *Cognitive therapy of borderline personality disorder.* Boston, MA: Allyn & Bacon.

Lazarus, R. S. (1966). *Psychological stress and coping process.* New York: McGraw-Hill.

Lazarus, R. S., & Folkman, S. (1984). Emotions: a cognitive-phenomenological analysis. In R. Plutchik & H. Kellerman (Eds.), *Theories of emotion* (pp. 189–217). New York: Academic Press.

Leahy, R. (2001). *Overcoming resistance in cognitive therapy.* New York: Guilford Press.

Leahy, R. (2007). Schematic mismatch in the therapeutic relationship. In P. Gilbert & R. Leahy (Eds.), *The therapeutic relationship in the cognitive behavioural psychotherapies* (pp. 229–254). London: Routledge.

Leith, W., McNiece, E. M. & Fusilier, B. B. (1989) *Handbook of supervision: a cognitive behavioral system.* Boston, MA: Little, Brown and Co.

Leucht, S., Hierl, S., Kissling, W., Dold, M., & Davis, J. M. (2012). Putting the efficacy of psychiatric and general medicine medication into perspective: review of meta-analyses. *British Journal of Psychiatry, 200*, 97–106.

Levinson, M. (2012). Working with 'diversity' in CBT. In W. Dryden & R. Branch (Eds.), *The CBT handbook* (pp. 162–178). Los Angeles, CA: Sage.

Lewis, C. C., Simons, A. D., & Kim, H. K. (2012). The role of early symptom trajectories and pretreatment variables in predicting treatment response to cognitive behavioral therapy. *Journal of Consulting and Clinical Psychology, 80*, 525–534.

Linehan, M. (1993). *Cognitive behavioral treatment of borderline personality disorder.* New York: Guilford Press.

Liness, S. (2014) Using outcome measures and feedback to enhance therapy and empower clients. In A. Whittington & N. Grey (Eds.), *How to become a more effective CBT therapist: mastering metacompetence in clinical practice* (pp. 255–283). London: Routledge.

Liness, S., & Muston, J. (2011). National curriculum for high intensity cognitive behavioural therapy courses. Kings College London. Retrieved from www.iapt. nhs.uk/silo/files/national-curriculum-for-high-intensity-cognitive-behavioural-therapy-courses.pdf (accessed 27 March 2015).

Little People UK. (2015). Retrieved from www.littlepeopleuk (accessed 6 April 2015).

Littrell, J., Lee-Borden, N., & Lorenz, J. (1979). A developmental framework for counselling supervision. *Counselor Education and Supervision, 19*, 129–136.

Lombardo, C., Milne, D., & Proctor, R. (2009). Getting to the heart of clinical supervision: a theoretical review of the role of emotions in professional development. *Behavioural and Cognitive Psychotherapy, 37*, 207–219.

Lowe, R. (2000). Supervising self-supervision: constructive inquiry and embedded narratives in case consultation. *Journal of Marital and Family Therapy, 26*, 511–521.

Lutz, W., Leon, S. C., Martinovich, Z., Lyons, J. S., & Stiles, W. B. (2007). Therapist effects in outpatient psychotherapy: a three-level growth curve approach. *Journal of Counseling Psychology, 54*, 32–39.

Lyon, A. R., Stirman, S. W., Kerns, S. E. U., & Bruns, E. J. (2011). Developing the mental health workforce: review and application of training approaches from multiple disciplines. *Administration and Policy in Mental Health and Mental Health Services Research, 38*, 238–253.

MacLellan, E. (1999). Reflective commentaries: what do they say about learning? *Educational Action Research, 7*, 433–449.

Marsden, C. (1999, 5 October). British prime minister tells Labour Party conference 'the class war is over'. Published by International Committee of the Fourth International (ICFI). Retrieved from www.wsws.org/en/articles/1999/10/uk-05o.html/ (accessed 4 June 2015).

Mead, N., & Bower, P. (2002). Patient-centred consultations and outcomes in primary care: a review of the literature. *Patient Education and Counselling, 48*, 51–61.

Martell, C. R., Dimidjian, S., & Herman-Dunn, R. (2010). *Behavioral activation for depression: a clinician's guide.* New York: Guilford Press.

Marton, F., & Booth, S. (1997). *Learning and awareness.* Mahwah, NJ: Lawrence Erlbaum Associates. (Cited in MacLellan, E. (2004). How reflective is the academic essay? *Studies in Higher Education, 29,* 75–89.)

Maslach, C. (1993). Burnout: a multidimensional perspective. In W. B. Schaufeli, C. Maslach & T. Marek (Eds.), *Professional burnout: recent developments in theory and research* (pp. 19–32). New York: Hampshire.

McEwen, B. (2008). Central effects of stress hormones in health and disease: understanding the positive and damaging effects of stress mediators. *European Journal of Pharmacology, 583,* 174–185.

McIntosh, P. (1998). White privilege and male privilege. In M. Andersen & P. Hill Collins (Eds.), *Race, class and gender* (3rd ed., pp. 94–105). Belmont, CA: Wadsworth.

Miller, S., Duncan, B., & Hubble, M. (2008). Supershrinks: what is the secret of their success. *Psychotherapy in Australia [online], 14,* 14–22.

Miller, S., Duncan, B., Sorrell, R., & Brown, G. (2005). The partners for change outcome management system. *Journal of Clinical Psychology, 61,* 199–208.

Milne, D. (2007). An empirical definition of clinical supervision. *British Journal of Clinical Psychology, 46,* 437–447.

Milne, D. (2009). *Evidence-based clinical supervision: principles and practice.* Chichester, UK: British Psychological Society/Blackwell.

Milne, D., Aylott, H., Fitzpatrick, H., & Ellis, M.V. (2012). How does clinical supervision work? Using a 'best evidence synthesis' approach to construct a basic model of supervision. *The Clinical Supervisor, 27,* 170–190.

Milne, D., & James, I. A. (2005). Clinical supervision: ten tests of the tandem model. *Clinical Psychology Forum, 151,* 6–9.

Milne, D., & Reiser, R. (2008). *Manual for the 'supervision: adherence & guidance evaluation' (SAGE) instrument.* Newcastle-Upon-Tyne: Newcastle University/Northumberland, Tyne & Wear NHS Foundation Trust.

Milne, D. L., Leck, C., & Choudhri, N. Z. (2009). Collusion in clinical supervision: literature review and case study in self-reflection. *The Cognitive Behaviour Therapist, 2,* 106–114.

Miranda, R., & Andersen, S. M. (2007). The therapeutic relationship: implications from a social cognition and transference. In P. Gilbert & R. Leahy (Eds.), *The therapeutic relationship in the cognitive behavioural therapies* (pp. 63–89). London: Routledge.

Montgomery, H., Croft, A. J., & Hackmann, A. (2010). Doing CBT through others. In M. Mueller, M. H. Kennerley, F. McManus, & D. Westbrook (Eds.), *Oxford guide to surviving as a CBT therapist* (pp. 199–214). Oxford: Oxford University Press.

Moon, J. (1999). *Learning journals: a handbook for academics students and professional development.* London: Kogan Page.

Moon, J. (2004). *A handbook of reflective and experiential learning: theory and practice.* London: Routledge.

Mooney, K. A., & Padesky, C. A. (2000). Applying client creativity to recurrent problems: constricting possibilities and tolerating doubt. *Journal of Cognitive Psychotherapy, 14,* 149–161.

Morgan, A. (2015). *Reading the world: confessions of a literary explorer.* London: Harvill Secker.

Morrissette, P. J. (2001). *Self-supervision: a primer for counselors and helping professionals.* New York: Brunner-Routledge.

Muse, K., McManus, F., Rakovshik, S., & Kennerley, H. (2014). Assessment of core cognitive behaviour therapy skills (ACCS). Oxford: Oxford Cognitive Therapy Centre.

New Zealand Psychologists' Board. (2014). *Core competencies for the practice of psychology in New Zealand.* Wellington: New Zealand Psychologists' Board.

NICE (2004a). *Depression: management of depression in primary and secondary care.* NICE Clinical Guideline 23. London: National Institute for Health and Clinical Excellence.

NICE (2004b). *Anxiety: management of anxiety (panic disorder, with and without agoraphobia and generalised anxiety disorder) in adults in primary, secondary and community care.* NICE Clinical Guideline 22. London: National Institute for Health and Clinical Excellence.

NICE (2011a). *Commissioning stepped care for people with common mental health disorders.* NICE Clinical Guideline 41. London: National Institute for Health and Clinical Excellence.

NICE (2011b). *Common mental health disorders: identification and pathways to care.* NICE Clinical Guideline 123. London: National Institute for Health and Clinical Excellence.

Nolen-Hoeksema, S., Wisco, B. E., & Lyubomirsky, S. (2008). Rethinking rumination. *Perspectives on Psychological Science, 3,* 400–424.

Norcross, J. C. (Ed.). (2002). *Psychotherapy relationships that work: therapist contributions and responsiveness to patients.* New York: Oxford University Press.

Norcross, J. C., & Guy, J. D. (2007). *Leaving it at the office: a guide to psychotherapist self-care.* New York: Guilford Press.

Okiishi, J. C., Lambert, M. J., Eggett, D., Nielsen, L., Dayton, D. D., & Vermeersch, D. A. (2006). An analysis of therapist treatment effects: toward providing feedback to individual therapists on their clients' psychotherapy outcome. *Journal of Clinical Psychology, 62,* 1157–1172.

Orlinsky, D., Norcross, J., Rønnestad, M., & Wiseman, H. (2005). Outcomes and impacts of the psychotherapist's own psychotherapy. In J. Geller, J. Norcross & D. Orlinsky (Eds.), *The psychotherapist's own psychotherapy: patient and clinician perspectives* (pp. 214–230). Oxford: Oxford University Press.

Orlinsky, D., Rønnestad, M. H., & Helge, M. (2005). *How psychotherapists develop: a study of therapeutic work and professional growth.* Washington, DC: American Psychological Association.

Ost, L. G. (2008). Cognitive behavior therapy for anxiety disorders: 40 years of progress. *Nordic Journal of Psychiatry, 62,* 5–10.

Oxford English Dictionary. (2015). Paraprofessional. Retrieved from www.oed.com/view/Entry/137609?redirectedFrom=paraprofessional#eid (accessed 30 May 2015).

Padesky, C. A. (1996). Developing cognitive therapist competency: teaching and supervision models. In P. M. Salkovskis (Ed.), *Frontiers of cognitive therapy* (pp. 266–292). New York: Guilford Press.

Padesky, C. A. (2005, June). The next phase: building positive qualities with cognitive therapy. Paper presented at the 5th International Congress of Cognitive Psychotherapy, Gotenburg, Sweden.

Padesky, C. A., & Mooney, K. A. (1990). Clinical tip: presenting the cognitive model to clients. *International Cognitive Therapy Newsletter, 6*, 13–14.

Papworth, M. (2013). Adapting LICBT for use with individuals from minority groups. In M. Papworth, T. Marrinan, B. Martin with D. Keegan & A. Chaddock, *Low intensity cognitive behaviour therapy: a practitioner's guide* (pp. 253–272). London: Sage.

Pearlman, L. A., & Saakvitne, K. W. (1995). Treating therapists with vicarious traumatisation and secondary traumatic stress disorders. In C. R. Figley (Ed.), *Compassion fatigue: coping with secondary traumatic stress disorder in those who treat the traumatised* (pp. 150–177). Levittown, PA: Brunner/Mazel.

Pedersen, P. B. (1990). The constructs of complexity and balance in multicultural counseling theory and practice. *Journal of Counseling and Development, 68*, 550–554.

Percevic, R., Lambert, M. J., & Kordy, H. (2006). What is the predictive value of responses to psychotherapy for its future course? Empirical explorations and consequences for outcome monitoring. *Psychotherapy Research, 16*, 364–373.

Persons, J. B. (1989). *Cognitive therapy in practice: a case formulation approach.* New York: W. W. Norton & Company.

Rai, L. (2006). Owning (up to) reflective writing in social work education. *Social Work Education, 25*, 785–797.

Rakovshik, S. G., & McManus, F. (2010). Establishing evidence-based training in cognitive behavioral therapy: a review of current empirical findings and theoretical guidance. *Clinical Psychology Review, 30*, 496–516.

Ramsden, P. (2003). *Learning to teach higher education* (2nd ed.). London: Routledge.

Richards, D., Farrand, P., & Chellingsworth, M. (2011). *National curriculum for the education of psychological wellbeing practitioners (PWP).* Improving Access to Psychological Therapies, NHS, UK. Retrieved from www.iapt.nhs.uk/silo/files/national-curriculum-for-the-education-of-psychological-wellbeing-practitioners-pwps-.pdf (accessed 30 May 2015).

Richards, D., & Whyte, M. (2009). *IAPT reach out: national programme educator materials to support the delivery of training for psychological wellbeing practitioners delivering low intensity interventions* (2nd ed.). London: Rethink.

Richards, D., & Whyte, M. (2011). *IAPT reach out: national programme educator materials to support the delivery of training for psychological wellbeing practitioners delivering low intensity interventions* (3rd ed.). London: Rethink.

Richards, D. A., Lovell, K., & McEvoy, P. (2003). Access and effectiveness in psychological therapies: self-help as a routine health technology. *Health and Social Care in the Community, 11*, 175–182.

Richardson, G., & Maltby, M. (1995). Reflection-on-practice: enhancing student learning. *Journal of Advanced Nursing, 22*, 235–242.

Richert, A. (1990). Teaching teachers to reflect: a consideration of programme structure. *Journal of Curriculum Studies, 22*, 509–527.

Rogers, C. R. (1965). *Client-centred therapy: its current practice, implications, and theory.* Boston, MA: Houghton Mifflin.

Rolfe, G., Freshwater, D., & Jasper, M. (2001). *Critical reflection for nursing and the helping professions: a user's guide.* Basingstoke: Palgrave.

Rønnestad, M. H., & Skovholt, T. M. (2001). Learning arenas for professional development: retrospective accounts of senior psychotherapists. *Professional Psychology: Research and Practice, 32*, 181–187.

Rønnestad, M. H., & Skovholt, T. M. (2003). The journey of the counsellor and therapist: research findings and perspectives on professional development. *Journal of Career Development, 30*, 5–44.

Roth, A., & Pilling, S. (2007a). *The competences required to deliver effective cognitive and behavioural therapy for people with depression and anxiety disorders*. London: Department of Health.

Roth, A., & Pilling, S. (2007b). *A competence framework for the supervision of psychological therapies*. Research Department of Clinical, Educational and Health Psychology, University College London. Retrieved from www.ucl.ac.uk/clinical-psychology/CORE/supervision_framework.htm (accessed 30 May 2015).

Rudd, M., & Joiner, T. (1997). Countertransference and the therapeutic relationship: a cognitive perspective. *Journal of Cognitive Psychotherapy, 11*, 231–249.

Russ, T. C., Stamatakis, E., Hamer, M., Starr, J. M., Kivimaki, M., & Batty, G. D. (2012). Association between psychological distress and mortality: individual participant pooled analysis of 10 prospective cohort studies. *British Medical Journal, 345*, e4933.

Ryan, A., Safran, J., Doran, J., & Muran, C. (2012). Therapist mindfulness, alliance and treatment outcome. *Psychotherapy Research, 22*, 289–297.

Safran, J. D. (Ed.). (1998). *Widening the scope of cognitive therapy*. Northvale, NJ: Jason Aronson.

Safran, J. D., & Muran, J. C. (2000). *Negotiating the therapeutic alliance: a relational treatment guide*. New York: Guilford Press.

Safran, J. D., & Segal, Z. V. (1990). *Interpersonal process in cognitive therapy*. New York: Basic Books.

Safran, J. D., & Segal, Z. V. (1996). *Interpersonal process in cognitive therapy*. London: Jason Aronson.

Saint Onge, J. M., Krueger, P. M., & Rogers, R. G. (2014). The relationship between major depression and nonsuicide mortality for US adults: the importance of health behaviors. *The Journals of Gerontology Series B: Psychological Sciences and Social Sciences, 69*, 622–632.

Samuels, M., & Betts, J. (2007). Crossing the threshold from description to deconstruction and reconstruction: using self-assessment to deepen reflection. *Reflective Practice, 8*, 269–283.

Savage, M., Devine, F., Cunningham, N., Taylor, M., Li, Y., Hjellbrekke, J., Le Roux, B., Friedman S., & Miles, A. (2013). A new model for social class: findings from the BBC's great British class survey. *Sociology, 47*, 219–250.

Saxon, D., & Barkham, M. (2012). Patterns of therapist variability: therapist effects and the contribution of patient severity and risk. *Journal of Consulting and Clinical Psychology, 80*, 535–546.

Sayyedi, M., & O'Bryne, K. (2003). Therapist: heal thyself. In J. Kottler & W. P. Jones (Eds.), *Doing better: improving clinical skills and professional competence* (pp. 233–247). New York: Brunner-Routledge.

Sburlati, E. S., & Bennett-Levy, J. (2014). Self-assessment of our competence as therapists. In E. S. Sburlati, H. J. Lyneham, C. A. Schniering, & R. M. Rapee (Eds.), *Evidence-based CBT for anxiety and depression in children and adolescents: a competencies-based approach* (pp. 25–35). Chichester, UK: John Wiley.

Scaife, J. (2010). *Supervising the reflective practitioner*. Abingdon: Routledge.

Schön, D. (1983). *The reflective practitioner: how professionals think in action*. Aldershot: Ashgate Arena.

Schulte, D., & Eifert, G. H. (2002). What to do when the manuals fail: the dual model of psychotherapy. *Clinical Practice, 9*, 312–328.

Segal, Z. V., Williams, M. G., & Teasdale, J. D. (2002). *Mindfulness-based cognitive therapy for depression: a new approach to preventing relapse*. New York: Guilford Press.

Segal, Z. V., Williams, J. M., & Teasdale, J. D. (2012). *Mindfulness-based cognitive therapy for depression* (2nd ed.). New York: Guilford Press.

Seligman, M. (2002). *Authentic happiness: using the new positive psychology to realise your potential for lasting fulfilment*. New York: Free Press.

Sheldon, O. J., Dunning, D., & Ames, D. R. (2015). Emotionally unskilled, unaware, and uninterested in learning more: reactions to feedback about deficits in emotional intelligence. *Journal of Applied Psychology, 99*, 125–137.

Shepard, D., & Morrow, G. (2003). Critical self-monitoring. In J. A. Kottler & W. P. Jones (Eds.), *Doing better: improving clinical skills and professional competence* (pp. 27–50). New York: Brunner-Routledge.

Shimokawa, K., Lambert, M. J., & Smart, D. W. (2010). Enhancing treatment outcome of patients at risk of treatment failure: meta-analytic and mega-analytic review of a psychotherapy quality assurance system. *Journal of Consulting and Clinical Psychology, 78*, 298–311.

Skinner, B. F., & Ferster, C. B. (1957). *Schedules of reinforcement*. New York: Appleton-Century-Crofts.

Skovholt, T. M., Rønnestad, M. H., & Jennings, L. (1997). Searching for expertise in counseling, psychotherapy, and professional psychology. *Educational Psychology Review, 9*, 361–369.

Smith, L. (2008). Positioning classism within counseling psychology's social justice agenda. *The Counseling Psychologist, 36*, 895–924.

Smith, M. L., Glass, G. V., & Miller, T. I. (1980). *The benefits of psychotherapy*. Baltimore, MD: Johns Hopkins University Press.

Smith, T. W., & Williams, P. (2013). Behavioral medicine and clinical health psychology. In M. J. Lambert (Ed.), *Handbook of psychotherapy and behavior change* (6th ed.). Hoboken, NJ: John Wiley & Sons.

Spafford, S., & Haarhoff, B. (2015). What are the conditions needed to facilitate online self-reflection for CBT trainees? *Australian Psychologist, 50*, 232–240.

Speight, S. L., Myers, L. J., Cox, C. I., & Highlen, P. S. (1991). A redefinition of multicultural counseling. *Journal of Counseling and Development, 70*, 29–36.

Spitzer, R. L., Kroenke, K., Williams, J., & Löwe, B. (2006). A brief measure for assessing generalised anxiety disorder. *Archives of Internal Medicine, 166*, 1092–1097.

Standing, G. (2011). *The precariat: the new dangerous class*. New York: Bloomsbury Academic.

Stott, R., Mansell, W., Salkovskis, P., Lavender, A., & Cartwright-Hatton, S. (2010). *Oxford guide to metaphors in CBT: building cognitive bridges*. Oxford: Oxford University Press.

Sue, D. W. (2010). *Microaggressions in everyday life: race, gender and sexual orientation*. Hoboken, NJ: John Wiley & Sons.

Sue, D. W. & Sue, D. (2008). *Counselling the culturally diverse: theory and practice*. Hoboken, NJ: John Wiley & Sons.

Sutton, L., Townend, M., & Wright, J. (2007). The experiences of reflective learning journals by cognitive-behavioural psychotherapy students. *Reflective Practice, 8*, 387–404.

Teasdale, J. D., Williams, M., & Segal, Z. (2014). *The mindful way workbook: an 8-week program to free yourself from depression and emotional distress*. New York: Guilford Press.

Thwaites, R., Bennett-Levy, J., Davis, M., & Chaddock, A. (2014). Using self-practice and self-reflection (SP/SR) to enhance competence and meta-competence. In A. Whittington & N. Grey (Eds.), *How to become a more effective CBT therapist: mastering metacompetence in clinical practice* (pp. 241–254). London: Routledge.

Thwaites, R., Bennett-Levy, J., & Haarhoff, B. (in press). Self-practice/self-reflection (SP/SR): contexts, challenges and ways forward. *Australian Psychologist, 5*, 344–349.

Thwaites, R., Cairns, L., Bennett-Levy, J., Johnston, L., Lowrie, R., Robinson, A., Turner, M., Haarhoff, B., & Perry, H. (2015). Developing metacompetence in low intensity CBT interventions: evaluating a self-practice/self-reflection program for experienced low intensity CBT practitioners. *Australian Psychologist, 50*, 311–321.

Todd, T. (1997). Self-supervision as a universal supervisory goal. In T. C. Todd & C. L. Storm (Eds.), *The complete systemic supervisors: context, philosophy and pragmatics* (pp. 17–25). Needham Heights, MA: Allyn & Bacon.

Townend, M. (2008). Clinical supervision in cognitive behavioural psychotherapy: development of a model for mental health nursing through grounded theory. *Journal of Psychiatric and Mental Health Nursing, 15*, 328–339.

Tracey, T., Wampold, B., Lichtenberg, J., & Goodyear, R. (2014). Expertise in psychotherapy: an elusive goal? *American Psychologist, 69*, 218–229.

Tummons, J. (2011). 'It sort of feels uncomfortable': problematising the assessment of reflective practice. *Studies in Higher Education, 36*, 471–483.

Turpin, G., & Wheeler, S. (2011). *Improving access to psychological therapies (IAPT) supervision* (revised March 2011). Retrieved from www.iapt.nhs.uk/silo/files/iapt-supervision-guidance-revised-march-2011.pdf (accesssed 29 March 2013).

Tyler, P., & Cushway, D. (1998). Stress and well-being in health-care staff: the role of negative affectivity and perception of job demand and discretion. *Stress Medicine, 14*, 99–107.

Ularntinon, S., & Friedberg, R. D. (2015). The SELF: a supervisory tool for enhancing residents' self-reflective learning in CBT with youth. *Academic Psychiatry, 38* (in press).

Ulrich, J. M., & Harris, A. L. (2003). *Essays on alternative youth (sub) culture: Gen X egesis*. Madison, WI: University of Wisconsin Press.

US Burden of Disease Collaborators. (2013). The state of US health, 1990–2010: burden of diseases, injuries, and risk factors. *Journal of the American Medical Association, 310*, 591–608.

Van, H. L., Schoevers, R. A., Kool, S., Hendriksen, M., Peen, J., & Dekker, J. (2008). Does early response predict outcome in psychotherapy and combined therapy for major depression? *Journal of Affective Disorders, 105*, 261–265.

van Grieken, R. A., Beune, E. J. A. J., Kirkenier, A. C. E., Koeter, M. W. J., van Zwieten, M. C. B., & Schene, A. H. (2014). Patients' perspectives on how treatment can impede their recovery from depression. *Journal of Affective Disorders, 167*, 153–159.

Vittengl, J. R., Clark, L. A., Thase, M. E., & Jarrett, R. B. (2013). Nomothetic and idiographic symptom change trajectories in acute-phase cognitive therapy for recurrent depression. *Journal of Consulting and Clinical Psychology, 81*, 615–626.

Vygotsky, L. S. (1978). *Mind in society: the development of higher psychological processes*. Cambridge, MA: Harvard University Press.

Walfish, S., McAlister, B., O'Donnell, P., & Lambert, M. J. (2012). An investigation of self-assessment bias in mental health providers. *Psychological Reports, 110*, 639–644.

Walker, A. (2014, 19 April) Dashed hopes and dreams (radio podcast). In Saturday Morning, New Zealand: National Radio. Retrieved from www.radionz.co.nz/national.

Waller, G. (2009). Evidence-based treatment and therapist drift. *Behaviour Research and Therapy, 47*, 119–127.

Wampold, B. (2001). *The great psychotherapy debate: models, methods and findings.* Mahwah, NJ: Lawrence Erlbaum Associates.

Wampold, B. E., & Brown, G. S. (2005). Estimating variability in outcomes attributable to therapists: a naturalistic study of outcomes in managed care. *Journal of Consulting and Clinical Psychology, 73*, 914–923.

Watson, J., & Rayner, R. (1920). Conditioned emotional reactions. *Journal of Experimental Psychology, 3*, 1–14.

Wenger, E. (1998). *Communities of practice: learning, meaning and identity.* Cambridge: Cambridge University Press.

Westbrook, D., Kennerley, H., & Kirk, J. (2011). *An introduction to cognitive behaviour therapy: skills and applications* (2nd ed.). London: Sage.

Whiteford, H. A., Degenhardt, L., Rehm, J., Baxter, A. J., Ferrari, A. J., Erskine, H. E., Charlson, F. J., Norman, R. E., Flaxman, A. D., Johns, N., Burstein, R., Murray, C. J. L., & Vos, T. (2013). Global burden of disease attributable to mental and substance use disorders: findings from the Global Burden of Disease Study 2010. *The Lancet, 382*, 1575–1586.

Whittington, A. (2014). Take control of your training for competence and meta-competence. In A. Whittington & N. Grey (Eds.), *How to become a more effective CBT therapist: mastering metacompetence in clinical practice* (pp. 284–299). London: Routledge.

Whittington, A., & Grey, N. (2014). Mastering metacompetence: the science and art of cognitive behavioural therapy. In A. Whittington & N. Grey (Eds.), *How to become a more effective CBT therapist: mastering metacompetence in clinical practice* (pp. 3–14). London: Routledge.

Wilde, O. (1965). *The importance of being Earnest.* In *The works of Oscar Wilde* (pp. 142–182). London: Spring Books.

Wiseman, S., & Scott, C. (2003). Hasta la vista, baby – I'm outta here: dealing with boredom in therapy. In J. A. Kottler & W. P. Jones (Eds.), *Doing better: improving clinical skills and professional competence* (pp. 85–103). New York: Brunner-Routledge.

Wolpe, J., & Lazarus, A. (1966). *Behavior therapy techniques.* Oxford: Pergamon Press.

Wood, D. H. (2014). Thematic analysis of factors influencing engagement with a self-practice/self-reflection (SP/SR) course. Empirical Paper, Unpublished MSc thesis, University of Lancaster, Lancaster, UK.

World Professional Association for Transgendered Health (WPATH). (2001). Standards of care of transgendered and gender nonconforming people (7th version). Retrieved from www.wpath.org.uk (accessed 4 June 2015).

Worrell, M. (2014). What to do when CBT isn't working? In A. Whittington & N. Grey (Eds.), *How to become a more effective CBT therapist: mastering metacompetence in clinical practice* (pp. 146–159). London: Routledge.

Young, J., & Beck, A. T. (1988). *The cognitive therapy rating scale manual* (revised ed.). Philadelphia, PA: Center for Cognitive Therapy, University of Pennsylvania.

Young, J. E. (1995). *Young compensation inventory*. New York: Cognitive Therapy Centre of New York.

Young, J. E., & Brown, G. (1990). *Young schema questionnaire*. New York: Cognitive Therapy Centre of New York.

Young, J. E., Klosko, J. S., & Weishaar, M. E. (2003). *Schema therapy: a practitioner's guide*. New York: Guilford Press.

Young, J. E., & Rygh, J. (1993). *Young-Rygh avoidance inventory*. New York: Cognitive Therapy Centre of New York.

Ziguras, C. (2004). *Self-care embodiment, personal autonomy and the shaping of health consciousness*. London: Routledge.

INDEX

Tables and Figures are indicated by page numbers in bold print. The abbreviation "bib" after a page number refers to bibliographical information in the Suggested Reading sections.